CANYON RANCH

Cooks

Copyright © 2001 CR License, LLC

Printed in China

Rodale Inc. makes every effort to use acid-free ⧖, recycled paper ♺.

Cover design by Joanna Williams

ISBN 1–57954–847–4

Distributed to the book trade by St. Martin's Press

2   4   6   8   10   9   7   5   3   hardcover

RODALE
WE INSPIRE AND ENABLE PEOPLE TO IMPROVE
THEIR LIVES AND THE WORLD AROUND THEM

FOR PRODUCTS & INFORMATION
WWW.RODALESTORE.COM
WWW.PREVENTION.COM
(800) 848-4735

CANYON RANCH

Cooks

Barry Correia, Scott Uehlein,
and the Kitchen Staff of Canyon Ranch

RODALE

ACKNOWLEDGEMENTS

EXECUTIVE CHEFS   Scott Uehlein
Barry Correia

The Kitchen Staff of Canyon Ranch in Tucson,
the Berkshires and SpaClub in Las Vegas

FOOD DEVELOPMENT   Jennifer Flora, M.S.
Marilyn Majchrzak, M.S., R.D.
Courtney E. Gambino, B.S.

NUTRITIONISTS   Lisa Powell, M.S., R.D.
Kathie Swift, M.S., R.D.

INTRODUCTORY TEXT   Kathleen Johnson, M.S., R.D.

FOOD AND BEVERAGE DIRECTOR   Ted Ent

RECIPE TESTING   Pamela Uehlein, Kathleen Johnson
and Laura Keen

EDITOR   Renée Downing

PROJECT MANAGER   Alyssa Cohen

PRODUCTION MANAGER   Lynne E. Brown

PROOFREADING   Lois Friedman, Ellen M. Hull and
Canyon Ranch Marketing Services Department

SENIOR ART DIRECTOR & DESIGNER   Carolyne Florez Jaeger

PHOTOGRAPHY   Jeff Green

FOOD STYLING   Trace Hayes

PHOTOSHOOT ASSISTANT   Jessica Bockman

PHOTOGRAPHY ASSISTANT   Sheri Bias-Green

PHOTO EDITING   Sian Goad

COLOR SEPARATIONS   Hollis Digital Imaging Systems, Inc.

TYPESETTING   Wendy Voorhees

Special thanks to Angela Wilke and Chris Haslett of American Home Furnishings for use of dinnerware.

Table of Contents

Canyon Ranch

Canyon Ranch Cooks is a celebration of food from the nutritionists, chefs and staff of the world's best health resort, where a passionate, informed commitment to good nutrition and great taste has evolved and been refined for more than 20 years. In this book, we think you'll find the tools and inspiration to eat well – in every sense.

Since its founding in 1979, Canyon Ranch has seen many changes in the concept of a healthy diet. Early in our history, the prevailing approach to weight loss influenced our approach to food and nutrition: We served very small portions of very low-fat foods. Our guests received 800 calories a day in our dining room and the major goal of our educational efforts was to make guests aware of calories from fat. As our understanding of nutrition and health has expanded, so has the nutrition focus of Canyon Ranch.

A balance of nutrients is more important than labeling some foods as unhealthy and others as healthy. We now know that virtually all nutrients, not just fat, need to be considered. In contrast to the days when we thought that all fat was "unhealthy," we now believe that some fats are necessary, and even health-protective, elements of a good diet.

We have always encouraged people to eat generous amounts of fruits and vegetables, but we've become even bigger advocates of plant foods as we've come to understand more clearly the disease-preventive powers of the antioxidants and other phytonutrients they contain.

In addition, we've become more aware of the importance of the quality and wholesomeness of the foods we eat. Avoiding unnecessary additives, minimizing exposure to antibiotics, hormones and pesticide residues is another aspect of eating for optimal health.

We also now understand that each individual has, in addition to the nutritional concerns common to all humans, some unique needs. There is no one way of eating that works for everyone. Genetic differences, health concerns, food sensitivities or allergies and personal preferences are all factors that influence what type of eating pattern works best for any individual.

Canyon Ranch has merged this new understanding of individual needs with a broad, comprehensive approach to optimizing health through nutrition. We call this concept Nutritional Intelligence.

Nutritional Intelligence will help you clear away confusion about healthy eating. In the sections that follow, you'll also find plenty of "kitchen intelligence," guidance on how to use this cookbook to plan and cook healthy meals that meet your unique needs. The wonder of cooking is that it can nourish you not only physically, but also creatively and spiritually. Enjoy.

Nutritional Intelligence

What is Nutritional Intelligence?

It is the Canyon Ranch philosophy that
integrates practical food and nutrition
knowledge with an understanding of
yourself. Developing your nutritional
intelligence can lead to long-term eating
strategies that work for you.

Guiding Principles

- **Honor your individuality**

  Your nutritional needs are your own. Many factors influence nutrient requirements – genetics, health and medical history, eating preferences, lifestyle and more. Your eating experiences are closely connected with your natural ability to make food choices that reflect your uniqueness.

- **Enjoy the sensual and social aspects of eating**

  Maximize your enjoyment of food by indulging your preferences for flavor and texture, and by treasuring the social pleasures of the table. Include pleasant conversation and create meaningful mealtime rituals. Eating should be a joyful experience that engages your physical and emotional senses. A meal with family or friends nourishes both body and spirit.

- **Consider the balance of your meals**

  Choose a variety of foods, including generous amounts of vegetables and fruits, moderate amounts of protein-rich foods and whole grains, and small amounts of healthy fats and oils. A balanced approach to eating energizes the body, stimulates the mind and enriches the spirit.

- **Eat to gently satisfy your appetite**

  Establish a pattern of eating regularly throughout the day to avoid extreme hunger. Learn to moderate your portions by eating with awareness and attention to your physical appetite.

- **Focus on clean and wholesome food**

  Choose fresh, seasonal vegetables and fruits, and foods free from preservatives, additives, hormones, antibiotics and other unnecessary chemicals. Shop for natural foods and discover great tastes and the rewards of supporting a cleaner and safer environment.

How to Eat Intelligently

■ **Begin by assessing personal needs or goals**

If possible, consult with a nutritionist to identify your nutritional needs. A nutritionist can guide you toward the diet that is best for you, derive nutritional meaning from lab tests, and evaluate types and amounts of supplements that may be important. A nutrition counselor will work with you to help you develop your healthiest relationship with food.

■ **Establish a pattern of eating regularly**

Nourish your body by eating regularly throughout the day to avoid extreme hunger. Try to eat every three to five hours. Work toward a pattern of breakfast, lunch and dinner with an afternoon snack, if necessary – especially if there is a long time between lunch and dinner. It's easy to forget to eat during a busy day, but regular meals may help you cope better with a demanding schedule.

A balanced approach to eating energizes the body, stimulates the mind and enriches the spirit.

■ **Be mindful of portion sizes**

Enjoy generous amounts of vegetables, and choose moderate portions of protein-rich food, starches, side dishes and fruit, and small amounts of healthy fats and oils. Learn to stop eating when your hunger is satisfied, and work on distinguishing between physical hunger and other reasons for eating such as stress, anxiety, boredom and emotional hunger. Develop strategies for eating out – share entrées or order a salad and appetizer. Remember, you're more likely to be satisfied with reasonable portions if you don't let yourself become ravenously hungry between meals.

■ **Eat 8 to 10 servings of vegetables and fruit daily**

These foods have the most power to prevent disease. Make major improvements in your diet by finding at least three new ways to conveniently add vegetables and fruit to your daily routine. Consider adding fruit to your breakfast, enjoy a medium-to-large salad once a day, be sure that each meal includes vegetables and/or fruit, and always include fruit or vegetables in your afternoon snack. Finally, choose organic produce whenever possible to minimize pesticide exposure.

■ **Emphasize whole grains**

Whole grains provide fiber and help stabilize blood sugar levels for several hours after eating. Other great carbohydrate sources include beans, sweet potatoes and pasta cooked al dente. Try hummus and other bean spreads, lentil and pea soups, and vegetarian chili. Learn how to prepare whole grains like quinoa, barley, and brown and wild rice.

■ **Focus on healthy fats & oils**

Fat is an essential part of a healthy diet. Canyon Ranch recommends a range of 20 to 30 percent of calories from fat for most people, with an emphasis on those fats with a positive impact on health. The latest word? The type of fat you consume may be as important for your health as the amount.

Emphasize monounsaturated fats

Choose extra virgin olive oil, canola oil, avocado, olives and nuts. Dress your salads lightly with an olive oil vinaigrette, using a delicious variety of vinegars or citrus juices. Sauté vegetables in olive oil and garlic. Eat small amounts of nuts each day and add avocado slices to sandwiches and salads.

Include a daily source of omega-3 fat in your diet

Omega-3 fat protects against heart attack and reduce inflammation. They're abundant in oily, deep-water fish, and in some nuts and seeds. You can get more omega-3 fat by adding freshly ground flax seeds to breads and muffins you bake at home, and by using fresh walnuts or pumpkin seeds on salads, in sauces or as snacks. Try eggs that contain higher amounts of omega-3 fat in the yolk, and enjoy fish – especially cold-water varieties such as salmon – several times a week.

Avoid trans-fat (hydrogenated oils)

We now know that trans-fat is as unhealthful as saturated fat from animals. Avoid using regular margarine as a spread or shortening when cooking; emphasize fats that are liquid at room temperature instead.

When you shop for baked or packaged goods, be on the lookout for hydrogenated or partially hydrogenated oils in the list of ingredients. If you see "hydrogenated" on the label, make another choice. Create consumer demand for healthier products in the supermarket. Also, keep in mind that many fast foods – especially those that are fried – are loaded with trans-fat.

Minimize saturated fat

Choose low-fat or nonfat dairy products like milk, yogurt and traditional low-fat cheeses such as feta, chèvre and part-skim mozzarella. Choose skinless chicken breasts and the leanest, best-trimmed cuts of red meat. Limit your consumption of foods made with butter and cream, and reduce your use of butter and full-fat cream cheese as spreads. Experiment with substitutes for full-fat dairy products in recipes.

The type of fat you consume may be as important to your health as the amount.

■ **Balance meals with some protein-rich food**

Include a protein-rich food with each meal to help control hunger and cravings, and stabilize energy levels. Our favorite sources of protein are beans, soy foods and fish, but there are many other plant and animal foods that can satisfy your protein needs. Don't overlook nut butters, low-fat or nonfat yogurt and cheeses, eggs and poultry.

■ **Limit sugar in your diet and avoid artificial sweeteners**

Savor the natural sweetness of whole foods such as fresh fruits, vegetables and nuts. If you must sweeten, go natural with small amounts of maple syrup, honey, brown rice syrup or unrefined sugar. Choose fruit for dessert, and stir fresh fruit or all-fruit preserves into plain yogurt for a quick breakfast or snack. You can also "sweeten" foods with cinnamon, vanilla and freshly grated nutmeg. Read labels to identify foods that are sweetened artificially, which inflates the desire for extreme sweetness.

■ **Be sensible about salt**

Gradually cut down on salt while pampering your palate with delectable, healing herbs and spices. These additions enhance the flavor of food while gently working their restorative magic. Rosemary is calming; cinnamon warms; ginger and chiles add pizzazz. Salt is also a flavor enhancer, but using it in moderation enhances your health.

■ **Drink plenty of clean water every day**

Your body is approximately 60 percent water. Because water is continuously used in nearly every life process, it's crucial to keep replenishing the supply. Proper hydration is also important for energy and hunger management – eight large glasses a day is a good rule. Make water your beverage of choice. Install a water cooler in your home or office, and use a beautiful, large tumbler as your glass. Add ice if you like, and a slice of lemon or lime to jazz up the flavor of nature's best beverage.

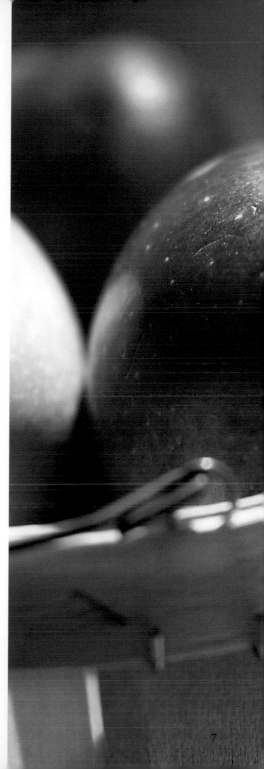

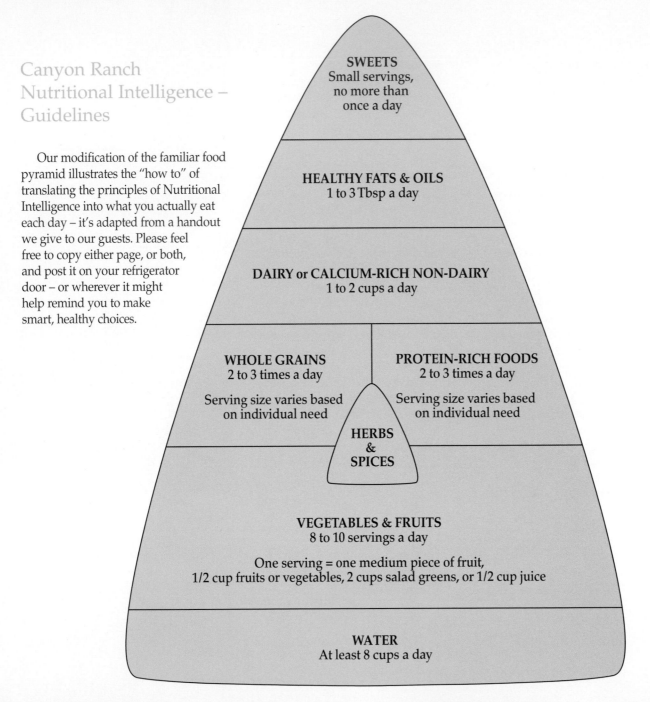

Canyon Ranch
Nutritional Intelligence –
Guidelines

Our modification of the familiar food pyramid illustrates the "how to" of translating the principles of Nutritional Intelligence into what you actually eat each day – it's adapted from a handout we give to our guests. Please feel free to copy either page, or both, and post it on your refrigerator door – or wherever it might help remind you to make smart, healthy choices.

SWEETS
Small servings,
no more than
once a day

HEALTHY FATS & OILS
1 to 3 Tbsp a day

DAIRY or CALCIUM-RICH NON-DAIRY
1 to 2 cups a day

WHOLE GRAINS
2 to 3 times a day

Serving size varies based
on individual need

PROTEIN-RICH FOODS
2 to 3 times a day

Serving size varies based
on individual need

**HERBS
&
SPICES**

VEGETABLES & FRUITS
8 to 10 servings a day

One serving = one medium piece of fruit,
1/2 cup fruits or vegetables, 2 cups salad greens, or 1/2 cup juice

WATER
At least 8 cups a day

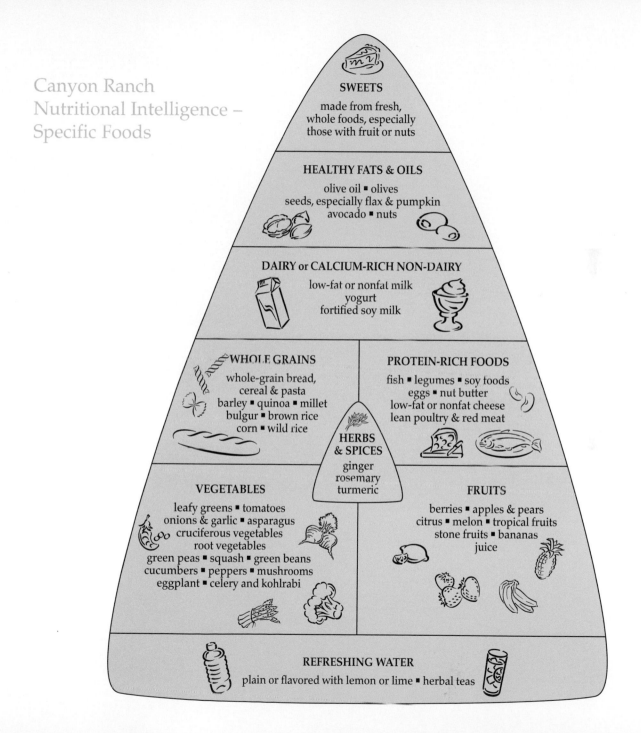

Canyon Ranch
Nutritional Intelligence –
Specific Foods

SWEETS
made from fresh,
whole foods, especially
those with fruit or nuts

HEALTHY FATS & OILS
olive oil ▪ olives
seeds, especially flax & pumpkin
avocado ▪ nuts

DAIRY or CALCIUM-RICH NON-DAIRY
low-fat or nonfat milk
yogurt
fortified soy milk

WHOLE GRAINS
whole-grain bread,
cereal & pasta
barley ▪ quinoa ▪ millet
bulgur ▪ brown rice
corn ▪ wild rice

PROTEIN-RICH FOODS
fish ▪ legumes ▪ soy foods
eggs ▪ nut butter
low-fat or nonfat cheese
lean poultry & red meat

**HERBS
& SPICES**
ginger
rosemary
turmeric

VEGETABLES
leafy greens ▪ tomatoes
onions & garlic ▪ asparagus
cruciferous vegetables
root vegetables
green peas ▪ squash ▪ green beans
cucumbers ▪ peppers ▪ mushrooms
eggplant ▪ celery and kohlrabi

FRUITS
berries ▪ apples & pears
citrus ▪ melon ▪ tropical fruits
stone fruits ▪ bananas
juice

REFRESHING WATER
plain or flavored with lemon or lime ▪ herbal teas

Ready Set Eat

Whether you want to transform your diet
or just fine-tune it, a step-by-step approach
to using this cookbook will be useful.

First, recognize just what you want to do,
based on an understanding of yourself and
your preferences. Then, you'll want to set up
(or spruce up) your kitchen, fill your pantry
and begin planning. We suggest you take it
one dish, one meal, one day at a time and
see what works for you.

Step by Step

- **First, recognize just what it is you want to do**

  Some people will pick up this cookbook because they love reading recipes. Others, who love cooking and are always looking for new recipes to try, will hunt through it for inspiration. Still others will open this book hoping to find a tool for improving the way they eat. We think they'll all find what they're looking for.

  Canyon Ranch has long inspired healthy eating in direct, practical ways, ranging from serving incredible meals in our dining rooms to providing individualized advice from our skilled nutritionists. No matter which type of reader you are, there's something for you in the sections that follow. Understanding your motivation will help you plan the approach that best meets your needs.

- **Do you want to eat cleaner, more wholesome foods?**

  The general safety and wholesomeness of our food supply is a growing concern for many of us. When you purchase and prepare your own food, you have significantly more control over the pesticide, antibiotic and hormone residues in your food. When you shop for and cook more of your meals, you can better avoid ingredients you'd rather not eat.

- **Do you want to improve your health by eating better?**

  You may want to lower your risk for a disease that runs in your family – heart disease, high blood pressure or osteoporosis – or control food allergies, achieve a healthier weight, or feel better and have more energy. Whatever your health and wellness concerns, the Canyon Ranch approach to healthy eating – not to mention our recipes – can help.

- **Do you want healthier choices than restaurants offer?**

  Although some restaurants serve healthy meals, the majority don't cater to health-conscious consumers. Whether the problem is portion sizes, unwelcome ingredients, excessive fats, or lack of fresh vegetables, eating out regularly presents challenges. Cook for yourself and you are in control.

- **Know your eating and cooking style**

  How you use this book depends on your relationship with food, both in the kitchen and at the table. At the Ranch, you'd probably hear someone say, "Start where you are." Take a look at the questions at right to help you figure out where you are now. It's always the first step in getting to where you want to be.

HOW DO YOU DESCRIBE YOURSELF WHEN IT COMES TO FOOD?

☐ I live to eat.

☐ I eat to live.

☐ My health concerns influence my eating.

☐ My weight concerns influence my eating.

☐ I like a lot of variety in my meals.

☐ I could eat the same thing every day and be happy.

☐ I like simple foods and basic flavors.

☐ I like complex, interesting foods and flavors.

HOW DO YOU DESCRIBE YOURSELF AS A COOK?

☐ I don't mind scrubbing vegetables and chopping.

☐ I hate / have no time for washing and chopping.

☐ I have a well-equipped kitchen.

☐ I have little kitchen equipment.

☐ I know my way around a grocery store.

☐ I have a good natural food store nearby.

☐ I have little experience shopping for food.

☐ I dislike / have no time for food shopping.

☐ I want to prepare most of my meals.

☐ I want to prepare just a few of my meals.

■ **Do you live to eat, or eat to live?**

In either case, if you're reading this you're clearly interested in eating in a nutritionally conscious way. Still, how much you care about taste is a real consideration. If you're an "eat to live" sort of individual, you may want to simply leave out some herbs and spices and garnishes in the fancier recipes and take a simple approach. A recipe is not set in stone after all, and the main ingredients and basic preparations will provide you with excellent nutrition. If, on the other hand, food is a major source of pleasure in your life, you'll want to try following the recipes to the letter. Our chefs create wonderful dishes.

Do you know how to cook?

If you have even a few cooking skills, making dishes from this cookbook will be a breeze. But if you are a newcomer to cooking, you'll be able to begin learning your way around the kitchen. Our instructions are detailed, and we point you in the right direction with recommendations for equipment, a shopping list for stocking your pantry and pointers to the easiest and quickest recipes in the book.

■ Do you like to cook?

This is a very different issue than whether you know how. If you can cook but it isn't your favorite pastime, you'll appreciate the simplicity of many of our recipes. If, on the other hand, you're an enthusiastic cook, you'll find delicious, healthy, inventive dishes that look and taste like you'd spent much more time than you really did. And you'll find amazing new tastes and interesting preparation ideas to get your creative juices flowing.

■ Do you have all the time in the world to cook?

Probably not. Time is such an issue these days that even if you're fired up with ambition to cook your own meals, you'll have to consider how much time you have to shop and cook. The staff of Canyon Ranch, who have years of experience helping people change their lives, believe that realistic goals are essential.

Begin by taking stock of what you're doing now for breakfast, lunch and dinner. We suggest you try tackling just one of the day's meals at a time. Ask yourself which one you'd like to change first.

For breakfast you might like to find simple, everyday alternatives to cereal or a bagel. A smoothie makes a delicious breakfast that's efficient enough for just about anyone. Or, if you're a crack-of-dawn type person, you might like to make one of our healthy quick breads. You may want to try something really special on the weekend.

Lunches are a wonderful opportunity to brownbag a healthy meal as an alternative to fast food or ordering in. You can get a two-for-one if you make extra at dinner the night before and lunch on healthy leftovers the next day.

If preparing more dinners is your goal, you may not need to plan and shop for seven full menus each week. Factor in the meals out that you enjoy with friends and the evenings when schedules don't allow a sit-down dinner with the family.

If you've been doing very little home cooking and have a realistic goal of making one or two dinners a week, perhaps you can cook on the weekend when you have the time. As you get more comfortable with the process, you can always expand your repertoire and the number of meals you make yourself.

Okay. You've pretty much determined your course of action. Let's get down to the details of how to get it done.

Lining Up Your Resources

Food shopping today in the United States offers more possibilities and sheer entertainment than ever before. From artisan bakeries and ethnic markets to well-stocked supermarkets and natural food stores, you have choices, and we encourage you to search out the best. Great meals begin with best-quality ingredients.

■ **Pick your markets well**

Convenience is nice, but cleanliness is at the top of our list. Stores should look spotless and smell good. Cleanliness means less risk of health problems and reflects a shopkeeper's attitude toward the merchandise.

■ **Get to know shopkeepers and managers**

Don't be afraid to ask a store to carry a new product you've heard about. If you primarily shop at supermarkets, get to know the managers of the meat and produce departments.

■ **Always shop with a list**

Whether you shop once a week or several times a week, a list is essential for efficiency, and will help you curb impulse shopping.

■ **Pick the best shop for the job**

Don't hesitate to limit your bread purchases to a bakery specializing in artisan loaves. Find out where you can buy the freshest fish. You may make more stops on a shopping trip, but the high quality of what you come home with is worth it.

■ **Consider all your alternatives:**

Natural food supermarkets

Many national and regional chains of natural food supermarkets are opening around the country. Some of these markets combine natural and gourmet foods. Look for attractive stores with a wide range of merchandise, salad and juice bars, and a section with prepared vegetables and healthy entrées. Many such stores have extensive dietary supplement departments.

Health food stores

These are a little more traditional and usually smaller than the natural food supermarkets, but can often serve as a source of staples like whole grains, beans and organic produce.

Supermarkets

Many conventional supermarkets now carry organic produce and natural products in addition to their regular merchandise. The grocery business is extremely competitive, and supermarkets want your business. You may find that the nearest supermarket is quite willing to stock items you ask for.

Farmer's markets and fruit stands

These are wonderful sources for the freshest seasonal produce. You may also find local specialties like honey, jams and chutneys.

Organic produce home delivery

For the busiest among us, this emerging service is a godsend. Many services provide a selection of whatever is ripe and available that week. This method of buying your produce allows you to be inspired – just like a restaurant chef – by the changing bounty of the seasons.

Co-ops

Some communities have organized groups that contract with a few organic growers in their area to buy their crops. This is a wonderful way to support smaller, organic farmers. Like home-delivery customers, co-op members get the freshest, but don't have much control over what they receive from week to week.

Bakeries

Artisan bakers are cropping up all over the country. All the breads and treats are wonderful; look for (or ask for) chewy, whole grain loaves.

Fish markets

Let your nose be your guide when choosing the best place to buy fish. If you don't live near the water, find out where you can buy the freshest fish locally. Learn when shipments arrive and plan your menus to take advantage of fish just as it arrives in town.

Butchers

Find a butcher who carries, or is willing to carry, some of the newly available, cleaner brands of beef and poultry that are free from growth hormones and antibiotics. You may want to ask how the animals are raised and fed. Once again, look for cleanliness.

Mail order

Mail order food shopping is not just limited to "fruit of the month" anymore. You can now purchase a wide variety of high-quality foods through the mail or on-line. Use this for the best of the best in fresh and dried fruit, jams, spices, condiments, teas, jellies and specialty items.

Choosing Your Ingredients

Our guidelines for choosing the ingredients for your cooking are seasoned with concern for your health, but also with concern for the environment. (Healthy people live on a healthy planet.) Notice our picks for products that will save you time without compromising your health.

■ **Vegetables and fruit**

Fresh

Fresh vegetables and fruit should be the mainstay of your marketing. We recommend buying seasonal, locally grown produce whenever possible – and organic, when available. By choosing organic, you provide the highest quality food for you and your family and help support an important movement for sustainable farming, wholesome food and low impact on the environment.

If you don't live in an area with organic farms, you can probably still find lovely organic produce in natural food markets and even supermarkets. If your supermarket doesn't carry some organic produce, ask them to.

If you can't purchase organic produce all the time, prioritize those vegetables and fruits that have been found to have the highest pesticide residues when conventionally farmed. At present, this list includes:

Strawberries	Grapes
Cherries	Apricots
Apples	Pears
Spinach	Frozen winter squash
Coffee	

The list changes often, however, as government agencies gather new data. *Consumer Reports* is a good source of current information on pesticide issues.

> **CONVENIENCE CUE:**
> - Bagged organic salad greens
> - Chopped vegetables and fruit ready to eat or cook

Frozen

Frozen vegetables are a great convenience for those days when you can't shop for fresh produce. Once again, we recommend choosing organic.

Canned or jarred

Contrary to popular opinion, some canned vegetables most definitely have a place in a health-conscious cook's pantry. The most important are tomato products; beans are also indispensable. Look for organic canned tomato sauce, paste, whole and crushed tomatoes and organic canned beans.

Dried

Unsulfured dried fruit is a great choice for cooking and snacking. Fruit treated with sulfur dioxide is prettier because the sulfur prevents browning. But because some individuals are quite sensitive to sulfur, we recommend buying untreated fruit. Unsulfured apples and apricots may look darker and "older," but they're just as moist and flavorful as treated fruit.

Clean-Eating Guidelines

PRODUCE

Buy a variety of seasonally fresh, locally grown and certified organic produce. You can further reduce your exposure to pesticides and bacteria by using these smart washing and peeling techniques:

- Prepare a vegetable wash solution using one teaspoon mild soap in one gallon of water, or use a prepared vegetable wash solution to wash all produce.

- Use a vegetable brush on potatoes, sweet potatoes, carrots and other hard produce with skin you plan to eat.

- Wash and peel non-organic fruit or vegetables with obvious wax coatings. (Likely candidates are cucumbers, apples, peppers and eggplants.) This will remove pesticides that often are sealed in the waxes.

- Discard the outer leaves of cabbage and head lettuce.

PROTEIN AND PACKAGED FOODS

Buy a variety of minimally processed foods. Whenever possible, use antibiotic- and hormone-free animal products. Avoid foods with additives such as artificial colorings, flavorings, sweeteners and preservatives.

FATS

Choose foods without "hydrogenated" or "partially hydrogenated" oils or altered fats like Olestra®.

WATER

If you have concerns about the water in your area, consider a water-purifying system for your home. Distillers are more expensive; reverse osmosis systems are good and cost less. Bottled water is another alternative – choose glass or hard plastic containers.

■ Fish

We strongly recommend fish as a source of protein for the healthy type of fat it provides. Virtually all fish contain some heart-protective omega-3 fatty acids, and population studies show health benefits from eating fish of all kinds. The fish with the most omega-3 fatty acids, though, are oily, coldwater varieties like salmon, trout, mackerel and sardines.

There are, however, safety and environmental concerns with some fish, both wild and farmed. The Audubon Society has warned against overfishing of many species and recommends care in your choices. The Society is also a good source of information about the safety and environmental impact of farmed fish and shellfish.

Mercury from industrial emissions contaminates water and consequently fish. The Environmental Working Group recommends eating fish with the lowest levels of mercury contamination, especially for women who are pregnant or nursing, and for young children. Fish with the lowest levels of mercury (at time of printing) include wild Pacific salmon, farmed trout, farmed catfish, summer flounder, croaker and haddock.

Poultry

Poultry, especially breast meat, has become a healthy staple in many households because it contains very little fat.

There are, however, factors other than nutritional value to consider when choosing poultry. Most of the poultry on the market has been raised on antibiotic-laced feed, and this overuse of antibiotics is thought by many to contribute to the evolution of antibiotic-resistant bacteria that cause food-borne illnesses.

Antibiotic-free poultry is now available, as well as free range and organic. We recommend that you look for it.

CONVENIENCE CUE:
- Flash-frozen skinless, boneless chicken breasts

Other meats

A variety of hormone- and pesticide-free meats are now available in natural food markets and some supermarkets. If your butcher doesn't provide information about where his meat comes from, ask.

Soy foods

Firm and soft tofu is available in refrigerated tubs and in bulk. Tofu bought in bulk from large barrels runs a greater risk of bacterial contamination. Silken tofu, a Japanese variation, is packaged in shelf-stable boxes. Organic tofu is available and recommended because of the high amount of pesticide residues found in regular soybeans.

Other considerations: Avoid tofu made from genetically modified soybeans (check the label), and if you are using tofu as a source of calcium, check the list of ingredients to be sure that calcium sulfate has been used as the coagulating agent.

Tempeh – a tender, chunky soybean cake – is commonly available in the frozen food section of a natural food store. Experiment with the different types of tempeh made from combinations of soybeans, grains and nuts. Choose organic whenever possible.

Edamame (green soybeans in their pods) and already-shelled "sweet" beans, make a great side dish, a fun-to-eat appetizer and a terrific snack. Look for them in the frozen food section.

Beans

Beans are one of our favorite foods and we recommend them often. Many people, however, shy away from using them regularly because they take so long to cook from scratch. While that is true for most beans – although not for lentils and split peas – there are cooking methods that take less time (pressure cooking) or virtually no effort (slow cooking).

Even more convenient, though, are canned beans. Dozens of types of beans are available and ready to use in recipes with no more work or time than it takes to open the can. Compare sodium levels in canned beans and look for organic brands.

CONVENIENCE CUE:
- Canned beans
- Dried bean flakes

You'll notice that we frequently recommend buying organic foods. It is true that consistent guidelines for labeling foods as organic are just being implemented and that the health benefits of eating organic foods are not well defined. We think, though, that minimizing exposure to pesticide residues and reducing the impact of farming on the environment are good ideas.

■ Dairy products

Whole milk and other full-fat dairy products are rich in saturated fat, which is associated with increased LDL cholesterol, a significant risk for cardiovascular disease. As a rule, choose low-fat or nonfat products.

Our choices are primarily low-fat versions of traditional cheeses. We use them in moderate amounts for flavor because their fat content – though reduced – is still quite saturated. We have found most nonfat cheeses lacking in flavor, texture and meltability, so we don't use them.

We do, however, make sparing use of some intensely flavored full-fat cheeses. Parmesan, feta and chèvre are so powerful that just a tablespoon or so adds incomparable flavor.

Many producers of milk and dairy products now state that they are not using milk from cows that have been treated with bovine growth hormone (BGH), and some producers are indicating this on their packaging. We recommend buying products without hormone residues. Organic milk and dairy products are also available.

■ Grains and grain products

Our blanket recommendation for this group of foods is to choose whole grains and whole-grain products. A good example of a whole grain that has not been milled and refined is brown rice. Whole-grain products – like whole-wheat bread, pasta and tortillas – are made from flour milled from whole grain.

We also suggest eating a variety of whole grains. Because wheat is the grain most commonly consumed in the United States, many people have developed sensitivities to it. Other grains such as amaranth, quinoa, barley and spelt provide new tastes and textures, as well as a break from the steady diet of wheat that triggers health problems for some people. We suggest that you keep grains and flours in tightly closed containers in the refrigerator or freezer.

Grains

Some grains that are very quick and easy to prepare as pilafs make delicious side dishes. Look for quinoa, whole-wheat couscous, bulgur, wild rice and the many different varieties of rice – jasmine, arborio and basmati.

Pasta

Wonderful whole-wheat pastas are available. They are chewier than their white flour counterparts and can be a nice alternative. For a change of pace, look for pastas made from quinoa, rice and corn – and even lentils.

Breakfast cereals

Choose cereals, both dry and cooked, made from whole grains, and consider trying some made from a variety of grains. Choose cereals free from unnecessary amounts of sugar or other sweeteners – no more than 2 teaspoons (8 grams) – per serving. Nuts and dried fruit add natural sweetness and variety of both taste and texture.

Breads and crackers

Choose breads and crackers made from whole-grain flours, and if you see "partially hydrogenated" on the label, make another choice. Even better are baked goods that have whole grains, seeds or nuts added to the dough or as toppings. If sensitivity to wheat or gluten is an issue, look for breads made without these ingredients, or try our gluten-free recipes (see Index).

■ Oils and other fats

A good deal of care is warranted in both purchasing and storing cooking oils – they're delicate, expensive and very important ingredients in healthy home cooking.

Our chefs use extra virgin olive oil and canola oil. Canola oil is appropriate when you want a flavorless oil, and when high temperatures are required, as in stir frying. For all other uses, we love olive oil for its healthy monosaturated nature and its depth of flavor. Be adventurous when buying olive oil: Flavor, color and fragrance vary dramatically from one region to another. Other oils, such as sesame and walnut, add flavor to dishes but are not recommended for cooking.

Oils should be purchased in small bottles and kept tightly closed in the refrigerator. (We always cringe when we see a lovely bottle of olive oil bottle sitting out on the kitchen counter. Yes, it's pretty, but the exposure to light is oxidizing the oil every minute of the day.) Olive oil becomes thick and cloudy in the refrigerator, but liquifies in a few minutes at room temperature.

Some of our recipes call for small amounts of butter when the flavor and texture of dish would be compromised by a substitute. We recommend that you buy good quality butter in small quantities and keep it frozen.

■ Nuts, seeds, nut butters

Nuts and seeds are wonderfully nutritious additions to your pantry, but there are a few considerations to be aware of. First is the issue of freshness. The naturally occurring oils in these foods can go rancid – rancidity, however, is usually detectable by your nose or tastebuds. (Rancid oil has been oxidized, and is not something you want to put in your body.)

Buy only fresh nuts and seeds, store them tightly covered in the refrigerator or freezer, and check them regularly for freshness. Throw away any that develop an off taste or smell.

Nut and seed butters are tasty and versatile ingredients. Buy the natural versions, that have no added ingredients except, if you want it, salt.

Use nut butters sparingly, since 1 teaspoon contains 5 grams of fat. Store in the refrigerator and check regularly for freshness.

■ Sweeteners

We use a variety of sweeteners, in small amounts, in our recipes. You'll find uses for sweeteners from maple syrup to brown sugar, molasses to honey. Although natural sweeteners are our first choice, if you must use non-nutritive sweeteners, you may want to try products such as stevia or sucralose (Splenda™).

■ Condiments

Some refrigerators are packed to the gills with bottles of every known type of mustard, bottled sauce and chutney. We encourage you to be selective in those you buy. Some are quite delicious and convenient; others are just well-marketed and don't compare to simple counterparts you can make from scratch. Read labels carefully and don't purchase products that contain additives or artificial colors. Throw out any condiments you've had for more than a year.

■ Spices and herbs

Small packages of fresh herbs are welcome newcomers to the produce aisle. Buy these on an as-needed basis – or start a fresh herb garden in a sunny window – and stock your pantry with a few spices, dried herbs and versatile mixes. Spices and dried herbs don't necessarily age well. Buy in small quantities and discard any that you've had for more than a year.

Setting Up Your Kitchen

Having the right equipment makes cooking easier and more fun. If you are just beginning to outfit your kitchen, begin with the basics, which we have identified in our list below (*). Add other items as you expand your repertoire. Be sure to read a recipe through before adding it to your menu plan, and if it requires equipment you don't have, consider how often you'll use the new item before investing. For best quality, visit your local restaurant supply house.

Obviously, you'll want to think a bit more about an indoor grill than a meat thermometer, but that fancy grill may open up new avenues of cooking creativity for you.

POTS AND PANS

- ☐ Sauté pans – small (8"), medium (10") and large (12"), with lids*
- ☐ Sauce pans – small (1 qt.), medium (1½ - 2 qt.) and large (2½ - 3 qt.), with lids*
- ☐ Double boiler (2 qt.)
- ☐ Stockpot (3 qt.) with colander insert and lid*
- ☐ Muffin tin (6 or 12 cups)
- ☐ Broiling or roasting pan (14"x10"x2")*
- ☐ Glass baking dishes or aluminum baking pans (8"x8"x2" & 13"x9"x2")*
- ☐ Baking sheet (15"x10"x1")*
- ☐ Cake pan (9")
- ☐ Tart pan (9")
- ☐ Springform pan (10")
- ☐ Custard cups (4 oz.)
- ☐ Pie plate (9")

WHAT TO LOOK FOR:

- – In sauce pans and sauté pans, look for sturdy, heavy-bottomed pots that can go from stovetop to oven.
- – Pots and pans made from copper or stainless steel conduct heat well, and a high quality nonstick finish will help you cook with little added oil. Stockpots need not be as heavy, but they should have sturdy handles that are easy to grasp.
- – Nonstick surfaces should be anodized – some other types can flake slowly into your food. Anodized aluminum is a good material for stock pots, because it weighs less than copper.
- – Note that if you have glass baking dishes, you'll need to reduce all temperatures by 25° – glass retains and conducts more heat than metal.
- – Broiling pans are easier to clean if they have a nonstick finish. The stovetop grill pans that are the most effective, though, are cast iron.

UTENSILS

- ☐ Spatula*
- ☐ Ladle*
- ☐ Large spoons*
- ☐ Large fork*
- ☐ Wire whip*
- ☐ Potato masher
- ☐ Digital thermometer
- ☐ Meat mallet
- ☐ Pastry cutter

WHAT TO LOOK FOR:

- – If you have nonstick pots and pans, don't buy metal utensils that will scratch the finish.
- – Try out the grip and buy utensils that fit your hand.
- – The handiest utensils hang from a rack within easy reach.

APPLIANCES

- ☐ Small grinder for flax seed and other seeds and spices
- ☐ Blender*
- ☐ Hand-held electric mixer
- ☐ Electric indoor grill
- ☐ Food processor

WHAT TO LOOK FOR:

One important consideration in choosing all appliances is ease of cleaning. From blenders to food processors to electric indoor grills, keep this in mind when you buy. If it's a pain in the neck to wash up, you won't want to use it.

OTHER

- ☐ Mixing bowls – small (3 c.), medium (1½ qt.) and large (2½ qt.)*
- ☐ Hand juicer
- ☐ Parchment paper
- ☐ Cheesecloth
- ☐ Colander*
- ☐ Kitchen oil spritzer*
- ☐ Measuring cups and spoons*

WHAT TO LOOK FOR:

Good quality stainless steel measuring cups and spoons are probably more accurate and will last longer than plastic.

GOOD KNIVES

- ☐ Chef's knife (5" - 12") – for slicing and chopping*
- ☐ Boning knife – for trimming fat off chicken, duck or meat*
- ☐ Paring knife   for small peeling and coring jobs*
- ☐ Serrated knife – for cutting bread*
- ☐ Steel with guard – for sharpening*

ADVICE FROM OUR CHEF ON BUYING KNIVES:

- – Go to a knife store for best selection.
- – Handle them to make sure they feel good and well-balanced in your hand.
- – Expect to pay for good knives – more expensive knives usually require less sharpening.
- – Store them where they don't touch each other to keep them sharp longer.

Stocking Your Pantry

We love fresh food and encourage its use every day, but a busy cook needs a "friendly," fall-back pantry that includes recipe ingredients that add flavor, save time and increase flexibility. Think in terms of the basics or the foundations of a recipe, the flavors and the baking cabinet. Included in our recommended pantry list are those ingredients that you'll find in our recipes, plus a few that are just good to have around.

For our purposes, pantry includes both unrefrigerated and refrigerated or frozen foods that you'll want to keep in stock.

THE BASICS

FISH
- [ ] Canned tuna (white albacore, water-packed)
- [ ] Canned salmon
- [ ] Canned sardines
- [ ] Frozen salmon
- [ ] Frozen shrimp

TOMATO PRODUCTS – CANNED OR BOXED
- [ ] Tomato sauce
- [ ] Tomato paste
- [ ] Diced tomatoes
- [ ] Pureed or crushed tomatoes
- [ ] Whole plum tomatoes
- [ ] Jarred marinara sauce

BEANS
- [ ] Canned black beans
- [ ] Canned garbanzo beans
- [ ] Canned white beans
- [ ] Canned pinto beans
- [ ] Canned vegetarian-style refried beans
- [ ] Dried lentils
- [ ] Other dried beans

SOY FOODS
- [ ] Tofu
- [ ] Tempeh
- [ ] Frozen edamame (green soy beans in the pod)

PASTA
- [ ] Whole-wheat or semolina pasta – spaghetti or linguini
- [ ] Shells or rigatoni
- [ ] Angel hair
- [ ] Lasagna noodles
- [ ] Rice noodles
- [ ] Couscous
- [ ] Corn, quinoa or lentil pasta

RICE AND OTHER GRAINS
- [ ] Brown rice – short or long-grain
- [ ] Wild rice
- [ ] Basmati rice
- [ ] Bulgur
- [ ] Barley
- [ ] Quinoa

WHOLE-GRAIN PRODUCTS
- [ ] Rolled Oats
- [ ] Multi-grain cereal
- [ ] Whole-wheat cold cereal
- [ ] Whole-wheat tortillas
- [ ] Whole-grain bread

STOCK OR BROTH – CANNED, BOXED OR FROZEN
- [ ] Chicken
- [ ] Vegetable
- [ ] Fish
- [ ] Clam juice (bottled or canned)

OTHER VEGETABLES AND FRUIT
- [ ] Frozen sweet corn, peas
- [ ] Frozen chopped organic spinach
- [ ] Canned or jarred artichoke hearts (in water)
- [ ] Frozen blueberries, raspberries and blackberries, and other frozen fruits
- [ ] Jarred roasted red peppers
- [ ] Canned chipotle, jalapeño and ancho chile peppers

FROZEN SKINLESS, BONELESS CHICKEN BREASTS

THE FLAVORS

OILS AND FATS
☐ Extra virgin olive oil
☐ Canola oil
☐ Sesame oil
☐ Butter

VINEGARS
☐ Distilled White
☐ Balsamic
☐ Rice
☐ Wine

ALCOHOL
☐ White and Red wine
☐ Sherry
☐ Mirin (rice) wine or sake

SWEETENERS
☐ Honey
☐ Brown sugar
☐ Molasses
☐ 100% maple syrup
☐ Sucralose or stevia (if desired)

FLAVORINGS
☐ Pure vanilla extract
☐ Almond extract

UNSULFURED DRIED FRUIT
☐ Raisins
☐ Currants
☐ Cherries
☐ Cranberries
☐ Apricots

PRESERVES
☐ Apricot
☐ All-fruit, organic, if possible

CONDIMENTS
☐ Capers, olives
☐ Salsa
☐ Mustard
☐ Miso paste
☐ Low-sodium tamari sauce
☐ Canola mayonnaise
☐ Soy mayonnaise

NATURAL NUT BUTTERS
☐ Tahini (sesame butter)
☐ Soy
☐ Almond
☐ Cashew
☐ Peanut

NUTS AND SEEDS
☐ Almonds
☐ Cashews
☐ Walnuts
☐ Pecans
☐ Flax seed

TEA
☐ Black, green & herbal

BOTTLED SALAD DRESSING
(minimal or no additives
or preservatives; no
hydrogenated oils)

SPICES AND HERBS
☐ Oregano
☐ Basil
☐ Thyme
☐ Rosemary
☐ Tarragon
☐ Red chili flakes
☐ Cumin
☐ Curry
☐ Cinnamon
☐ Nutmeg
☐ Ginger
☐ Cardamom
☐ Turmeric
☐ Black pepper

FRUIT JUICE CONCENTRATES
☐ Frozen
☐ Boxed

THE BAKING CABINET

☐ Whole-wheat flour
☐ Whole-wheat pastry flour
☐ Stone-ground cornmeal or polenta

☐ Bread flour
☐ All-purpose flour
☐ Sugar
☐ Sea salt

☐ Cornstarch
☐ Arrowroot
☐ Tapioca
☐ Baking soda

☐ Baking powder
☐ Unsweetened cocoa powder
☐ Unsweetened baking chocolate

Planning Your Strategy–A Quick Overview

Menu planning requires just that – some planning. Even though you certainly have experience planning one thing or another, walking through the steps involved in planning a menu is valuable. It may seem daunting to add another task to your already busy life, but if you want to take more control over what you eat, and do it efficiently, planning is the answer.

If you are a cook, it may seem silly to see these steps spelled out like this – you know how to plan a menu and roast a sweet potato, for heaven's sake. However, if it has been a while since you took a systematic approach to menu planning if your life has changed significantly since you last cooked much, or if you are new to the kitchen, read along.

■ The first step

To begin, we suggest a little fun preliminary research. Browse through the recipes in the book. Imagine the flavors of each dish and read through the techniques involved. Mark the dishes you and your family would like and that you would be willing to cook. Use sticky tabs or dog-ear the pages if you like. It's your book. **Use it!**

Decide how many meals you want to plan for one week. If you're doing this for the first time, you'll probably just want to plan one or two.

■ The second step

Next, plan the menu for each meal. There are two ways you can do this. One is to start with a main dish; the other is to begin with seasonal vegetables.

The main dish approach is more traditional. Main dishes usually provide the protein in a meal. Remember that beans (including soybeans) and fish are at the top of our list. After picking a recipe for a main dish, round out the menu with side dishes. Our chefs suggest sides for every entrée. You can use these or pick your own – perhaps a family favorite or a super-convenient option like frozen vegetables or a bagged salad.

Vegetables warrant some extra discussion. Eating a generous amount of vegetables each day is a powerful way to protect yourself against disease. If you like vegetables and have cooked them before, check our recipes for new vegetable entrées, salads and side dishes. Pick a few you'd like to try.

If your relationship with vegetables is just beginning, spend some time reading our simple instructions for basic preparation. Roasting and steaming are the two basic methods. Learning to make salads and salad dressings will give you the skills you need to transform virtually any vegetable into an integral part of a menu.

The seasonal vegetable approach to planning a menu is appealing for many reasons. You go to the market and pick out the best and most delectable vegetables of the season. This approach requires you to be somewhat spontaneous in your shopping: You may be surprised by the unexpected showing of Russian kale, for example. Other seasonal offerings are predictable enough to allow you to go to the store with a list – tender asparagus in the spring, sweet corn in midsummer, pumpkins and other winter squash in the fall.

The vegetables can either be prepared as side dishes and accompanied by a simple main dish or used in the main dish itself. You can use whatever seasonal vegetables you find in many of our vegetarian entrées. Just substitute one leafy vegetable for another, one root vegetable for another, one cabbage-family vegetable for another, and so on.

Whether you plan your meal around the entrée or the vegetables round out every menu with all the components – protein, whole grains, healthy fats, fruits and vegetables.

■ The third step

The next task is to generate a shopping list. It is not a bad idea to begin by writing the complete list of all the ingredients you'll need for the entire menu. "Shop" your refrigerator, freezer and pantry first. Cross those ingredients you already have off the list. Then head to the market for the rest. If time is not a factor, or if you can efficiently shop once a week, you may want to visit specialty stores like your favorite produce market, bakery or natural food store.

Parting Words

Eating is one of the fundamental pleasures of life, and for many of us, cooking is another. We wish for you not only the health benefits of a busy, health-conscious kitchen, but all the fun and satisfaction of making good things. Cooking can be creative and wild, or soothing and meditative; the market can be a place of discovery and a pleasant social center; the kitchen can be the heart of the home, an alchemist's laboratory, an artist's studio, a place of refuge or a gathering place for friends and family. We hope this book helps you make your cooking, and your kitchen, exactly what you desire.

Now go cook.

Sample Menus

Here are a few days of balanced, healthy selections. You can, indeed, eat well, in both senses of the phrase, at the same time.

DAY 1

Breakfast:

Migas, page 38

Fresh Fruit Plate*

½ cup Fruited Yogurt**

Lunch:

Black Bean Soup with
    Red Onion Salsa, page 80

Cashew Chicken Salad,
    page 132

Apple Strudel, page 278

Dinner:

1 cup mixed greens with
    2 tablespoons Grapefruit
    and Sage Dressing, page 155

Beef Tenderloin with
    Adobado Paste, page 236

Chipotle Whipped Potatoes,
    page 113

Calabacitas, page 110

Fresh Fruit Plate*

DAILY NUTRITION
INFORMATION

Calories: 1745
Carbohydrate: 246 gm.
Fat: 44 gm.
Protein: 105 gm.
Sodium: 1726 mg.
Fiber: 40 gm.
Calcium: 864 mg.

DAY 2

Breakfast:

Flax Seed Apple Batter
    French Toast with Fresh Fruit,
    page 48

Breakfast Sausage, page 39

½ cup Fruited Yogurt**

Lunch:

Southwest Roasted Pepper and
    Avocado Salad, page 146

Mexican Pizza, page 265

Fresh Fruit Plate*

Dinner:

Cold Peach Soup, page 69

Macadamia-Crusted Mahi Mahi,
    page 194

½ cup Himalayan red rice,
    page ii (Basic Food Prep 318)

½ cup steamed baby carrots,
    page iv (Basic Food Prep 320)

Lime Pots De Créme, page 284

DAILY NUTRITION
INFORMATION

Calories: 1740
Carbohydrate: 251 gm.
Fat: 45 gm.
Protein: 96 gm.
Sodium: 1979 mg.
Fiber: 31 gm.
Calcium: 931 mg.

Note: Daily nutrition information assumes serving size indicated in each recipe.

* Fresh Fruit Plate equates to about 1 cup sliced fruit or berries or 100 to 120 calories.

** Fruited yogurt is made by mixing 1/2 cup nonfat plain yogurt with 1 tablespoon all-fruit preserves or 2 tablespoons sliced fresh fruit. It's a great source of calcium.

Sample Menus

DAY 3

Breakfast:

Spinach Eggs Benedict,
    page B-2

Fresh Fruit Plate*

Lunch:

New England
    Clam Chowder, page S-20

Fish Tacos, page F-24

Fresh Fruit Plate*

Dinner:

Spicy Crab Cakes, page A-4

Arugula Salad with
    Roasted Tomatoes,
    page SD-20

Vegetarian Jambalaya,
    page V-8

French Vanilla
    Cheesecake, page D-8

DAILY NUTRITION
INFORMATION

Calories: 1625
Carbohydrate: 221 gm.
Fat: 47 gm.
Protein: 91 gm.
Sodium: 2813 mg.
Fiber: 37 gm.
Calcium: 904 mg.

DAY 4

Breakfast:

Whole-wheat Buttermilk
    Pancakes with Fruit and
    Maple Syrup, page B-10

Breakfast Sausage,
    page B-5

½ cup Fruited Yogurt**

Lunch:

Spinach and Pear Salad,
    page SD-22

Turkey and Swiss
    Sandwich, page P-22

Chocolate Polenta Cake,
    page D-4

Dinner:

Spanish Onion Soup, page S-10

Poached Salmon with
    Orange Basil Relish, page F-6

½ cup roasted Yukon Gold potatoes,
    page iii (Basic Food Prep 101)

½ cup roasted or steamed asparagus,
    page iv (Basic Food Prep 101)

Fresh Fruit Plate*

DAILY NUTRITION
INFORMATION

Calories: 1755
Carbohydrate: 217 gm.
Fat: 52 gm.
Protein: 103 gm.
Sodium: 2335 mg.
Fiber: 27 gm.
Calcium: 1119 mg.

About the Recipes

■ Our first and most important advice is to read the recipe all the way through before you begin. Do you have the time to make the dish, and all the equipment and ingredients on hand? Nothing's more frustrating than suddenly realizing, halfway through, that you're missing a key ingredient.

■ Our ingredient lists provide the quantity of prepared vegetables and fruits in cups, tablespoons, etc. Occasionally, to make shopping easier, we follow with the whole vegetables you will need for this amount. Quantities of meats, poultry and fish are, of course, specified by weight.

■ When we call for a whole egg, we always mean a large egg.

■ To peel or not to peel is a matter of how a vegetable will eventually be used – and your personal judgement. When our chefs would peel, we say so.

■ When we advise you to lightly coat or spray a pan with oil, the oil is not listed in the ingredients and is not figured into the nutritional analysis. We do mean "lightly," so the amount of oil used should be negligible.

■ Although we simply specify olive oil in the recipes, our choice is extra virgin, cold-pressed olive oil – the purest, least processed and most flavorful kind.

■ We just say to use salt, but our chefs prefer sea salt – in fact, Mediterranean sea salt – for its clean, crisp flavor. Sea salt often has less sodium than regular salt.

NOTEWORTHY FEATURES

30 MIN – 30 minutes or less symbol. This appears on recipes that you can put on the table within a half-hour from the moment you start.

– Nutritional analysis under each recipe. A per-serving analysis of key nutrients is included for each recipe, just as it is on the menus in the Ranch dining rooms.

– Meal Suggestion. For the poultry, fish and meat recipes, we offer our chefs' vegetable and starch recommendations for a perfect balance of flavors and textures. Recipes in this book are capitalized.

– Gluten-free and dairy-free recipes. Lists on pp. 341–342 in the back identify recipes for people with special food needs. Dairy-free recipes contain no milk, cream, butter, cheese, ice cream, sour cream, cottage cheese, cream cheese or other milk-based ingredients. Gluten-free recipes contain no wheat, barley, rye, oats or spelt.

Breakfast, Breads & Smoothies

MORE GREAT TASTES

Yes, it is the most important meal of the day. Why? Just for starters, eating breakfast helps you maintain a healthy weight. Breakfast tells your body that you're not in the midst of a famine and it's going to have all the fuel it needs to run. You burn more calories throughout the day when you take the time to eat first thing.

One good breakfast strategy is to keep the makings of a smoothie on hand. Peel a banana, throw it into the blender with some frozen fruit, ice, fruit juice, yogurt, etc., hit the "puree" button, pour it into your commuter cup and you're gone. Kids love smoothies, and love making them, too.

You can boost the protein content of your on-the-go meal by adding a scoop of protein powder: Look for a basic protein powder made from whey, egg, soy or rice that contains at least 17 grams of protein per serving.

On days when you have more time, nothing says "weekend" like a big, home-cooked breakfast or brunch. French toast, waffles, sausage, eggs – now we're talking great food. Our versions of the standard components give them a healthy twist: Our Breakfast Sausage is low in fat and free from nitrates and nitrites, while our Flax Seed Apple Batter French Toast contains no animal products.

Lox and Cream Cheese Frittata

Ingredients

3 whole eggs
3 egg whites
Pinch salt
1 tablespoon chopped chives
½ cup 2% milk
1 teaspoon canola oil
½ cup Neufchâtel cheese
2 ounces diced lox

1. Preheat oven to 400°. In a large bowl, combine eggs, egg whites, salt, chives and milk and mix well.

2. Place canola oil in a nonstick, oven-proof sauté pan. Swirl to distribute the oil as you heat pan over medium for 30 seconds. Add egg mixture. Using a spatula, move egg mixture so that it cooks evenly for about 30 seconds, or until eggs begin to set. Remove from heat.

3. Spoon Neufchâtel cheese by table-spoons evenly over egg mixture. Top with diced lox.

4. Place pan in oven and bake until slightly browned all over, about 15 to 20 minutes.

5. Remove from oven and cut into 4 equal wedges.

MAKES 4 SERVINGS
EACH SERVING CONTAINS APPROXIMATELY:
160 calories | 4 gm. carbohydrate
10 gm. fat | 186 mg. cholesterol
14 gm. protein | 348 mg. sodium | Trace fiber

Cook's Note:

For a lighter taste, use whipped cream cheese.

Created by Barry Correia

8 cups washed fresh spinach leaves, well drained

1½ teaspoons Mrs. Dash® or other salt-free seasoning

4 whole-wheat English muffins

FOR THE HOLLANDAISE SAUCE:

3 egg yolks

1 teaspoon fresh lemon juice

Pinch cayenne pepper

Pinch salt

4 tablespoons melted butter

3 egg whites

Pinch cream of tartar

FOR THE POACHED EGGS:

1 tablespoon white vinegar

4 cups water

8 whole eggs

Created by Barry Correia

Spinach Eggs Benedict

Few kitchen ballets are as compelling as Eggs Benedict. This is one for the weekend, and preferably for an admiring stove-side audience – and perhaps a reliable helper or two. The results are more than worth the effort. If asparagus is in season, you can substitute it for the spinach.

1. Lightly coat a large sauté pan with canola oil and sauté spinach over medium-high heat until wilted. Season with Mrs. Dash®. Cover and set aside.

2. Split English muffins in half and toast.

3. Bring a large saucepan of water to boil.

4. In a medium stainless steel mixing bowl, combine egg yolk, lemon juice, cayenne pepper and salt. Place stainless steel bowl over (not touching) boiling water in pan and whisk egg mixture with a wire whip until thickened. Place mixture in blender container and blend at high speed for 5 seconds. Reduce to medium speed and slowly add butter.

5. In a medium bowl, beat egg whites and cream of tartar until mixture forms stiff peaks. Fold egg yolk mixture into egg white mixture until blended. Set aside.

6. Add vinegar to water in a medium saucepan, bring to a boil again and reduce to simmer. To poach eggs, gently crack each shell just above the surface and let the egg slip into the water. As eggs cook, use a spoon to corral whites around the yolks. Cook until whites are firm and opaque, but yolk is still soft. As you lift each egg from the pot with a slotted spoon, let it drip for a second or two.

7. For each serving, place an English muffin half on a plate and top with ¼ cup spinach, one poached egg and 2 tablespoons hollandaise sauce.

MAKES 8 SERVINGS
EACH SERVING CONTAINS APPROXIMATELY:
210 calories | 16 gm. carbohydrate
12 gm. fat | 254 mg. cholesterol
11 gm. protein | 400 mg. sodium | 3 gm. fiber

Cook's Note:

Spinach is a lovely but notoriously muddy vegetable. To be sure there's no grit in spinach, either buy pre-washed organic leaves in bags, or wash by swishing in a sink-full of cool water and then lifting into a colander before draining the sink. Very muddy spinach sometimes needs two immersions, but if you rinse the sink between dunkings, you can be confident that it's clean and crunch-free.

Spinach Eggs Benedict

2 large whole-wheat tortillas

1 tablespoon canola oil

1 medium tomato, diced

1/3 cup diced red onion

1/3 cup diced canned green chiles

1/4 teaspoon salt

6 whole eggs, beaten

1/2 cup shredded mozzarella cheese

Migas

The authentic version of migas involves frying tortilla strips in oil. We bake our tortillas until crisp and add them when the eggs are almost cooked, so that the crispiness of the tortillas remains.

1. Preheat oven to 400°. Lightly coat a baking sheet with canola oil.

2. Cut tortillas into 1-inch pieces. Spread evenly over baking sheet and bake until lightly brown and crisp, about 5 minutes. Be careful not to burn. Set aside.

3. Heat canola oil in a large sauté pan over medium heat. Sauté tomato, onion and green chiles until onion is translucent. Season with salt. Add eggs and lightly scramble with vegetables until eggs are half-cooked. Fold in tortillas and finish cooking eggs. Divide egg and tortilla mixture into 4 portions. Place each serving on plate and top with 2 tablespoons mozzarella cheese.

MAKES 4 SERVINGS
EACH SERVING CONTAINS APPROXIMATELY:
240 calories | 26 gm. carbohydrate
9 gm. fat | 226 mg. cholesterol
17 gm. protein | 264 mg. sodium | 3 gm. fiber

Nutrition Note:

Mozzarella cheese is naturally low in fat. If you use another type of cheese for this recipe, choose low-fat or reduced-fat varieties.

Created by Frank Cañez

Breakfast Sausage

This fresh, homemade sausage handily combines several of the best flavors of breakfast.

1. In a medium bowl, combine ground chicken with all other ingredients and mix well.

2. Make patties, using ⅓ cup meat mixture for each.

3. Place in a large sauté pan. Sauté over medium heat until cooked through, about 3 to 5 minutes on each side or until golden brown.

MAKES 6 SERVINGS
EACH SERVING CONTAINS APPROXIMATELY:
140 calories | 4 gm. carbohydrate
6 gm. fat | 44 mg. cholesterol
18 gm. protein | 440 mg. sodium | Trace fiber

Ingredients

1 pound ground chicken breast
⅓ cup peeled and diced red apple
2 tablespoons olive oil
2 tablespoons diced onions
1 tablespoon maple syrup
2 teaspoons dried sage
1 teaspoon salt
½ teaspoon black pepper
½ teaspoon minced fresh garlic

Cook's Note:

If you can't find ground chicken breast, place 1 pound skinless chicken breast, boned and defatted and cut into 1" cubes, in a food processor with all other ingredients. Pulse until the mixture is finely chopped.

Created by Scott Uehlein

FOR THE PÂTE BRISÉE:

1 cup all-purpose flour

1 teaspoon sugar

¼ teaspoon salt

3 tablespoons butter

4 tablespoons cold water

FOR THE FILLING:

½ cup diced shallots

1 cup shredded spinach

½ cup shredded arugula

1 cup sliced mushrooms

1 tablespoon olive oil

¾ cup 2% milk

¾ cup half and half

2 whole eggs

2 egg whites

¾ teaspoon salt

1 teaspoon black pepper

½ teaspoon ground or grated nutmeg

1 teaspoon minced lemon peel

⅓ cup shredded mozzarella cheese

¼ cup whole-wheat bread crumbs

¼ cup grated Parmesan cheese

Created by Touria Semingson

Springtime Quiche

1. Preheat oven to 350°.

2. In a small bowl, combine flour, sugar and salt. Mix well. Using a pastry cutter, blend in butter until mixture is crumbly and pea-sized. Add cold water, 1 tablespoon at a time and mix gently and briefly with a fork after each addition. Mixture should begin to bind together after the last tablespoon of water is added. If too dry, add 1 more tablespoon water. Gather mixture into a ball and let rest for 5 minutes in the refrigerator.

3. Lightly flour a flat surface and roll dough into a large circle, 12 to 14 inches in diameter. Gently press into a 9" pie pan and flute edges. Bake for 10 minutes or until crust is just beginning to turn golden brown.

4. In a large sauté pan, sauté shallots, spinach, arugula and mushrooms in olive oil over medium heat until tender, about 2 minutes. Set aside.

5. In a large bowl, combine milk, half and half and eggs and beat until well combined. Add salt, pepper, nutmeg, lemon peel, cheeses, bread crumbs and sautéed vegetables.

6. Pour into baked pie shell and bake for 30 minutes or until filling is set. A knife inserted in the center will come out clean. Let cool slightly and cut into 8 slices.

MAKES 8 SERVINGS
EACH SERVING CONTAINS APPROXIMATELY:
230 calories | 20 gm. carbohydrate
13 gm. fat | 97 mg. cholesterol
11 gm. protein | 509 mg. sodium | 2 gm. fiber

Cook's Note:

Serve quiche for breakfast, lunch or dinner, or as an appetizer. For appetizers, bake quiche in an 8" x 8" square pan. Cut into small squares.

Springtime Quiche

FOR THE PANCAKES:

1 cup whole-wheat flour

½ cup yellow cornmeal

½ teaspoon salt

½ teaspoon baking soda

4 egg whites

1 cup cooked brown rice

2 cups buttermilk

1 tablespoon canola oil

FOR THE CHERRY MAPLE SYRUP:

¾ cup maple syrup

½ cup chopped dried cherries

Brown Rice & Cornmeal Pancakes

1. In a medium bowl, combine flour, cornmeal, salt and baking soda.

2. In a medium stainless steel mixing bowl, beat egg whites with an electric mixer until they form soft peaks. Stir in cooked rice, buttermilk and oil and mix thoroughly. Fold egg mixture into dry ingredients, being careful not to over mix.

3. In a small saucepan, heat maple syrup to a slow boil. Add cherries and simmer until cherries are plump, about 5 minutes.

4. Lightly coat a griddle or large sauté pan with a small amount of canola oil. Place on burner over medium heat until hot. Spoon 3 tablespoons per pancake onto the griddle. Cook until the top of each pancake is covered with tiny bubbles and the bottom is brown. Turn and brown the other side. Repeat with remaining batter.

5. Serve 3 pancakes with 2 tablespoons of syrup.

MAKES 6 SERVINGS

EACH 3 PANCAKE SERVING CONTAINS APPROXIMATELY:

310 calories | 45 gm. carbohydrate

5 gm. fat | 4 mg. cholesterol

12 gm. protein | 515 mg. sodium | 6 gm. fiber

Cook's Note:

To see if your griddle is hot enough for pancakes, flick a few drops of water on it. If they dance on the surface, the griddle is ready.

Created by Dave Joyner

Sweet Potato Pancakes

Perfect for the morning after Thanksgiving – leftover sweet potatoes do fine.

1. In a medium bowl, combine cooled sweet potatoes, butter, egg white and milk. Beat until blended. Add flour, baking powder and salt. Stir until smooth.

2. Lightly coat a griddle or large sauté pan with canola oil. Place on burner over medium heat until hot. Pour ¼ cup of batter onto griddle. Cook until the top of each pancake is covered with tiny bubbles and the bottom is golden brown. Turn and brown the other side.

MAKES 4 SERVINGS
EACH 2 PANCAKE SERVING CONTAINS APPROXIMATELY:
190 calories | 36 gm. carbohydrate
3 gm. fat | 7 mg. cholesterol
6 gm. protein | 179 mg. sodium | 4 gm. fiber

Ingredients

1 cup cooled, mashed sweet potatoes

1½ teaspoons melted butter

1 medium egg white, lightly beaten

¾ cup 2% milk

¼ cup whole-wheat flour

½ cup all-purpose flour

½ teaspoon baking powder

¼ teaspoon salt

¾ cup bread flour

¾ cup whole-wheat flour

3 tablespoons sugar

¼ teaspoon salt

2½ teaspoons baking powder

1 teaspoon baking soda

1 tablespoon maple syrup

1 whole egg

1 cup buttermilk

¾ cup 2% milk

2½ tablespoons canola oil

1 cup berries or chopped fruit

Whole-Wheat Buttermilk Pancakes with Fruit

Blueberries and bananas work well in this recipe.

1. In a large bowl, combine all dry ingredients. In a medium bowl, combine remaining ingredients, except berries, and mix well. Add wet ingredients to dry ingredients and mix until smooth.

2. Lightly coat a griddle or large sauté pan with canola oil. Place on burner over medium heat until hot. Pour 3 tablespoons batter on griddle and sprinkle with 1 tablespoon berries. Cover berries with 1 additional tablespoon batter and cook until bubbles form. Turn and cook until bottom is brown.

MAKES 6 SERVINGS
EACH 3 PANCAKE SERVING CONTAINS APPROXIMATELY:
335 calories | 59 gm. carbohydrate
8 gm. fat | 48 mg. cholesterol
8 gm. protein | 572 mg. sodium | 4 gm. fiber

Cook's Note:

This recipe may also be used for waffles. For successful waffles, use a nonstick waffle iron and spray thoroughly with canola oil. Start with ¾ cup batter.

If you want to prepare this recipe the day before making the pancakes, simply mix all of the dry ingredients and all of the wet ingredients separately. Cover the wet ingredients and store overnight in the refrigerator. Mix them together just prior to using.

Created by
Jayne Shaulis/Touria Semingson

Whole-Wheat Buttermilk Pancakes with Fruit

FOR THE MUFFINS:

1 cup all-purpose flour

½ cup whole-wheat pastry flour

2 teaspoons baking powder

½ teaspoon salt

1 whole egg

⅓ cup 2% milk

⅓ cup nonfat plain yogurt

2 tablespoons canola oil

⅓ cup sugar

1 cup peeled and chopped
fresh fruit, or fresh berries

FOR THE TOPPING:

Pinch cinnamon

2 tablespoons sugar

Fruit Muffins

1. Preheat oven to 350°. Lightly coat cups of a 12-cup muffin tin with canola oil.

2. In large bowl, combine flours, baking powder and salt.

3. In a medium bowl, combine egg, milk, yogurt and oil. Add sugar and mix well.

4. Pour egg mixture into dry ingredients and stir until all ingredients are moistened. Add fruit and stir until just mixed.

5. Place ¼ cup batter in each muffin cup and bake for 15 to 20 minutes or until muffins are golden and toothpick inserted into center comes out clean.

6. To prepare topping, mix together cinnamon and sugar. Sprinkle ½ teaspoon over each warm muffin. Cool and remove from tins.

MAKES 12 MUFFINS
EACH MUFFIN CONTAINS APPROXIMATELY:
135 calories | 24 gm. carbohydrate
3 gm. fat | 15 mg. cholesterol
3 gm. protein | 87 mg. sodium | 2 gm. fiber

Cook's Note:

Whole-wheat pastry flour is finer textured than regular whole-wheat flour and results in a more tender muffin.

Try the fruit-and-seasoning combinations suggested for Fruit Crisp (see recipe) in these wholesome muffins.

Created by
Jayne Shaulis/Touria Semingson

Gluten-Free Fruit Muffins

1. Preheat oven to 375°. Lightly coat the cups of a 12-cup muffin tin with canola oil.

2. In a large bowl, combine flours, salt, baking powder and cinnamon and mix well and set aside.

3. In a blender container combine rice milk, applesauce, pureed prunes, fruit sweetener, vanilla extract, ground flax seed and banana and puree until mixed well, about 30 seconds. Pour into dry ingredients and mix well. Fold in blueberries until evenly distributed.

4. Fill muffin tin cups ⅔ full and bake for 20 to 25 minutes or until golden brown.

MAKES 12 MUFFINS

EACH MUFFIN CONTAINS APPROXIMATELY:
170 calories | 35 gm. carbohydrate
3 gm. fat | 0 mg. cholesterol
3 gm. protein | 142 mg. sodium | 3 gm. fiber

Ingredients

⅔ cup brown rice flour
⅔ cup white rice flour
¼ cup potato starch
3 tablespoons tapioca flour
½ teaspoon salt
2 teaspoons baking powder
½ teaspoon ground cinnamon
⅔ cup rice milk
⅓ cup unsweetened applesauce
3 tablespoons baby food pureed prunes
⅔ cup fruit sweetener (see note page B-17)
½ teaspoon pure vanilla extract
½ cup ground flax seed
½ medium banana
1½ cups fresh blueberries

Cook's Note:

You can use other fresh berries or chopped fruit. If fruit is very wet, it must be well drained. Nuts and seeds may also be added; however, the calories and fat grams will change.

Oriental markets carry a very fine white rice flour that performs well in this recipe.

Created by Richard Castonguay

FOR THE FRUIT COMPOTE:

¼ cup orange juice

¼ cup pineapple juice

¼ cup diced fresh pineapple

¼ cup peeled and diced apple

1 teaspoon grated orange peel

1 teaspoon chopped fresh mint leaves

FOR THE FRENCH TOAST:

1 tablespoon ground flax seeds

3 tablespoons apple butter

¾ cup soy milk

Pinch ground or grated nutmeg

Pinch ground cinnamon

Pinch salt

1 teaspoon canola oil

4 large slices multigrain bread (about ¾-inch thick)

Created by Frank Cañez

Flax Seed Apple Batter French Toast with Fruit Compote

1. In a medium saucepan, bring juices to a boil. Add pineapple, apple and orange peel and cook until fruit is soft. Add mint. Set aside.

2. Combine ground flax seeds, apple butter, soy milk, nutmeg, cinnamon and salt in a blender and mix until smooth. Transfer to shallow pan.

3. Heat a large sauté pan over medium and add canola oil. Dip both sides of bread into soy milk mixture and transfer to hot pan. Repeat for remaining slices. Cook until golden brown on both sides.

4. Reheat fruit compote and serve ¼ cup with 1 slice french toast.

MAKES 4 SERVINGS
EACH SERVING CONTAINS APPROXIMATELY:
205 calories | 37 gm. carbohydrate
5 gm. fat | 0 mg. cholesterol
6 gm. protein | 214 mg. sodium | 4 gm. fiber

Nutrition Note:

Flax seeds are a great source of heart healthy omega-3 fatty acids and are naturally high in fiber. Use the ground form and store in the refrigerator to preserve freshness or buy whole seeds and grind your own just before using.

Flax Seed Apple Batter French Toast with Fruit Compote

2¼ cups warm water (90° to 105°)

1 tablespoon brown sugar

2 tablespoons molasses

1 tablespoon (1 package) active dry yeast

1 cup ground flax seeds

2 tablespoons wheat bran

1½ teaspoons salt

½ cup nonfat dry milk

3 tablespoons vital wheat gluten

½ cup high gluten flour

3 cups whole-wheat flour

1 tablespoon canola oil

Whole-Wheat Flax Seed Bread

1. In large bowl, combine water, brown sugar, molasses, yeast, ground flax seed and wheat bran. Let sit for 15 minutes or until bubbly.

2. In a medium bowl, combine remaining ingredients except for oil. Mix well. Add half of dry mixture to yeast mixture and stir to combine. Stir in oil. Add remaining half of flour mixture and mix on low speed with an electric mixer dough hook or by hand until all ingredients are well combined, about 1 minute. Knead with dough hook or by hand for 5 minutes or until dough is smooth and elastic and lightens in color.

3. Place dough in a large greased bowl and cover with a towel. Let sit in a warm place until double in size. Punch down and divide in half. Form into 2 balls and gently roll to form cylinders the length of the bread pans.

4. Lightly coat two 8½" x 4 ½" x 2½" bread pans with canola oil. Place dough in pans, cover with a cloth and let rise until doubled in size again, about 1 to 1½ hours.

5. Preheat oven to 375°.

6. Bake for 15 minutes, reduce heat to 325° and bake for 30 minutes longer. Turn breads out of pans immediately and let cool on a rack. Cut each loaf into 16 slices, as needed.

MAKES 2 LOAVES
EACH SLICE CONTAINS APPROXIMATELY:
105 calories | 16 gm. carbohydrate
3 gm. fat | 0 mg. cholesterol
6 gm. protein | 122 mg. sodium | 3 gm. fiber

Cook's Note:

Vital wheat gluten gives the bread more structure – you can find it in the baking section of natural food markets.

This loaf freezes well. Double-wrapped and airtight, and it will keep up to 3 months.

Created by Jayne Shaulis

Rice Bread

1. In a small bowl, dissolve yeast in warm water. Add 2 tablespoons fruit sweetener and let sit until bubbly, about 5 minutes.

2. In a medium bowl combine water, 4 tablespoons fruit sweetener, rice vinegar, olive oil and ground flax seed. Mix well, about 1 minute, and set aside for 10 minutes.

3. In the bowl of an electric mixer, combine remaining ingredients. Add yeast and flax seed mixtures to dry ingredients and beat on high for three minutes using a paddle attachment. (If a paddle attachment is not available, use an electric mixer with beaters and mix on low speed.) The dough should be the consistency of thick cake batter. Cover bowl with a towel and let rise in a warm place, about 45 minutes.

4. Preheat oven to 400°. Lightly coat two 8½" x 4½" x 2½" bread pans with olive oil.

5. When dough has doubled in size, beat again for 2 minutes. Divide dough evenly between the two pans. Let rise in warm place, uncovered, until dough just reaches the rim of the pan. Carefully transfer to oven and bake for 15 minutes. Cover with foil and bake for 40 minutes more. Remove foil and bake for another 5 minutes. Total baking time should be 1 hour.

6. Remove loaves from pans and cool on a rack. Slice each loaf into 16 slices, as needed.

MAKES 2 LOAVES
EACH SLICE CONTAINS APPROXIMATELY:
165 calories | 29 gm. carbohydrate
5 gm. fat | 0 mg. cholesterol
3 gm. protein | 269 mg. sodium | 1 gm. fiber

Cook's Note:

Fruit sweeteners are syrups made from fruit juices. We use a sweetener made from pear, apple and grape juice. Look for these sweeteners in natural food stores.

Ingredients

- 2 tablespoons active dry yeast (2 packages)
- ½ cup warm water (90° to 105°)
- 6 tablespoons fruit sweetener
- 3¼ cups water
- 1 tablespoon rice vinegar
- ½ cup olive oil
- 1 cup ground flax seed
- 2½ cups brown rice flour
- 2½ cups white rice flour
- 1¼ cups potato starch
- 1¼ cups tapioca flour
- 1 tablespoon salt
- 1 tablespoon unflavored gelatin
- 1 teaspoon fruit pectin

Created by Richard Castonguay

5 tablespoons sugar

Pinch salt

2 tablespoons nonfat dry milk

3 tablespoons butter

1 whole egg

⅓ cup water

½ cup skim milk

½ cup yellow cornmeal

1¼ cups all-purpose flour

2 teaspoons baking powder

Corn Bread

1. Preheat oven to 325°. Lightly coat a 9" square baking pan with canola oil.

2. Combine sugar, salt, dry milk and butter in the bowl of an electric mixer. Mix on low speed until well blended.

3. Add egg, water and skim milk. Mix until smooth.

4. In a small bowl, combine cornmeal, flour and baking powder. Add to milk mixture and mix until just smooth.

5. Pour batter into greased baking pan. Bake for 35 minutes or until a knife comes out clean when inserted in the middle.

6. Remove from oven, turn out of pan and let cool on a rack.

7. Cut into 24 pieces.

MAKES 24 SERVINGS
EACH SERVING CONTAINS APPROXIMATELY:
55 calories | 9 gm. carbohydrate
1 gm. fat | 5 mg. cholesterol
1 gm. protein | 115 mg. sodium | 1 gm. fiber

Created by Touria Semingson

Banana Bread

Coffee and spices perk up a familiar quick bread.

1. Preheat oven to 350°. Lightly coat an 8½" x 4½" x 2½" bread pan with canola oil and dust with flour.

2. In a small bowl, combine bananas, coffee and orange peel and mix well. Set aside.

3. In a medium bowl, mix sugar, brown sugar and applesauce. Add egg and mix well. Add to banana mixture and mix until smooth.

4. In a small bowl, sift together dry ingredients. Add to banana mixture and mix until all ingredients are just combined. Fold in walnuts. Pour into prepared pan and bake for 1 hour or until toothpick inserted in center comes out clean. Remove from oven and let cool on a rack for 5 minutes. Remove from pan and slice when cooled completely.

MAKES 12 SERVINGS
EACH SERVING CONTAINS APPROXIMATELY:
135 calories | 27 gm. carbohydrate
2 gm. fat | 18 mg. cholesterol
3 gm. protein | 146 mg. sodium | 2 gm. fiber

Ingredients

3 small, very ripe bananas, mashed – about 1 cup

¼ cup brewed coffee

1 teaspoons grated orange peel

½ cup sugar

¼ cup brown sugar

¼ cup unsweetened applesauce

1 whole egg

1 cup whole-wheat flour

¼ cup bread flour

¾ teaspoon baking soda

¼ teaspoon salt

¼ teaspoon baking powder

½ teaspoon ground allspice

⅓ cup chopped walnuts

Cook's Note:

Feel free to substitute other nuts for the walnuts in this recipe.

Created by Maggie Flowers

2 small zucchini, finely grated, approximately 1 cup

¼ cup olive oil

¼ cup baby food prune puree

½ cup raisins

¼ cup unsweetened applesauce

1 cup whole-wheat flour

1 cup all-purpose flour

1 tablespoon baking soda

2 teaspoons baking powder

¼ teaspoon salt

2 teaspoons ground cinnamon

½ teaspoon ground cloves

½ teaspoon ground cardamom

⅓ cup ground flax seed

2 whole eggs

½ cup sugar

1 teaspoon pure vanilla extract

Zucchini Bread

1. Preheat oven to 350°. Lightly coat a 8 ½" x 4 ½" x 2 ½" bread pan with canola oil.

2. In a medium bowl, combine zucchini, olive oil, prune puree, raisins and applesauce. Mix gently. Set aside.

3. In a small bowl, combine all flours, baking soda and baking powder, salt, cinnamon, cloves and cardamom. Stir in flax seed and mix well.

4. In a medium bowl, beat eggs with sugar until fluffy. Stir in vanilla extract. Add zucchini mixture and mix well. Add dry ingredients and mix until just combined. Do not overmix.

5. Pour into bread pan and bake for 45 minutes, or until bread springs back when touched in the center. Cool completely on a rack. Remove from pan and cut into 18 slices.

MAKES 18 SLICES
EACH SLICE CONTAINS APPROXIMATELY:
150 calories | 24 gm. carbohydrate
5 gm. fat | 22 mg. cholesterol
4 gm. protein | 271 mg. sodium | 2 gm. fiber

Created by Touria Semingson

Breads

Ingredients

1 cup almond butter

1 cup brown rice syrup

¾ cup chopped walnuts

1 cup dried cherries

1⅔ cups puffed millet

1⅔ cups puffed rice

¼ cup pumpkin seeds

¾ cup sunflower seeds

⅓ cup quinoa flakes

Trail Bars

1. Lightly coat a 9" x 13" baking pan with canola oil.

2. In a large saucepan, heat almond butter with brown rice syrup over low heat until bubbles form. Quickly stir in remaining ingredients and mix well.

3. When cool enough to handle, press into baking pan. Cool completely. Cut into 40 bars. Wrap pan tightly.

MAKES 40 SERVINGS
EACH SERVING CONTAINS APPROXIMATELY:
130 calories | 15 gm. carbohydrate
7 gm. fat | 0 mg. cholesterol
3 gm. protein | 2 mg. sodium | 1 gm. fiber

Cook's Note:

Quinoa flakes can be found in natural food markets in the cooked cereal or baking section. Of all the grains, quinoa is one of the most balanced sources of protein and complex carbohydrates.

Created by Laurie Erickson

Granola

1. Preheat oven to 250°. Lightly coat a baking sheet with canola oil.

2. Combine oats, oat flour, brown sugar, cashews, cinnamon and salt in a medium bowl and mix well. Combine apple juice concentrate, pineapple juice concentrate, coconut milk, honey, vanilla extract, cashew butter and maple syrup in a small bowl and mix well. Add to dry mixture and mix until ingredients are moist.

3. Spread mixture onto baking sheet and bake for 45 minutes to 1 hour, stirring after 25 minutes to allow for even cooking. Remove from oven and cool. Break apart while still slightly warm and add dried fruit and remaining nuts.

MAKES 12 SERVINGS
EACH ¼ CUP SERVING CONTAINS APPROXIMATELY:
200 calories | 32 gm. carbohydrate
6 gm. fat | 0 mg. cholesterol
4 gm. protein | 36 mg. sodium | 3 gm. fiber

Ingredients

1½ cups rolled oats

½ cup oat flour

1 tablespoon brown sugar

3 tablespoons cashews, chopped in large pieces

Pinch ground cinnamon

Pinch salt

2 tablespoons apple juice concentrate

1 tablespoon pineapple juice concentrate

¼ cup light coconut milk

2 tablespoons honey

1 tablespoon pure vanilla extract

¾ teaspoon cashew butter

1 tablespoon maple syrup

¼ cup golden raisins

¼ cup dried cranberries

⅓ cup dried cherries

¼ cup dried blueberries

⅓ cup almonds, chopped in large pieces

⅓ cup hazelnuts, chopped in large pieces

Cook's Note:

Feel free to substitute almond or peanut butter for cashew butter.

You can make oat flour in the food processor from regular or quick rolled oats.

Created by Jayne Shaulis/Scott Uehlein

Ingredients

FOR THE FRUIT CRISP:

- 4 cups peeled and thinly sliced fresh fruit such as pears, peaches, apples, berries or cherries
- ½ cup all-purpose flour
- ¼ cup unsweetened apple juice concentrate, thawed

FOR THE TOPPING:

- ⅓ cup all-purpose flour
- ¾ cup rolled oats
- ¼ teaspoon baking soda
- Pinch salt
- ⅓ cup brown sugar
- 1 teaspoon grated orange peel
- 1 teaspoon orange juice concentrate, thawed
- ¾ teaspoon ground cinnamon
- Dash ground or grated nutmeg
- 4 tablespoons melted butter or canola oil

Created by
Jayne Shaulis/Touria Semingson

Fruit Crisp

A wholesome, delectably old-fashioned treat. This is a Ranch favorite, and we make it year-round with seasonal fruits.

1. Preheat oven to 300°. Lightly coat an 8" square baking pan with canola oil.

2. In a small bowl combine fruit, ½ cup all-purpose flour and apple juice concentrate and toss until fruit is well coated. Pour into prepared pan and set aside.

3. For the topping, combine remaining flour, oats, baking soda, salt, brown sugar, orange peel, juice and spices in another small bowl. Gradually stir in melted butter or oil and mix until mixture resembles coarse crumbs. Sprinkle evenly over fruit.

4. Bake 30 minutes or until topping is lightly browned.

MAKES 8 SERVINGS
EACH SERVING CONTAINS APPROXIMATELY:
200 calories | 35 gm. carbohydrate
6 gm. fat | 0 mg. cholesterol
3 gm. protein | 182 mg. sodium | 2 gm. fiber

Cook's Note:

Fruit combinations along with added spices and flavorings add variety to this recipe. Here are some of our favorites:

Cherry and pear with almond extract	Blueberry and fresh lemon juice	Mixed berries (raspberries, blueberries and blackberries) with orange extract
Peach and fresh ginger	Apple and fig	
Apricot and raspberry	Apple and cranberry	

ADDITIONAL TIPS FOR CREATING YOUR OWN CRISPS:
Cinnamon, nutmeg, ginger and cardamom are versatile spices that can be included in all combinations.

Apple juice concentrate adds sweetness without changing the balance of flavors.

Orange juice concentrate can be substituted for apple juice concentrate to vary the flavor; try grated orange or lemon peel in the topping.

Apricot Raspberry Smoothie

 30 MIN

Combine all ingredients in a blender and puree until smooth.

MAKES I SERVING
EACH SMOOTHIE CONTAINS APPROXIMATELY:
130 calories | 32 mg. carbohydrate
Trace fat | 0 mg. cholesterol
2 gm. protein | 7 mg. sodium | 5 gm. fiber

Ingredients

½ cup fresh or water-packed apricots, drained
¼ cup frozen raspberries
⅓ cup unsweetened apple juice
¼ medium banana
¼ cup crushed ice

Created by Rebecca Poage

Pineapple Coconut Smoothie

30 MIN

Combine all ingredients in a blender and puree until smooth.

MAKES I SERVING
EACH SMOOTHIE CONTAINS APPROXIMATELY:
210 calories | 43 gm carbohydrate
3 gm. fat | Trace cholesterol
5 gm. protein | 60 mg. sodium | 2 gm. fiber

Ingredients

¾ cup pineapple juice
½ medium banana
2 tablespoons low-fat coconut milk
⅓ cup nonfat plain yogurt

Created by Frank Cañez

Cherry and Blackberry Smoothie

30 MIN

Combine all ingredients in a blender and puree until smooth.

MAKES I SERVING
EACH SMOOTHIE CONTAINS APPROXIMATELY:
150 calories | 35 gm. carbohydrate
Trace fat | 0 mg. cholesterol
2 gm. protein | 5 mg. sodium | 5 gm. fiber

Ingredients

⅔ cup frozen sweet dark cherries
½ cup fresh or frozen blackberries
⅓ cup orange juice

Cook's Note:

If you use fresh fruit, you may want to add more orange juice.

Created by Rebecca Poage

Tropical Shake

30 MIN

Ingredients

½ cup diced fresh or frozen pineapple

¼ cup diced fresh or frozen mango

¼ cup apple juice

2 tablespoons low-fat coconut milk

2 tablespoons orange juice

Created by Scott Uehlein

Combine all ingredients in a blender and puree until smooth.

MAKES 1 SERVING
EACH SHAKE CONTAINS APPROXIMATELY:
160 calories | 34 gm. carbohydrate
4 gm. fat | 0 mg. cholesterol
1 gm. protein | 6 mg. sodium | 3 gm. fiber

Cook's Note:
You may substitute fresh or frozen papaya for mango.

Kiwi Banana Strawberry Shake

30 MIN

Ingredients

1 medium banana

¼ cup peeled and chopped kiwi

⅓ cup chopped fresh or frozen organic strawberries

¼ cup apple juice

¼ cup chopped ice

Created by Scott Uehlein

Combine all ingredients in a blender and puree until smooth.

MAKES 1 SERVING
EACH SHAKE CONTAINS APPROXIMATELY:
180 calories | 45 gm. carbohydrate
1 gm. fat | 0 mg. cholesterol
2 gm. protein | 6 mg. sodium | 6 gm. fiber

Peach Mango Raspberry Smoothie

30 MIN

Ingredients

¼ cup chopped fresh or frozen peaches

¼ cup chopped fresh or frozen mango

¼ cup fresh or frozen raspberries

¼ cup nonfat plain yogurt

½ cup apple juice

Created by Frank Cañez

Combine all ingredients in a blender and puree until smooth.

MAKES 1 SERVING
EACH SMOOTHIE CONTAINS APPROXIMATELY:
170 calories | 39 gm. carbohydrate
Trace fat | Trace cholesterol
4 gm. protein | 42 mg. sodium | 5 gm. fiber

Smoothies

Strawberry Banana Smoothie

Combine all ingredients in a blender and puree until smooth.

MAKES 1 SERVING
EACH SMOOTHIE CONTAINS APPROXIMATELY:
190 calories | 44 gm. carbohydrate
Trace fat | Trace cholesterol
5 gm. protein | 61 mg. sodium | 4 gm. fiber

Ingredients

¼ cup fresh or frozen organic strawberries

1 small banana

½ cup apple juice

⅓ cup nonfat plain yogurt

Created by Frank Cañez

Date Banana Yogurt Smoothie

Combine all ingredients in a blender and puree until smooth.

MAKES 1 SERVING
EACH SMOOTHIE CONTAINS APPROXIMATELY:
275 calories | 64 gm. carbohydrate
Trace fat | 2 mg. cholesterol
8 gm. protein | 103 mg. sodium | 6 gm. fiber

Ingredients

¼ cup chopped dates

½ medium banana

⅓ cup nonfat plain yogurt

⅓ cup skim milk

¼ cup crushed ice

Created by Frank Cañez

Kumquat Blueberry Shake

30 MIN

Combine all ingredients in a blender and puree until smooth.

MAKES 1 SERVING
EACH SHAKE CONTAINS APPROXIMATELY:
220 calories | 53 gm. carbohydrate
Trace fat | 0 mg. cholesterol
6 gm. protein | 96 mg. sodium | 4 gm. fiber

Ingredients

1 tablespoon grated kumquat peel

¾ cup nonfat blueberry yogurt

¼ cup fresh or frozen blueberries

½ banana

2 tablespoons diced fresh pineapple

2 tablespoons apple juice

Created by Scott Uehlein

Cook's Note:

Kumquats look like tiny, oval oranges. The rind or peel is sweet and the flesh inside is tart.

If you can't find kumquats, use finely grated orange peel instead.

Soups & Stocks

MORE GREAT TASTES

Soups are the original one-dish meal, and they're among the most satisfying and nourishing of foods.

Here are a few tips to help you get the most enjoyment out of your stockpot:

- Don't add salt, sugar or tomatoes to beans at the beginning of the cooking process: They won't get soft.

- You can use canned stocks instead of home-made. Select brands that are low in sodium and, preferably, organic.

- Many of our soups are pureed at some point. Let hot mixtures cool a bit before transferring them to the blender, don't fill the container more than two-thirds full, be sure to put the lid on and always start blending at low speed.

- Most soups can be frozen. Tips for freezing: Freeze in small portions – about 2 to 3 servings. A convenient way to freeze soup is to put a freezer-weight bag in a bowl, pour cooled soup in and then set the whole thing in the freezer. When the soup is solid, seal the bag, take it out of the bowl and return it to the freezer for up to 3 months.

Cream of Asparagus Soup

 30 MIN

Ingredients

1¼ pounds chopped asparagus
spears

2 teaspoons olive oil

2 cups diced leeks

3 cups Vegetable Stock (see
recipe)

1 cup soy milk

½ teaspoon salt

Pinch black pepper

1. In a large sauté pan, sauté asparagus in oil, over medium heat, until slightly browned. Stir in leeks and cook briefly, about 1 minute, until translucent.

2. Add vegetable stock and simmer until asparagus is soft, about 10 to 15 minutes. Remove from heat. Cool slightly.

3. Transfer soup to a blender and puree until smooth. Strain soup through a fine-mesh strainer into a saucepan. Discard any solids.

4. Stir in soy milk, salt and pepper and heat through.

MAKES 4 SERVINGS

EACH ¾ CUP SERVING CONTAINS APPROXIMATELY:
130 calories | 19 gm. carbohydrate
4 gm. fat | 0 mg. cholesterol
7 gm. protein | 124 mg. sodium | 5 gm. fiber

Cook's Note:

Substitute 2% milk for soy milk, if desired.

3 tablespoons diced onions

½ teaspoon olive oil

1 tablespoon maple syrup

½ teaspoon honey

1 tablespoon peeled and minced fresh ginger

1 cup peeled and chopped carrots, about 6 ounces

3 cups Vegetable Stock (see recipe)

¼ cup peeled and diced sweet potato

1 teaspoon salt

¼ teaspoon black pepper

¼ teaspoon dried thyme

¼ teaspoon minced fresh garlic

Carrot and Ginger Soup

Serve hot or cold.

1. In a medium saucepan, sauté onions in olive oil over low heat, until onions are translucent. Add maple syrup, honey and ginger. Cook until onions begin to turn golden brown, about 10 minutes.

2. Add the remaining ingredients, cover and simmer for 10 minutes or until carrots and sweet potato are soft.

3. Cool slightly, transfer mixture to a blender container and puree until smooth.

4. Pour soup into a saucepan and warm over medium heat before serving.

MAKES 4 SERVINGS
EACH ¾ CUP SERVING CONTAINS APPROXIMATELY:
60 calories | 13 gm. carbohydrate
Trace fat | 0 mg. cholesterol
1 gm. protein | 318 mg. sodium | 1 gm. fiber

Carrot and Ginger Soup

2 acorn squash, halved, strings and seeds discarded, about 2 pounds

1 tablespoon olive oil

1 cup peeled and chopped carrots

1 cup chopped celery

1 cup chopped onions

1/2 cup leeks, white and pale green part only, washed and chopped

3 cups Chicken Stock (see recipe)

1/2 teaspoon ground cinnamon

1/4 teaspoon ground or grated nutmeg

1/4 cup maple syrup

1/4 cup half and half

Acorn Squash Soup

1. Preheat oven to 450°. Lightly coat a shallow baking pan with olive oil.

2. Arrange squash in baking pan, cut side down, with 1 cup water. Bake covered with foil for 45 minutes or until soft.

3. Remove from pan and spoon out pulp. Transfer pulp to a blender container and puree until smooth.

4. Heat olive oil in a large saucepan. Add remaining vegetables and cook over medium-low heat until they begin to soften, about 5 minutes. Add stock, squash puree, cinnamon and nutmeg and simmer, covered for 40 minutes.

5. Stir in maple syrup and half and half. Simmer, uncovered for 5 minutes more.

MAKES 6 SERVINGS

EACH 3/4 CUP SERVING CONTAINS APPROXIMATELY:
115 calories | 21 gm. carbohydrate
3 gm. fat | 5 mg. cholesterol
2 gm. protein | 33 mg. sodium | 3 gm. fiber

Cook's Note:

For superior flavor, use freshly ground or grated nutmeg. You can buy whole nutmegs at natural food supermarkets, keep them for months in a jar and quickly grate a little whenever you need nutmeg.

To convert this to a vegan recipe, replace chicken stock with vegetable stock and half and half with soy milk.

Cold Peach Soup

A lovely hot-weather dish, this makes a delectably light and refreshing dessert.

1. In a large bowl, thaw peaches and retain juice.

2. Place peaches and juice, preserves, lemon juice, cinnamon and yogurt in a blender container and puree until smooth.

3. Pour into a pitcher and cover. Chill for 2 to 4 hours.

MAKES 4 SERVINGS
EACH ¾ CUP SERVING CONTAINS APPROXIMATELY:
145 calories | 35 gm. carbohydrate
Trace fat | 0 mg. cholesterol
4 gm. protein | 51 mg. sodium | 3 gm. fiber

Ingredients

1 pound frozen or fresh peaches, peeled and sliced

½ cup all-fruit apricot preserves

1 tablespoon fresh lemon juice

1 teaspoon cinnamon

1 cup nonfat plain yogurt

Cook's Note:

You can substitute apricots or nectarines for the peaches. To peel these fruits easily, put them in a bowl, cover with boiling water and let sit for a minute. Pour off hot water and let cool. The skins will slide right off. (This also works with tomatoes.)

¾ cup diced onions

¾ cup diced leeks

½ cup chopped scallions

2 tablespoons olive oil

1 teaspoon minced fresh garlic

2½ cups frozen green peas, thawed

5 cups Vegetable Stock (see recipe)

½ cup chopped chives

1 teaspoon chopped fresh mint

½ teaspoon salt

¼ teaspoon black pepper

Pea Soup

The use of mint in this recipe is a fine example of how an unexpected herb or spice can add freshness and complexity of flavor to a familiar dish. Spearmint is easy to grow, makes a delightful garnish and combines happily with a galaxy of other ingredients. In short, mint makes life better – use it freely and see.

1. In a large saucepan, sauté onions, leeks and scallions in olive oil until onions are translucent. Add garlic and peas and sauté for 2 minutes. Add vegetable stock and bring to a boil. Reduce heat and simmer for 30 minutes.

2. Add chives and mint and cook 5 minutes. Remove from heat and transfer to a blender container and puree until smooth. Add salt and pepper.

MAKES 8 SERVINGS
EACH ¾ CUP SERVING CONTAINS APPROXIMATELY:
80 calories | 13 gm. carbohydrate
2 gm. fat | 0 mg. cholesterol
4 gm. protein | 161 mg. sodium | 4 gm. fiber

Created by Scott Uehlein

Pea Soup

2   cloves elephant garlic, peeled

1   cup chopped button
    mushrooms

¼   cup peeled and chopped
    parsnips

½   cup chopped leeks, white part
    only

1½ tablespoons olive oil

⅓   cup white wine

3   cups Chicken Stock (see
    recipe)

1½ tablespoons heavy cream

1   teaspoon salt (optional)

½   teaspoon black pepper

2   tablespoons thinly sliced
    scallions

Elephant Garlic Soup

1. Preheat oven to 350°. Place elephant
   garlic on a small baking pan and
   cover with aluminum foil. Roast for
   15 minutes or until soft.

2. In a large saucepan, sauté mushrooms,
   parsnips and leeks in olive oil over
   medium heat until translucent. Add
   wine and cook until almost dry.

3. Add chicken stock and bring to a
   boil. Reduce heat and simmer
   until vegetables are tender, about
   15 minutes. Add garlic, transfer to
   blender container and puree. Stir
   in heavy cream, salt and pepper.
   Stir in scallions.

MAKES 6 SERVINGS
EACH ¾ CUP SERVING CONTAINS APPROXIMATELY:
90 calories | 8 gm. carbohydrate
5 gm. fat | 5 mg. cholesterol
2 gm. protein | 379 mg. sodium | 1 gm. fiber

Cook's Note:

Elephant garlic is not a true
garlic (as a member of the
leek family, it's actually a
cousin), but is so named for
its mild garlic flavor and
because it looks like a wildly
outsized garlic. One clove is
about the size of a whole
bulb or "head" of true garlic.

Cauliflower and Kale Soup

Ingredients

½ cup diced onions

1 tablespoon minced fresh garlic

1½ teaspoons olive oil

½ cup white wine

1 head cauliflower, washed, cored and chopped

3½ cups Vegetable Stock (see recipe)

1 cup thinly sliced kale, lightly packed

1 teaspoon chopped fresh tarragon

1 teaspoon salt

½ teaspoon pepper

1. In a large saucepan, sauté onions and garlic in olive oil until onions are translucent.

2. Add wine and reduce by half. Add cauliflower and vegetable stock. Bring to a boil, reduce heat to medium-low and cook until cauliflower is soft, about 20 minutes. Add kale and simmer for 5 minutes. Remove from heat and cool. Transfer to a blender container and puree until smooth.

3. Return soup to saucepan and bring to a simmer. Add tarragon, salt and pepper.

MAKES 8 SERVINGS
EACH ¼ CUP SERVING CONTAINS APPROXIMATELY.
50 calories | 8 gm. carbohydrate
1 gm. fat | 0 mg. cholesterol
2 gm. protein | 338 mg. sodium | 2 gm. fiber

Cook's Note:

Kale, a member of the cabbage family, is one of the most nutrient-rich vegetables around. Choose small, deep-colored, springy bunches, store in the coldest part of the refrigerator and use within a day or two – elderly kale loses nutrients and has a strong, unpleasant flavor. Throw the fibrous center stalk away.

Created by Justin Morrow

1 tablespoon olive oil
1½ cups sliced yellow onion
½ cup sliced red onion
¼ cup chopped shallots
1¼ teaspoons minced fresh garlic
¼ cup white wine
2½ teaspoons all-purpose flour
½ teaspoon dried thyme
1¾ cups Chicken Stock
(see recipe)
1¾ cups Vegetable Stock
(see recipe)
½ teaspoon salt
1 teaspoon black pepper
1½ teaspoons butter
2 corn tortillas, thinly sliced
Dash paprika

Spanish Onion Soup

1. Heat oil in a large saucepan over medium-low and add onions. Cook until onions are browned and caramelized, about 10 minutes. Add shallots and garlic and cook until shallots are translucent. Add wine and simmer until wine is reduced by half. Add flour and thyme and simmer briefly.

2. Add chicken stock and vegetable stock and bring to a boil. Reduce heat and simmer for 30 to 40 minutes. Add salt, pepper and butter.

3. Preheat oven to 375°. Lightly coat a sheet pan with canola oil. Place tortilla strips on sheet pan and sprinkle with paprika. Bake in oven until crisp, about 5 minutes.

4. Serve ¾ cup soup and garnish with tortilla strips.

MAKES 8 SERVINGS
EACH ¾ CUP SERVING CONTAINS APPROXIMATELY:
80 calories | 12 gm. carbohydrate
2 gm. fat | 6 mg. cholesterol
3 gm. protein | 213 mg. sodium | 2 gm. fiber

Cook's Note:

If your onions aren't very sweet, add a pinch of sugar.

Created by Guillermo Ortiz

Spanish Onion Soup

¼ cup chopped onions

¼ cup chopped shallots

1 teaspoon minced fresh garlic

1½ teaspoons canola oil

1½ tablespoons chopped pistachios

½ medium potato, peeled and diced

½ teaspoon curry powder

Pinch ground turmeric

2 cups Vegetable Stock (see recipe)

2 cups chopped broccoli

½ teaspoon salt

Pinch white pepper

1 teaspoon minced pistachios (for garnish)

Cream of Broccoli Soup

1. In a medium saucepan, sauté onions, shallots and garlic in oil until translucent. Add pistachios. Add potato, curry powder and turmeric and cook over low heat for 5 minutes.

2. Deglaze pan with vegetable stock and bring to a boil. Add broccoli and simmer over medium heat for 15 minutes. Cool slightly.

3. Transfer mixture to a blender container and puree until smooth. Add salt and pepper.

4. Garnish each bowl with ¼ teaspoon minced pistachios.

MAKES 4 SERVINGS
EACH ¾ CUP SERVING CONTAINS APPROXIMATELY:
100 calories | 13 gm. carbohydrate
4 gm. fat | 0 mg. cholesterol
5 gm. protein | 266 mg. sodium | 3 gm. fiber

Nutrition Note:

Turmeric, a pungent, intensely orange powder from a plant related to ginger, is the main ingredient in the curry mixtures so essential to Indian cooking. (It's also used to make American mustard yellow.) It's valuable as a flavoring, a coloring and as a medicine – turmeric is an anti-inflammatory and aids digestion.

Creamy Turnip Soup

 30 MIN

Ingredients

1½ teaspoons butter
1 cup diced leeks
½ cup diced shallots
3 cups peeled and diced turnips
5 cups Chicken Stock (see recipe)
¾ cup whole milk
¾ teaspoon salt
½ teaspoon black pepper

1. Melt butter in a large saucepan on low heat. Add leeks and shallots and sauté for approximately 4 to 5 minutes. Add turnips and sauté for 2 additional minutes.

2. Add chicken stock and bring to a simmer, cover the pan and cook until the turnips are tender, approximately 15 minutes.

3. Remove saucepan from heat, cool slightly and transfer ingredients to a blender container, two cups at a time and puree until smooth.

4. Transfer ingredients back into the saucepan and return to a simmer. Stir in milk, salt and pepper.

MAKES 6 SERVINGS
EACH ¼ CUP SERVING CONTAINS APPROXIMATELY:
90 calories | 16 gm. carbohydrate
2 gm. fat | 7 mg. cholesterol
3 gm. protein | 335 mg. sodium | 3 gm. fiber

Cook's Note:

Turnips get a bad rap for being bitter. If, when you peel them, you pare them down past the faint dark line inside the peel, you'll never be disappointed in their flavor. Throw out any turnips that are woody or stringy inside.

2 teaspoons butter

⅓ cup diced onions

1⅓ cups peeled and diced carrots

⅓ cup diced celery

1 cup quartered red bliss potatoes

¾ teaspoon paprika

½ teaspoon thyme

Pinch black pepper

⅓ cup white wine

1½ teaspoons tomato paste

1 cup diced tomatoes

1 cup clam juice

¼ cup all-purpose flour

2 cups 2% milk

6 ounces chopped shrimp, peeled and deveined

4 ounces chopped scallops

1 tablespoon sherry wine

1 tablespoon chopped fresh parsley

Shellfish Chowder

1. In a large saucepan, melt butter over medium heat.

2. Add onions, carrots and celery. Cover and cook for 15 minutes, stirring occasionally.

3. Add potatoes, paprika, thyme, pepper, white wine, tomato paste, diced tomatoes and clam juice. Bring to a boil. Cover again and reduce heat. Simmer for 20 to 25 minutes or until potatoes are tender.

4. Place flour in a medium bowl. Slowly add milk, blending with a wire whip. Slowly stream milk mixture into chowder. Continue cooking over medium heat until thickened, about 5 minutes, stirring constantly to prevent scorching.

5. Stir in shrimp, scallops, sherry and parsley. Bring to a simmer – not a boil – and cook for approximately 2 to 3 minutes, or until seafood is cooked through.

MAKES 8 SERVINGS
EACH ¾ CUP SERVING CONTAINS APPROXIMATELY:
130 calories | 16 gm. carbohydrate
3 gm. fat | 44 mg. cholesterol
11 gm. protein | 167 mg. sodium | 2 gm. fiber

Created by Linda Stewart

Shellfish Chowder

1 cup dry black beans

FOR THE RED ONION SALSA:

1 tablespoon minced fresh garlic

2 teaspoons chopped fresh cilantro

¼ cup diced red onion

2 teaspoons red wine vinegar

FOR THE SOUP:

1 medium red bell pepper, seeded and quartered

½ cup diced onions

½ cup peeled and diced carrots

¼ cup diced celery

1 tablespoon minced fresh garlic

2 quarts Vegetable Stock (see recipe)

¼ teaspoon ground cumin

½ teaspoon salt

1 teaspoon chopped fresh oregano

2 teaspoons chopped fresh parsley

Created by James Boyer

Black Bean Soup with Red Onion Salsa

Black or turtle beans are favorites throughout Latin America, where they're often served with rice. They make a fabulous soup, and most supermarkets stock them.

1. In a large saucepan, cover black beans with at least 3 cups of water and soak overnight.

2. In a small bowl combine salsa ingredients. Mix well, cover and refrigerate.

3. Preheat oven to 400°. Lightly coat a baking sheet with olive oil. Lay peppers skin side up on baking sheet and roast in oven 10 to 15 minutes or until skins have blackened. Remove from oven and rinse under cold water to peel away skins. Dice.

4. Rinse beans in a colander with fresh water and drain.

5. Lightly spray a large saucepan with olive oil. Sauté onions, carrots, celery, diced roasted red pepper and garlic. Add vegetable stock and black beans. Bring to a boil, reduce heat and simmer for 1 hour.

6. When beans are tender, pour into blender container or food processor and puree. Add cumin, salt, oregano and parsley. Garnish with 1 tablespoon salsa.

MAKES 6 SERVINGS
EACH ¾ CUP SERVING CONTAINS APPROXIMATELY:
140 calories | 27 gm. carbohydrate
Trace fat | 0 mg. cholesterol
8 gm. protein | 182 mg. sodium | 5 gm. fiber

Cook's Note:

If you prefer to use canned beans, substitute 2 to 1 for dry beans. One 15-ounce can contains about 2 cups of cooked beans. Canned beans will already be tender, of course, but you don't want to reduce cooking time – the flavors still need time to "marry."

Navy Bean and Leek Soup

1. Drain and rinse beans. If using canned, drain and rinse beans, as well.

2. In a large saucepan, sauté leeks, onions and garlic in olive oil until the onions are translucent. Add beans and vegetable stock, thyme and bay leaf and simmer for 30 minutes.

3. Remove thyme sprigs and bay leaf. Stir in salt and pepper. Garnish each bowl with a teaspoon of chives.

MAKES 8 SERVINGS,
EACH ¾ CUP SERVING CONTAINS APPROXIMATELY:
125 calories | 24 gm. carbohydrate
Trace fat | 0 mg. cholesterol
7 gm. protein | 72 mg. sodium | 4 gm. fiber

Ingredients

3 cups cooked navy beans
1 cup julienne leeks
½ cup minced red onion
2 cloves fresh garlic, minced
2 teaspoons olive oil
5 cups Vegetable Stock (see recipe)
2 sprigs thyme
1 bay leaf
1 teaspoon salt
¼ teaspoon black pepper
3 tablespoons chopped chives

Cook's Note:

If you're using dry navy beans, start with 1½ cups.

Ingredients

- 1 cup diced onions
- 2 teaspoons curry powder
- ¾ teaspoon cayenne pepper or to taste
- ¾ teaspoon Old Bay® seasoning (optional)
- 1 tablespoon olive oil
- 1 tablespoon minced fresh garlic
- 3½ cups Chicken Stock (see recipe)
- 1¼ cups diced turkey breast
- 2 Roma tomatoes, peeled and diced
- 2 tablespoons chopped fresh cilantro
- 2 tablespoons currants
- ¼ cup low-fat coconut milk
- 1 teaspoon salt (optional)

Curried Turkey Soup

1. In a large saucepan, sauté onions and seasonings in olive oil until onions are translucent. Add garlic and sauté briefly, about 30 seconds. Add ½ cup chicken stock and turkey and bring to a simmer. Cook for 3 to 5 minutes or until turkey is cooked through. Cool.

2. Place mixture in food processor and pulse briefly until turkey is slightly shredded. Return to saucepan and add remaining stock. Cook for 1 hour over low heat. Add tomatoes, cilantro, currants and coconut milk. Bring to a boil and simmer 1 minute. Season with salt.

MAKES 6 SERVINGS

EACH ¾ CUP SERVING CONTAINS APPROXIMATELY:
125 calories | 11 gm. carbohydrate
5 gm. fat | 23 mg. cholesterol
10 gm. protein | 339 mg. sodium | 2 gm. fiber

Cook's Note:

A perfect use for diced leftover turkey – cooked meat works just as well.

Created by James Boyer

Curried Turkey Soup

Ingredients

- 2 tablespoons olive oil
- 2 cups diced onions
- ¾ teaspoon dried thyme
- 1 cup diced celery
- 6 cups clam juice
- 2 small potatoes, peeled and diced
- ½ teaspoon black pepper
- 2 tablespoons cornstarch
- 2 tablespoons water
- 1 cup chopped clams
- ½ cup heavy cream
- ½ teaspoon salt (optional)

New England Clam Chowder

 30 MIN

As easy and fast as it is good, chowder is even better reheated after a night in the refrigerator.

1. Heat olive oil in a large saucepan. Add onions, thyme and celery. Sauté on low heat until onions are translucent.

2. Add clam juice and bring to a boil. Add potatoes and pepper. Reduce heat and simmer 15 to 20 minutes.

3. Combine cornstarch with water to make a thin paste. Add to potato-clam juice mixture and cook 1 minute. Add clams and cook 1 more minute. Remove from heat and stir in heavy cream. Season with salt.

MAKES 12 SERVINGS
EACH ¾ CUP SERVING CONTAINS APPROXIMATELY:
105 calories | 10 gm. carbohydrate
5 gm. fat | 33 mg. cholesterol
6 gm. protein | 332 mg. sodium | 1 gm. fiber

Cook's Note:

The saltiness of clam juice varies, so you'll want to taste this soup before salting.

Created by Justin Morrow

Albóndigas

Albóndigas is Spanish for "meatball." The soup with the same name is traditionally made with beef broth and ground beef. We have created a healthier version using chicken stock and ground turkey.

1. Preheat oven to 325°. Lightly coat a baking sheet with olive oil.

2. Combine all ingredients for meatballs in a large bowl. Mix well. Portion about 2 tablespoons, about 1 ounce, and form into a ball with wet hands. Place on baking sheet and bake for 12 to 15 minutes until cooked through. Do not overcook.

3. Heat chicken stock in a large saucepan. Add pureed salsa and simmer for 20 to 30 minutes. Add vegetables, cilantro, salt and meatballs. Cook until vegetables are tender, about 10 minutes.

4. Serve 1 cup soup with 2 meatballs per serving.

MAKES 10 SERVINGS
EACH 1 CUP SERVING CONTAINS APPROXIMATELY:
135 calories | 13 gm. carbohydrate
1 gm. fat | 63 mg. cholesterol
17 gm. protein | 319 mg. sodium | 2 gm. fiber

Ingredients

FOR THE MEATBALLS:

1 pound ground turkey

½ cup cooked white rice

2 tablespoons chopped fresh mint

1 tablespoon minced fresh garlic

⅓ cup breadcrumbs

1 whole egg

¼ cup minced yellow onion

½ teaspoon salt

FOR THE SOUP:

1½ quarts Chicken Stock (see recipe)

¾ cup Pico de Gallo, pureed (see recipe)

1 cup peeled and diced potatoes

1 cup peeled and diced carrots

1 cup diced celery

⅓ cup chopped fresh cilantro

1 teaspoon salt

Created by Frank Cañez

FOR THE SOUP:

2 cups Chicken Stock (see recipe)

1½ cups Vegetable Stock (see recipe)

1 skinless chicken breast half, boned and defatted

Pinch red chili flakes (optional)

½ teaspoon Mrs. Dash® or other non-salt seasoning

½ teaspoon minced fresh garlic

½ teaspoon salt

Pinch black pepper

1 small carrot, chopped

½ cup cauliflower florets

½ cup broccoli florets

½ cup sliced mushrooms

½ cup diced celery

FOR THE DUMPLINGS:

½ cup all-purpose flour

2 tablespoons water

1 whole egg

FOR THE GARNISH:

1 tablespoon chopped fresh parsley

1 tablespoon chopped scallions

1 tablespoon chopped chives

Created by Bob Vykulil

Bohemian Chicken Soup with Dumplings

Every cuisine, and nearly every region, has its dumpling. These delicate and fun-to-make miniatures, similar to German spaetzle, are from the Czech Republic.

1. In a large saucepan, bring chicken stock and vegetable stock to a boil. Dice chicken breast and add to stock. Reduce heat to medium-low and simmer until chicken is cooked, about 10 minutes.

2. Add pepper flakes, Mrs. Dash®, garlic, salt and pepper. Continue to cook for 5 minutes. Add vegetables and simmer until tender, about 15 to 20 minutes.

3. In a small bowl, combine flour, water and egg. Mix until a very soft dough forms. Dough should be slightly thicker than pancake batter. Position a colander with large holes over a saucepan and press dough through holes into simmering soup. Cook at least 5 more minutes, stirring occasionally to create tiny dumplings Garnish with parsley, scallions and chives.

MAKES 6 SERVINGS
EACH ¾ CUP SERVING CONTAINS APPROXIMATELY:
70 calories | 9 gm. carbohydrate
1 gm. fat | 34 mg. cholesterol
7 gm. protein | 208 mg. sodium | 1 gm. fiber

Cook's Note:

The size of the holes in your colander determines the size of your dumplings.

Bohemian Chicken Soup with Dumplings

2 to 4 pounds chicken parts, except the liver

3 quarts cold water

2 carrots, peeled and chopped

2 celery ribs without leaves, chopped

1 large onion, cut into quarters

4 fresh garlic cloves, cut into halves

1 bay leaf

12 whole peppercorns

Chicken Stock

1. Place chicken bones and parts in a shallow baking dish and bake in a 350° oven until golden brown, approximately 35 to 45 minutes. Drain off and discard excess fat.

2. Place browned bones and parts in a large pot, add cold water and bring to a boil. Add remaining ingredients. Reduce heat and simmer **uncovered** for 2 to 2½ hours, skimming off any foam that comes to the surface. **Do not stir, and do not allow to boil again.** Let stock cool slightly for easier handling.

3. Line a kitchen strainer or colander with a double thickness of cheesecloth and set over a large bowl or pot in the kitchen sink. Strain stock through cheesecloth, **pouring slowly and steadily** so as not to stir up sediments. Discard the dregs. Cool.

4. Refrigerate until fat is solid on the surface. Remove fat.

5. Refrigerate or store in small portions in the freezer.

MAKES 8 SERVINGS
EACH 1 CUP SERVING CONTAINS APPROXIMATELY:
10 calories | 3 gm. carbohydrate
Trace fat | 1 mg. cholesterol
Trace protein | 48 mg. sodium | Trace fiber

Beef or Veal Stock

1. Preheat oven to 425°. Place bones in a roasting pan and roast in oven for 30 minutes. **Do not allow to burn.** Add carrots, onions and celery and roast for 15 to 20 minutes longer, or until browned but not burned.

2. Bring water to a boil in a large stock pot. Add bones and vegetables and bring to a boil. Reduce heat and simmer **uncovered** for 1 hour, skimming off any foam that comes to the surface. Add sachet and simmer for another hour. **Do not stir, and do not allow to boil again.** Let stock cool slightly for easier handling.

3. Line a kitchen strainer or colander with a double thickness of cheesecloth and set over a large bowl or pot in the kitchen sink. Strain stock through cheesecloth, **pouring slowly and steadily** so as not to stir up sediments. Discard the dregs. Cool.

4. Refrigerate or store in the freezer in small portions.

MAKES 4 SERVINGS
EACH 1 CUP CONTAINING APPROXIMATELY:
15 calories | 3 gm. carbohydrate
Trace fat | 2 mg. cholesterol
Trace protein | 21 mg. sodium | Trace fiber

Ingredients

5 pounds beef or veal bones
1 large carrot, peeled and chopped
1 large onion, chopped
1 celery stalk, chopped
1 gallon water
1 sachet of parsley, bay leaf and black peppercorns

Cook's Note:

Beef stock has a stronger, richer flavor than stock made from veal bones.

Ingredients

2 medium leeks, washed and chopped

4 onions, chopped

6 carrots, peeled and chopped

1 small bunch celery, chopped

1 small bunch parsley, chopped

3 bay leaves

2 teaspoons dried leaf marjoram

½ teaspoon dried thyme

1½ gallons cold water

Vegetable Stock

1. Combine all ingredients in a large stock pot, and bring to a boil. Reduce heat and simmer **uncovered** for 1 hour, skimming off any foam that comes to the surface. **Do not stir, and do not allow to boil again.** Let stock cool slightly for easier handling.

2. Line a kitchen strainer or colander with a double thickness of cheesecloth and set over a large bowl or pot in the kitchen sink. Strain stock through cheesecloth, **pouring slowly and steadily** so as not to stir up sediments. Discard the dregs. Cool.

3. Refrigerate or store in the freezer in small portions.

MAKES 16 SERVINGS
EACH 1 CUP CONTAINING APPROXIMATELY:
10 calories | 3 gm. carbohydrate
Trace fat | 0 mg. cholesterol
Trace protein | 21 mg. sodium | Trace fiber

Cook's Note:

For sweeter stock, add bell peppers, zucchini and yellow squash. Do not add cabbage, lettuce or eggplant – they cause bitterness.

Consommé

1. In a large stock pot, combine all ingredients cold, then slowly bring to a boil over medium heat. When simmering, reduce heat to medium-low. **Do not stir, and do not allow to boil again.** A "raft" of floating meat, egg whites, spices, and vegetable bits will form on the surface in 30 minutes to an hour.

2. Continue to gently simmer for 1 hour longer until consommé is clear. Let stock cool slightly for easier handling.

3. Line a kitchen strainer or colander with a double thickness of cheesecloth and set over a large bowl or pot in the kitchen sink. Gently clear an area of raft debris. Pour consommé through this area, through the cheesecloth, pouring slowly and steadily so as not to stir up sediments. Most of the raft should remain in the pot. Discard the dregs. Cool.

4. Refrigerate until fat is solid on the surface. Remove fat.

5. Refrigerate or store in the freezer in small portions.

6. The strained consommé may be reheated before serving.

MAKES 8 SERVINGS
EACH ¾ CUP SERVING CONTAINS APPROXIMATELY:
15 calories | 7 gm. carbohydrate
Trace fat | 0 mg. cholesterol
2 gm. protein | 75 mg. sodium | Trace fiber

- 2 quarts Chicken Stock (see recipe)
- 4 ounces ground raw chicken
- ½ cup chopped onions
- ⅓ cup peeled and chopped carrots
- ⅓ cup chopped celery
- 2 tablespoons chopped tomatoes
- 1 sachet of peppercorns, thyme, parsley and bay leaf
- 1 teaspoon fresh lemon juice
- 4 egg whites
- Pinch salt

⅓ cup minced shallots

½ teaspoon sesame oil

3 tablespoons miso paste

1 quart Vegetable Stock (see recipe)

3 tablespoons sliced scallions (optional)

¼ cup diced firm organic tofu (optional)

Miso Soup

1. In a medium sauce pan, over medium heat, sauté shallots in sesame oil until translucent.

2. Add miso paste and stir well. Add vegetable stock and bring to a simmer. Reduce heat to low and simmer 10 to 15 minutes.

3. Garnish with tofu and scallions, if desired.

MAKES 4 SERVINGS
EACH ¾ CUP SERVING CONTAINS APPROXIMATELY:
45 calories | 6 gm. carbohydrate
1 gm. fat | 0 mg. cholesterol
Trace protein | 322 mg. sodium | Trace fiber

Cook's Note:

Miso paste loses nutritional value when allowed to boil; always simmer miso over low heat.

Appetizers & Accompaniments

MORE GREAT TASTES

LAUGHTER IS BRIGHTEST,

IN THE PLACE WHERE THE FOOD IS

– Irish Proverb

This is our catch-all section for everything that surrounds the entrée: Appetizers (to have before), side-dishes (to go with) and condiments (to enhance). All are delicious enough to establish your reputation as a cook while providing great nutrition. In fact, this chapter reveals the central principle of Canyon Ranch cuisine: Every element of every meal adds nutritional value – and the result is food that's not only better for you, it tastes better, too.

Take any of our three fresh salsas, for example. Spoon them over steak or a baked potato, add them to scrambled eggs or beans, scoop them up with baked corn chips – nothing but great flavor and brilliant color, right? Wrong. Each zippy bite is also packed with disease-fighting vitamins and nutrients. You'll never find a tastier way to eat your vegetables.

Chicken Satay with Apple Curry Sauce

1. Slice chicken into 1-inch strips. In a large glass bowl, combine apple juice, curry powder, sweet garlic paste, seasoned rice vinegar and red chili flakes. Add chicken and marinate covered in refrigerator for 8 hours or overnight.

2. Lightly coat a small sauté pan with canola oil and sauté onions until translucent. Add apple juice and bring to a boil. Add applesauce and reduce heat to medium. Stirring constantly, add curry powder and mint. Cook until mixture begins to thicken, about 10 minutes. Cool slightly.

3. In a small bowl, combine all ingredients for red pepper relish.

4. Preheat grill or broiler. Soak 8" wooden skewers in water for 10 to 15 minutes. Skewer marinated chicken strips and grill or broil until cooked through, about 2 to 3 minutes on each side.

5. Serve 1½ ounces chicken with 2 tablespoons red pepper relish and 1 tablespoon apple curry sauce.

MAKES 8 APPETIZER SERVINGS
EACH SERVING CONTAINS APPROXIMATELY:
115 calories | 5 gm. carbohydrate
2 gm. fat | 48 mg. cholesterol
18 gm. protein | 62 mg. sodium | Trace fiber

Cook's Note:

To serve as an entrée, double the serving size and add accompaniments.

Ingredients

- 4 skinless chicken breast halves, boned and defatted
- ⅓ cup apple juice
- ¾ teaspoon curry powder
- ¾ teaspoon Sweet Garlic Paste (see recipe)
- 1 tablespoon seasoned rice vinegar
- Pinch red chili flakes

FOR THE APPLE CURRY SAUCE:

- 2 teaspoons minced red onion
- ½ cup apple juice
- 2 tablespoons unsweetened applesauce
- 1 teaspoon curry powder
- ½ teaspoon fresh mint

FOR THE RED PEPPER RELISH:

- ½ cup diced red bell pepper
- 2 teaspoons chopped fresh cilantro
- 1 teaspoon chopped fresh mint
- 3 tablespoons peeled and finely diced carrots
- 3 tablespoons diced pineapple
- 2 tablespoons chopped scallions

Created by Frank Cañez

FOR THE WASABI SOY SAUCE:

¾ cup water

2 tablespoons peeled and sliced fresh ginger

1 tablespoon minced fresh garlic

1 tablespoon minced lemon grass

1 tablespoon low-sodium tamari sauce

1 tablespoon seasoned rice vinegar

1 tablespoon fresh lemon juice

1 teaspoon wasabi powder (Japanese horseradish)

FOR THE CHICKEN:

1 4-ounce sliced skinless chicken breast, boned and defatted

1 tablespoon peeled and minced fresh ginger

1 tablespoon Sweet Garlic Paste (see recipe)

2 tablespoons chopped scallions

1 egg white

½ teaspoon black pepper

Pinch salt (optional)

2 teaspoons olive oil

24 wonton skins

Chicken Gyoza with Wasabi Soy Sauce

"Pot-stickers" make terrific party food.

1. In a small saucepan, bring water to a boil and add ginger and garlic. Reduce heat and simmer for 15 to 20 minutes. Add lemon grass and tamari. Cook until liquid measures about ⅓ cup. Strain and cool.

2. Pour cooled liquid into a small bowl and add seasoned rice vinegar, lemon juice and wasabi powder. Whisk until wasabi is completely dissolved.

3. In a food processor, chop chicken breast at high speed, until finely chopped. Add minced ginger, garlic paste and scallions. Add egg white, pepper and oil and mix well.

4. Arrange wonton skins on a flat surface. Place 1 heaping teaspoon of chicken mixture in center of each wonton. Brush edges with water. Fold in half and lightly pinch edges together to ensure a good seal. (May be frozen at this time for future use.)

5. Lightly spray a large sauté pan with canola oil. Arrange stuffed wontons in a single layer in sauté pan. Sear bottoms only to a golden brown color. Transfer to steamer and steam for 3 to 5 minutes. Serve 6 chicken gyoza with 2 tablespoons wasabi soy sauce.

MAKES 4 SERVINGS
EACH SERVING CONTAINS APPROXIMATELY:
185 calories | 26 gm. carbohydrate
4 gm. fat | 44 mg. cholesterol
11 gm. protein | 367 mg. sodium | Trace fiber

Cook's Note:

If your wonton skins are square, cut them into circles with a biscuit cutter.

Created by Frank Cañez

Chicken Gyoza with Wasabi Soy Sauce

Spicy Crab Cakes with Tomato Herb Coulis

FOR THE TOMATO HERB COULIS:

4 tablespoons minced fresh garlic

1 tablespoon olive oil

6 Roma tomatoes, about 8 ounces, chopped

1 cup diced red onion

2 tablespoons chopped fresh basil

2 tablespoons chopped fresh thyme

2 tablespoons chopped fresh parsley

1 teaspoon salt

1 teaspoon pepper

FOR THE CRAB CAKES:

1 pound lump crabmeat

½ cup minced shallots

3 tablespoons chopped fresh parsley

⅓ cup Sweet Garlic Paste (see recipe)

2 tablespoons diced scallions

¼ cup minced red bell pepper

½ teaspoon cayenne pepper

1 egg plus 1 egg white, beaten

2 tablespoons low-sodium tamari sauce

1 cup bread crumbs

1 teaspoon canola oil

1. In a medium saucepan, sauté garlic with olive oil over medium heat for about 30 seconds. Add tomatoes, bring to a simmer and cook until tomatoes begin to break apart, about 5 minutes. Add remaining ingredients, reduce heat to low and simmer for 20 minutes. Remove from heat, allow to cool slightly and transfer to a blender container. Puree until smooth.

2. Combine all ingredients for crab cakes in a large bowl and mix well. Form ¼-cup portions into 2-inch patties.

3. Heat a sauté pan until hot over medium heat. Lightly coat with canola oil. Place crab cakes in pan and cook until golden brown, about 3 to 5 minutes. Turn and continue to cook to golden brown.

4. Serve 3 crab cakes with 2 tablespoons coulis.

MAKES 8 APPETIZER SERVINGS
EACH SERVING CONTAINS APPROXIMATELY:
160 calories | 15 gm. carbohydrate
5 gm. fat | 102 mg. cholesterol
18 gm. protein | 376 mg. sodium | 3 gm. fiber

Cook's Note:

To serve as an entrée, double the serving size and add accompaniments.

Created by Frank Cañez

Spicy Crab Cakes with Tomato Herb Coulis

½ cup julienne onion

1 teaspoon olive oil

2½ cups sliced red cabbage

1 small bay leaf

Pinch ground cloves

Pinch salt

¼ teaspoon black pepper

¼ teaspoon caraway seed

2 tablespoons red wine

1 tablespoon red wine vinegar

2 tablespoons water

½ cup julienne red apple

1 tablespoon honey

Braised Red Cabbage

A classic accompaniment for game and other meats – but good all on its own.

1. In a medium sauté pan, sauté onions in olive oil over medium heat until golden. Add the red cabbage. Cover and cook for about 2 minutes.

2. Add bay leaf, cloves, salt, pepper, caraway seed, red wine, red wine vinegar and water. Mix well.

3. Cook over medium-low heat, covered, for 25 minutes.

4. Remove bay leaf and add sliced apple and honey. Mix well and cook for an additional 10 minutes.

MAKES 4 SERVINGS
EACH ¾ CUP SERVING CONTAINS APPROXIMATELY:
55 calories | 10 gm. carbohydrate
trace fat | 0 mg. cholesterol
1 gm. protein | 71 mg. sodium | 4 gm. fiber

Ginger-Spiced Carrots

 30 MIN

Ingredients

1 tablespoon olive oil

1½ cups finely diced onion

2 tablespoons fresh minced ginger

1 teaspoon ground cumin

4 tablespoons sugar

4 cups peeled sliced carrots

2 cups Vegetable Stock (see recipe)

Pinch salt

2 tablespoons fresh chopped dill

1. In a large sauté pan, cook onions in olive oil over medium heat until onions begin to caramelize, about 5 to 10 minutes.

2. Add remaining ingredients except for salt and dill. Simmer until carrots are tender and most of liquid has evaporated.

3. Remove from heat and let cool for 5 minutes. Add salt and dill and mix well.

MAKES 6 SERVINGS

EACH ½ CUP SERVING CONTAINS APPROXIMATELY:
110 calories | 26 gm. carbohydrate
Trace fat | 0 mg. cholesterol
2 gm. protein | 95 mg. sodium | 2 gm. fiber

Sautéed Mustard Greens

Turnip greens, spinach and kale are also terrific prepared this way.

Ingredients

½ cup thinly sliced onions

1 tablespoon olive oil

1 pound mustard greens, washed and torn into large pieces, stems removed

¼ teaspoon salt

¼ teaspoon pepper

1. In a large sauté pan, cook onions in olive oil over medium heat until golden brown and caramelized, about 5 to 10 minutes.

2. Add mustard greens and briefly cook until wilted. Season with salt and pepper.

MAKES 4 SERVINGS
EACH ½ CUP SERVING CONTAINS APPROXIMATELY:
60 calories | 4 gm. carbohydrate
4 gm. fat | 0 mg. cholesterol
2 gm. protein| 161 mg. sodium | 2 gm. fiber

Nutrition Note:

Mustard greens, a popular side-dish since Roman times, are a superb source of vitamins A and C, thiamine and riboflavin, and a good source of calcium. Look for crisp, young, intensely green leaves.

Roasted Beets

Ingredients

4 medium beets, about 3 ounces each

1. Preheat oven to 350°.

2. Wash beets thoroughly. Wrap individually in foil, place on sheet pan and roast for 2 hours.

3. Unwrap, cool, peel and slice.

MAKES 4 SERVINGS
EACH SERVING CONTAINS APPROXIMATELY:
35 calories | 8 gm. carbohydrate
Trace fat | 0 mg. cholesterol
1 gm. protein | 64 mg. sodium | 2 gm. fiber

Cook's Note:

Beets range in appearance from red to white and can be found year round. Small to medium beets are generally more tender than large ones. Look for firmness and smooth skins.

Mongolian BBQ Sauce

30 MIN

This can be used as a marinade for fish, chicken or even tofu. It also works well as a stir-fry sauce.

1. In a large saucepan, combine ½ cup tamari sauce, sugar, rice vinegar, sesame oil, sake and ⅓ cup water and bring to a boil. Add ketchup, coriander, ground ginger and red chili flakes. Simmer for 10 minutes. Remove from heat.

2. In a small bowl, combine leeks, garlic, fresh ginger, 2 tablespoons water and 2 tablespoons tamari sauce. Add to cooked mixture and stir until combined. Pour into a jar.

3. Cover and store in refrigerator up to 2 weeks.

MAKES 16 SERVINGS
EACH 2 TABLESPOON SERVING CONTAINS
APPROXIMATELY:
35 calories | 4 gm. carbohydrate
Trace fat | 0 mg. cholesterol
Trace protein | 288 mg. sodium | Trace fiber

Ingredients

½ cup low-sodium tamari sauce
2 tablespoons sugar
¼ cup rice vinegar
1 tablespoon sesame oil
½ cup sake
⅓ cup water
⅓ cup ketchup
Pinch ground coriander
Pinch ground ginger
¼ teaspoon red chili flakes
¼ cup minced leeks
2 teaspoons minced fresh garlic
2 teaspoons peeled and minced fresh ginger
2 tablespoons water
2 tablespoons low-sodium tamari sauce

Cook's Note:

This is one of our most requested recipes at Canyon Ranch, Tucson. Head chef Scott Uehlein recalls that "A very kind chef in Japan gave me this recipe, reminding me that 'There are no secrets in cooking.'"

Adapted by Scott Uehlein

2 teaspoons canola oil

¾ cup snow peas

¼ cup sliced red onion

¼ cup thinly sliced red and
    yellow bell peppers, mixed

¼ cup stemmed and sliced
    shiitake mushrooms

½ cup broccoli florets

1 cup shredded Napa cabbage

½ cup Mongolian BBQ Sauce
    (see recipe)

Japanese Stir-fry Vegetables

1. Heat wok until hot and add oil. Add
   vegetables and cook for 30 seconds to
   1 minute until vegetables are crisp,
   but tender.

2. Add BBQ sauce and toss to coat
   vegetables.

MAKES 4 SERVINGS,
EACH ½ CUP SERVING CONTAINS APPROXIMATELY:
65 calories | 8 gm. carbohydrate
2 gm. fat | 0 mg. cholesterol
2 gm. protein | 275 mg. sodium | 2 gm. fiber

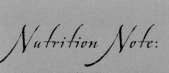

Nutrition Note:

The range of brilliant colors
of vegetables in this recipe
is a sure sign that every serving is packed with a wide
variety of beneficial phytonutrients. The compounds
that give fruits and vegetables their color also fight
disease and slow aging.

Japanese Stir-fry Vegetables

Caramelized Onions

Great over salads, with meats and on sandwiches.

In a large sauté pan, cook onions in olive oil over medium heat for 5 minutes. When onions begin to brown, reduce heat to low and cook 5 more minutes or until sugars are released. Season with salt and pepper.

MAKES 8 SERVINGS
EACH ¼ CUP SERVING CONTAINS APPROXIMATELY:
50 calories | 5 gm. carbohydrate
3 gm. fat | 0 mg. cholesterol
Trace protein | 64 mg. sodium | 1 gm. fiber

Ingredients

2 large yellow or red onions, thinly sliced

2 tablespoons olive oil

¼ teaspoon salt (optional)

Pinch pepper (optional)

Celery Root and Potato Puree

1. In a large stock pot, bring vegetable stock to a boil.

2. Reduce heat and add celery root and potatoes. Cover and simmer until vegetables are tender, about 10 to 15 minutes.

3. Transfer vegetables and stock to a blender container and add milk and salt. Puree until smooth.

MAKES 8 SERVINGS
EACH ½ CUP SERVING CONTAINS APPROXIMATELY:
95 calories | 21 gm. carbohydrate
Trace fat | 0 mg. cholesterol
3 gm. protein | 65 mg. sodium | 2 gm. fiber

Ingredients

4 cups Vegetable Stock (see recipe)

2 cups diced celery root (about 1 pound)

4 cups diced, peeled potatoes (about 1½ pounds)

½ cup 2% milk

½ teaspoon salt

White Corn Polenta

 30 MIN

1. In a large saucepan, sauté onion in butter over medium heat until translucent. Add corn and sauté briefly, about 30 seconds. Add milk and bring to a boil. Using a wire whip, lightly whisk in polenta, salt, pepper and sugar. Cook until thickened, about 3 minutes.

2. Add cheese and stir until melted. Serve ⅓ cup.

MAKES 4 SERVINGS
EACH ⅓ CUP SERVING CONTAINS APPROXIMATELY:
100 calories | 12 gm. carbohydrate
4 gm. fat | 13 mg. cholesterol
4 gm. protein | 179 mg. sodium | Trace fiber

Ingredients

3 tablespoons finely minced onion

1 tablespoon butter

3 tablespoons white corn, cut from the cob

1¼ cups 2% milk

¼ cup quick-cooking dry polenta

¼ teaspoon salt

Pinch pepper

1¼ teaspoons sugar

2 tablespoons freshly grated Parmesan cheese

Created by Justin Morrow

Glazed Baby Carrots

30 MIN

1. Place carrots in a vegetable steamer or in a large saucepan of rapidly boiling water and cook for 5 to 7 minutes, until tender. Drain.

2. In a medium saucepan, combine remaining ingredients and simmer until sauce reduces to ¼ cup. Add carrots and carefully coat with sauce.

MAKES 4 SERVINGS
EACH ½ CUP SERVING CONTAINS APPROXIMATELY:
80 calories | 17 gm. carbohydrate
Trace fat | 0 mg. cholesterol
Trace protein | 147 mg. sodium | Trace fiber

Ingredients

12 ounces baby carrots, peeled, stem intact

3 tablespoons frozen concentrated orange juice

3 tablespoons water

¼ teaspoon cinnamon

¼ teaspoon ground cumin

2 tablespoons honey

2 teaspoons maple syrup

¼ teaspoon salt

¼ teaspoon pepper

Created by Scott Uehlein

Ingredients

- 2 teaspoons olive oil
- ¾ cup chopped onion
- ¾ cup peeled and chopped carrot
- ¾ cup chopped celery
- 1 teaspoon minced fresh garlic
- 2 cups cooked cannellini beans
- ½ teaspoon each chopped fresh sage, rosemary and oregano
- 2 teaspoons grated lemon peel
- 1 cup Chicken Stock (see recipe)
- ¾ teaspoon salt
- ¼ teaspoon black pepper
- 2 tablespoons freshly grated Parmesan cheese

Tuscan Beans

Florence is the capitol of Tuscany, and people there are so fond of beans that citizens of other regions call them I Mangiafagioli – "bean-eaters." The Florentines, a self-confident lot for centuries, choose to take it as a compliment. This dish is typical of the uncomplicated, profoundly good cooking of central Italy.

1. In a large sauté pan, sauté onions, carrots and celery in olive oil for 2 minutes. Add garlic, and sauté for 1 minute more.

2. Lightly stir in beans, herbs, lemon peel, chicken stock, salt and pepper. Let simmer until stock is reduced by half, about 10 to 15 minutes.

3. Finish by stirring in Parmesan cheese.

MAKES 6 SERVINGS
EACH ½ CUP SERVING CONTAINS APPROXIMATELY:
125 calories | 20 gm. carbohydrate
2 gm. fat | 3 mg. cholesterol
8 gm. protein | 225 mg. sodium | 5 gm. fiber

Created by Steve Matson

Tuscan Beans (foreground) and Calabacitas

- 1 small zucchini, sliced ½-inch thick in half-moon shapes
- 1 small yellow squash, sliced ½-inch in half-moon shapes
- 1 Roma tomato, diced
- 1 small onion, diced
- ½ cup frozen corn
- 1 teaspoon chopped fresh oregano
- 1 teaspoon black pepper
- ½ teaspoon salt

Calabacitas

A delicious Southwestern treatment of the delectable, small squash of summer. The name (call-ah-bah-SEE-tas) means "little squash" or "little pumpkins" – and equates with the English term "summer squash."

1. Preheat oven to 425°. Lightly coat a sheet pan with canola oil.

2. Lay zucchini and yellow squash on sheet pan and roast in oven for 5 to 10 minutes or until golden brown.

3. Lightly coat a sauté pan with canola oil. Add roasted squash, tomatoes, onions and corn. Sauté over medium heat until just soft, about 5 minutes. Add oregano and pepper and salt. Serve immediately.

MAKES 4 SERVINGS
EACH ½ CUP SERVING CONTAINS APPROXIMATELY:
30 calories | 7 gm. carbohydrate
Trace fat | 0 mg. cholesterol
1 gm. protein | 205 mg. sodium | 2 gm. fiber

Created by Frank Cañez

Charro Beans

Charro means "cowboy" in Spanish, and this dish uses the typical seasonings and the favorite bean of the Southwest and of northern Mexico, the pinto.

1. In a medium saucepan, sauté onions and garlic in olive oil over medium heat until onions are translucent.

2. Add remaining ingredients and bring to a boil. Reduce heat and simmer for 15 minutes or until liquid has reduced by three-quarters.

MAKES 6 SERVINGS

EACH ⅓ CUP SERVING CONTAINS APPROXIMATELY:
70 calories | 14 gm. carbohydrate
Trace fat | 0 mg. cholesterol
4 gm. protein | 295 mg. sodium | 2 gm. fiber

Cook's Note:

Pinto beans take 3 to 4 hours to cook after soaking, so canned beans are a real time-saver in this recipe. Just drain and rinse.

Ingredients

⅓ cup diced onions

½ teaspoon minced fresh garlic

½ teaspoon olive oil

1¼ cups cooked pinto beans

1 cup Vegetable Stock (see recipe)

Pinch ground oregano

3 tablespoons canned green chiles, diced

⅓ cup diced tomato

1 tablespoon chopped fresh cilantro

¾ teaspoon salt

¼ teaspoon black pepper

Barbecue Beans

1. In a large bowl soak beans overnight, covering with at least 3 inches of water. Drain and rinse.

2. Place beans and stock in a large saucepan and cook until tender, about 2 hours.

3. Lightly coat a saucepan pan with a small amount of canola oil. Sauté onions until translucent. Add beans, tomatoes, molasses, salt and tomato juice to onions. Cook over low to medium heat until half of the liquid is absorbed.

4. Stir in tomato paste, brown sugar and pepper, and continue cooking until mixture has thickened.

MAKES 8 SERVINGS

EACH ½ CUP SERVINGS CONTAINS APPROXIMATELY:
135 calories | 29 gm. carbohydrate
Trace fat | 0 mg. cholesterol
6 gm. protein | 190 mg. sodium | 4 gm. fiber

Ingredients

2 cups kidney beans

4½ cups Vegetable Stock (see recipe)

¾ cup diced onion

½ cup diced tomatoes

½ tablespoon blackstrap molasses

½ teaspoon salt

1½ cups low-sodium tomato juice

½ cup tomato paste

½ cup brown sugar

½ teaspoon black pepper

Ingredients

2 cups water
1 cup Pico de Gallo (see recipe)
½ teaspoon salt
1 cup basmati rice

Mexican Rice

1. In a large saucepan, combine water, Pico de Gallo and salt. Bring to a boil and add rice.

2. Stir, cover and simmer for 20 minutes. Remove from heat and let sit for 5 minutes.

3. Fluff with a fork.

MAKES 6 SERVINGS
EACH ½ CUP SERVING CONTAINS APPROXIMATELY:
130 calories | 29 gm. carbohydrate
Trace fat | 0 mg. cholesterol
3 gm. protein | 257 mg. sodium | 1 gm. fiber

Created by Steve Matson

Ingredients

½ cup basmati rice
2 tablespoons diced onions
1½ teaspoons olive oil
1 cup Vegetable Stock or Chicken Stock (see recipes)
¼ teaspoon saffron
¼ teaspoon salt
2 tablespoons diced tomato
2 teaspoons chopped fresh parsley

Saffron Rice

1. In a medium saucepan, sauté rice and onions in olive oil until rice is lightly toasted. Add stock, saffron and salt and bring to a boil. Cover, reduce heat and simmer 20 minutes or until water is absorbed and rice is fluffy.

2. Fold in tomatoes and parsley.

MAKES 4 SERVINGS
EACH ⅓ CUP SERVING CONTAINS APPROXIMATELY:
105 calories | 21 gm. carbohydrate
2 gm. fat | 0 mg. cholesterol
2 gm. protein | 151 mg. sodium | Trace fiber

Cook's Note:

Saffron, the dried stigmas from a small crocus, is easily the world's most expensive spice. It must be harvested by hand, flower by flower, and it takes 14,000 stigmas to make an ounce. Its intense yellow-red color and pungent flavor go a long way, and are worth every penny in rice dishes, baked goods and paella. Buy whole saffron in tiny quantities; powdered saffron doesn't keep well and is often adulterated.

Mashed Sweet Potatoes

 30 MIN

1. Place sweet potatoes in 6 cups boiling water. Cook for 10 minutes or until potatoes are tender. Turn off heat and drain. Place saucepan back on burner for 30 seconds more to dry potatoes.

2. Add remaining ingredients and mash with a potato masher until all ingredients are mixed well. Potatoes will be slightly lumpy.

MAKES 8 SERVINGS
EACH ½ CUP SERVING CONTAINS APPROXIMATELY:
110 calories | 25 gm. carbohydrate
Trace fat | 0 mg. cholesterol
2 gm. protein | 250 mg. sodium | 4 mg. fiber

Cook's Note:

Mashed Sweet Potatoes can be made ahead of time and frozen in a sealed container. Warm in a microwave.

Ingredients

2 medium sweet potatoes, washed, peeled and cut in 1-inch cubes

2 tablespoons frozen concentrated orange juice

½ teaspoon salt

¼ teaspoon black pepper

¼ teaspoon ground cinnamon

½ teaspoon pure vanilla extract

Created by Scot Uehlein

Chipotle Whipped Potatoes

 30 MIN

1. Place potatoes in 6 cups boiling water. Cook for 10 minutes or until potatoes are tender. Turn off heat and drain. Place saucepan back on burner for 30 seconds more to dry potatoes.

2. Add remaining ingredients and mash with a potato masher until all ingredients are mixed well. Potatoes will be slightly lumpy.

MAKES 4 SERVINGS
EACH ½ CUP SERVING CONTAINS APPROXIMATELY:
110 calories | 25 gm. carbohydrate
Trace fat | 1 mg. cholesterol
3 gm. protein | 175 mg. sodium | 3 gm. fiber

Ingredients

3 medium russet potatoes, peeled and chopped

¼ cup scallions, chopped

2 tablespoons frozen corn, thawed

3 tablespoons chopped Roma tomatoes

2 tablespoons Sweet Garlic Paste (see recipe)

2 tablespoons nonfat milk

1 teaspoon chipotle chili powder

½ teaspoon salt

½ teaspoon black pepper

Created by Frank Cañez

3 medium russet potatoes, thinly sliced (about 3 cups)

¾ cup thinly sliced onions

1 cup 2% milk

1 tablespoon all-purpose flour

½ teaspoon salt

¼ teaspoon freshly ground black pepper

1½ teaspoons melted butter

Scalloped Potatoes

1. Preheat oven to 425°. Lightly coat a 9" square baking dish with a small amount of canola oil.

2. Place half of the potatoes in the dish and cover with onions. Top with remaining sliced potatoes.

3. In a blender, combine milk, flour, salt, pepper and butter. Blend until well mixed. Pour over the potatoes evenly.

4. Bake, covered, for 45 minutes. Remove cover and bake an additional 15 minutes or until potatoes reach desired crispness on top. Cut into 6 equal servings.

MAKES 6 SERVINGS

EACH SERVING CONTAINS APPROXIMATELY:
90 calories | 15 gm. carbohydrate
3 gm. fat | 7 mg. cholesterol
3 gm. protein | 241 mg. sodium | 2 gm. fiber

2 medium sweet potatoes or yams, about 12 ounces each

¼ teaspoon salt

Pinch pepper

Baked Sweet Potato

1. Preheat oven to 375°.

2. Slice ends off sweet potatoes and cut in half. Lightly season cut side with salt and pepper.

3. Double-wrap each sweet potato half in foil and place in oven. Bake for 40 to 45 minutes or until soft.

MAKES 4 SERVINGS

EACH SERVING CONTAINS APPROXIMATELY:
170 calories | 40 gm. carbohydrate
Trace fat | 0 mg. cholesterol
3 gm. protein | 114 mg. sodium | 5 gm. fiber

Cook's Note:

Look for small to medium sweet potatoes with smooth, unbruised skins. Sweet potatoes and yams are similar in many ways and are often confused with one another, but they actually come from different plant families. True yams are not widely marketed and are seldom grown in the United States.

Scalloped Potatoes

Ingredients

- 3 medium yukon gold or red bliss potatoes, scrubbed and chopped
- 2 tablespoons chopped fresh cilantro
- 3 tablespoons nonfat sour cream
- 1 tablespoon fresh lime juice
- 1 tablespoon butter
- ¼ teaspoon chipotle chili powder, or ½ teaspoon minced chipotle pepper
- ½ teaspoon salt
- Pinch black pepper

Created by Jim Massey

Lime Cilantro Mashed Potatoes   30 MIN

1. Place potatoes in 6 cups boiling water. Cook for 10 to 15 minutes or until potatoes are tender. Turn off heat and drain water. Place saucepan back on burner for 30 seconds to dry potatoes.

2. Add remaining ingredients and mash with a potato masher until all ingredients are mixed well. Potatoes will be slightly lumpy.

MAKES 4 SERVINGS
EACH ½ CUP SERVING CONTAINS APPROXIMATELY:
105 calories | 17 gm. carbohydrate
3 gm. fat | 9 mg. cholesterol
2 gm. protein | 171 mg. sodium | 2 gm. fiber

Cook's Note:

For smoother potatoes, peel before cooking and beat with an electric mixer on a low setting until smooth. We prefer to leave the skins on for heartier flavor, more interesting texture and better nutrition.

Ingredients

- 3 medium russet potatoes, peeled and chopped
- 3 tablespoons buttermilk
- 3 tablespoons 2% milk
- ¼ cup scallions, finely chopped
- 2 teaspoons butter
- ¼ teaspoon pepper
- ¼ teaspoon salt

Created by Scott Uehlein

Scallion Mashed Potatoes   30 MIN

1. Place potatoes in 6 cups boiling water. Cook for 10 minutes or until potatoes are tender. Turn off heat and drain. Place saucepan back on burner for 30 seconds more to dry potatoes.

2. Add remaining ingredients and mash with a potato masher until all ingredients are mixed well. Potatoes will be slightly lumpy.

MAKES 4 SERVINGS
EACH ½ CUP SERVING CONTAINS APPROXIMATELY:
115 calories | 22 gm. carbohydrate
2 gm. fat | 6 mg. cholesterol
3 gm. protein | 178 mg. sodium | 2 gm. fiber

Sweet Garlic Paste

30 MIN

1. In a small pot, bring chicken stock to a boil. Add garlic, reduce heat and simmer until most of liquid is evaporated and garlic has formed a paste.

2. Transfer to blender container and puree until smooth. May be stored in refrigerator for up to 1 week.

MAKES 8 SERVINGS
EACH 1 TABLESPOON SERVING CONTAINS
APPROXIMATELY:
55 calories | 12 gm. carbohydrate
Trace fat | 0 mg. cholesterol
2 gm. protein | 10 mg. sodium | Trace fiber

Ingredients

1½ cups Chicken Stock (see recipe)
4 ounces garlic, peeled and chopped

Sweet and Sour Sauce

30 MIN

Serve over shrimp or chicken or use as a sauce for stir-frying. The strawberries give the sauce a rosy color and added nutritional value.

1. In a small bowl, combine cornstarch and pineapple juice. Set aside.

2. In a small saucepan, combine strawberries and apple juice and bring to a boil. Add brown sugar and vinegar. Add pineapple/cornstarch mixture, reduce heat to low and simmer until mixture thickens.

3. Cool to room temperature, cover tightly and refrigerate. May be stored 4 to 5 days.

MAKES 6 SERVINGS
EACH 2 TABLESPOON SERVING CONTAINS
APPROXIMATELY:
20 calories | 5 gm. carbohydrate
Trace fat | 0 mg. cholesterol
Trace protein | 1 mg. sodium | Trace fiber

Ingredients

1 teaspoon cornstarch
2 tablespoons pineapple juice
¼ cup pureed fresh or frozen organic strawberries
½ cup apple juice
¾ teaspoon brown sugar
1 tablespoon cider vinegar

Pico de Gallo

Pico de gallo (PEE-ko day GUY-o) is Spanish for "rooster's beak," and the name seems to indicate that it was once a finger-food. The story is that picking up pieces of finely chopped vegetables with the thumb and forefinger was thought to resemble a rooster's pecking beak.

1. Place all ingredients in a food processor and mix briefly – vegetables should remain chunky.

2. Pour in a bowl with a cover and refrigerate. May be stored up to a week.

MAKES 3 CUPS
EACH 2 TABLESPOON SERVING
CONTAINS APPROXIMATELY:
10 calories | 2 gm. carbohydrate
Trace fat | 0 mg. cholesterol
Trace protein | 122 mg. sodium | Trace fiber

Ingredients

4 medium tomatoes, diced
1½ cups diced canned tomatoes
½ cup diced red onion
3 tablespoons chopped scallions
½ cup diced yellow bell pepper
1 tablespoon seeded and diced jalapeño pepper
¼ cup chopped fresh cilantro
1½ tablespoons fresh lime juice
1 teaspoon salt
¼ teaspoon black pepper
½ teaspoon dried oregano leaves
¼ teaspoon garlic powder

Created by Scott Uehlein

Yellow Pepper Salsa

Use as an alternative to regular salsa with chips or on quesadillas. The bright yellow color also makes this a pretty garnish.

1. Combine all ingredients in a medium bowl and mix well.

2. Cover tightly and refrigerate. May be stored up to 5 days.

MAKES 32 SERVINGS
EACH 2 TABLESPOON SERVING
CONTAINS APPROXIMATELY:
20 calories | 5 gm. carbohydrate
Trace fat | 0 mg. cholesterol
Trace protein | 21 mg. sodium | 1 gm. fiber

Ingredients

1 large yellow bell pepper, diced
½ cup peeled and diced jicama
½ cup chopped scallions
¼ cup orange juice
½ teaspoon minced, canned chipotle pepper
Pinch salt
Pinch pepper

Created by Frank Cañez

Nutrition Note:

Peppers are loaded with vitamins A and C, beneficial antioxidants that slow the aging process.

Canyon Ranch Salsas

1 15-ounce can whole
   tomatoes, drained

¼ cup diced red onion

1 clove garlic, minced

1 teaspoon dried oregano

1 tablespoon chopped cilantro

¼ teaspoon minced canned
   chipotle pepper

½ teaspoon salt

1 teaspoon red wine vinegar

1 teaspoon white wine vinegar

Pinch red chili flakes

Chipotle Salsa

30 MIN

A touch of smoky chipotle pepper adds complexity to classic Southwestern salsa.

1. Place all ingredients in a blender
   container or bowl of a food processor
   and blend until smooth. Pour in a jar.

2. Store covered in refrigerator up to
   1 week.

MAKES 16 SERVINGS
EACH 2 TABLESPOON SERVING CONTAINS
APPROXIMATELY:
10 calories | 2 gm. carbohydrate
Trace fat | 0 mg. cholesterol
Trace protein | 152 mg. sodium | Trace fiber

Cook's Note:

Canned tomatoes (we
recommend organic)
are traditionally used
for this salsa.

Salads & Salad Dressings

MORE GREAT TASTES

We adore salads because they're so versatile, so good and so very good for us – a big entrée salad, all by itself, can furnish three or four servings of the fresh fruits and vegetables that fight aging and disease. Our salads will open your eyes and fire your imagination.

Our spectacular salad recipes call for fresh, homemade dressing, but why would you bother making your own when the shelves of markets groan with bottled dressings and sauces?

Glad you asked.
When you make your own dressing, you know exactly what's in it.

The prepared dressings that crowd market shelves typically contain preservatives, additives, thickeners and gums that contribute nothing to good nutrition. And the flavor of bottled dressing cannot compare to a home-made dressing whisked up from fresh, high-quality ingredients.

Finally, making dressings and sauces is one of the most entertaining parts of cooking: The mad-chemist aspect of concocting them is just plain fun.

Chinese 7-Vegetable Salad

1. In a medium saucepan, combine all ingredients for sauce and bring to a boil. Reduce heat and simmer until sauce is reduced to ½ cup.

2. Heat canola oil in wok over high heat. Add carrots, red onion and broccoli and stir-fry for about 30 seconds. Add snow peas, zucchini, squash and mushrooms and stir-fry 30 more seconds. Add bok choy and sauce and stir-fry until all vegetables are tender, but still crisp.

3. Divide lettuce into 4 equal portions and place on large plate. Top with 2 cups stir-fry vegetables. Drizzle each with ¼ cup Lemon Miso Dressing.

MAKES 4 SERVINGS
EACH SERVING CONTAINS APPROXIMATELY:
200 calories | 28 gm. carbohydrate
9 gm. fat | 0 mg. cholesterol
9 gm. protein | 613 mg. sodium | 9 gm. fiber

Ingredients

FOR THE SAUCE:
1½ cups water
3 tablespoons peeled, minced ginger
1 tablespoon minced fresh garlic
1 tablespoon minced lemon grass
2 tablespoons low-sodium tamari sauce

FOR THE SALAD:
1 tablespoon canola oil
1½ cups sliced carrots
1½ cups sliced red onion
1½ cups broccoli florets
1 cup snow peas
1 cup sliced zucchini
1 cup sliced yellow squash
1 cup sliced mushrooms
1½ cups chopped bok choy
1½ heads romaine lettuce, torn into bite-size pieces
1 cup Lemon Miso Dressing (see recipe)

Cook's Note:

Garnish with our crispy baked wontons – see recipe for Cashew Chicken Salad.

FOR THE DRESSING:

2 tablespoons red wine vinegar

½ teaspoon salt

¾ teaspoon black pepper

2 tablespoons olive oil

FOR THE SALAD:

1 large head romaine lettuce, chopped

½ cup peeled and diced cucumber

½ cup diced red bell pepper

¼ cup diced yellow bell pepper

¼ cup peeled and diced carrots

¼ cup diced red onion

¼ cup diced black olives

¾ teaspoon chopped fresh oregano

2 teaspoons chopped fresh basil

¾ cup diced tomato

¾ cup cooked white beans

½ cup cooked garbanzo beans

½ cup chopped hearts of palm

Created by Touria Semingson

Chopped Vegetable and Bean Salad

1. In a small bowl, combine red wine vinegar, salt and pepper. Add olive oil and beat well with a wire whip.

2. In a large bowl, combine salad ingredients. Add salad dressing and toss lightly. Divide equally into large salad bowls.

MAKES 4 SERVINGS

EACH SERVING CONTAINS APPROXIMATELY:
235 calories | 33 gm. carbohydrate
8 gm. fat | 0 mg. cholesterol
10 gm. protein | 449 mg. sodium | 8 gm. fiber

Cook's Note:

Canned beans are fine for this satisfying salad. You'll also need to go to the canned goods section for hearts of palm: In this country, fresh hearts of palm are usually only available in Florida. Once the can is opened, transfer unused hearts to a covered, non-metal container and refrigerate in their own liquid. They keep for about a week.

Chopped Vegetable and Bean Salad

FOR THE SOUVLAKIA:

2 teaspoons chopped fresh rosemary

2 teaspoons minced fresh garlic

½ teaspoon salt

½ teaspoon fresh lemon juice

½ teaspoon black pepper

1 pound boneless lamb roast

3 slices lavosh bread, cut in half

FOR THE TZATZIKI:

¾ cup peeled and diced cucumber

¾ teaspoon chopped fresh rosemary

½ teaspoon chopped fresh dill

Pinch salt

4 cloves roasted garlic, chopped

¾ cup nonfat plain yogurt

FOR THE SALAD DRESSING:

3 tablespoons red wine vinegar

3 tablespoons olive oil

¾ cup water

1 tablespoon Dijon mustard

1½ teaspoons chopped fresh thyme

½ teaspoon salt

FOR THE SALAD:

6 cups chopped romaine lettuce

6 tablespoons feta cheese

6 tablespoons chopped kalamata olives

¾ cup diced tomatoes

6 thin slices red onion

Created by Barry Correia

Greek Souvlakia Salad

Creamy, cooling Tzatziki sauce and seasoned roast lamb are a traditional and delicious pairing.

1. Preheat oven to 350°.

2. In a small bowl, combine rosemary, garlic, salt, lemon juice and pepper. Rub lamb roast with seasonings and place in a roasting pan. Bake lamb for 30 to 40 minutes, until medium rare, or until internal temperature reaches 140°. Allow lamb to cool for 15 minutes, then slice very thin.

3. In a small bowl, combine all ingredients for tzatziki. Mix well, cover and refrigerate.

4. In a blender container, combine red wine vinegar, olive oil, water, mustard, thyme and salt. Puree until smooth.

5. In a large bowl, combine lettuce with salad dressing. Place 1 cup of lettuce on plate. Top with 1 tablespoon each of feta cheese and olives, 2 tablespoons tomato and 1 onion slice.

6. To assemble souvlakia, place ½ slice lavosh bread on a flat surface. Top with 2 ounces lamb and 2 tablespoons tzatziki, tuck one end in and roll into a wrap sandwich. Serve over salad.

MAKES 6 SERVINGS

EACH SERVING CONTAINS APPROXIMATELY:
280 calories | 19 gm. carbohydrate
13 gm. fat | 45 mg. cholesterol
21 gm. protein | 317 mg. sodium | 4 gm. fiber

Cook's Note:

For a simple Greek salad, just use the second part of the recipe. Try pita bread or a soft tortilla as an alternative to soft lavosh.

Feta Cheese Salad with Roasted Vegetable Medley and Tomato Vinaigrette

1. Preheat oven to 375°. Lightly coat a baking sheet with olive oil.

2. Slice bread into 1-inch pieces. Spread onto baking sheet and spray or brush bread pieces lightly with olive oil. Sprinkle with minced fresh herbs (oregano, basil or rosemary) if desired. Bake for 5 to 10 minutes or until golden brown. Remove croutons from pan.

3. Lightly coat baking sheet again with olive oil. Distribute tomatoes, asparagus, red peppers and red onion evenly and roast for 15 to 20 minutes or until edges begin to turn brown. Cool and remove skins from tomatoes and peppers. Slice peppers.

4. To prepare dressing, combine tomato, balsamic vinegar, olive oil and salt in a blender container and puree until smooth.

5. Divide leaf lettuce among 4 large salad plates. Top each salad with 2 slices tomato, 2 slices onion and 4 spears of asparagus. Drizzle 2 tablespoons dressing over each salad and garnish with roasted pepper slices and 2 tablespoons feta cheese.

MAKES 4 SERVINGS

EACH SERVING CONTAINS APPROXIMATELY:
280 calories | 43 gm. carbohydrate
8 gm. fat | 15 mg. cholesterol
12 gm. protein | 336 mg. sodium | 6 gm. fiber

Ingredients

FOR THE VEGETABLE MEDLEY:

1 2-ounce French roll

2 large tomatoes, sliced in 8 slices

8 ounces fresh asparagus spears, cleaned and blanched, about 16 spears

1 medium red bell pepper, cut into quarters

1 medium red onion, sliced

FOR THE TOMATO VINAIGRETTE:

1 medium tomato, peeled and chopped, about 4 ounces

1 teaspoon balsamic vinegar

2 teaspoons olive oil

¼ teaspoon salt

FOR THE SALAD:

1 head green leaf lettuce, cleaned and torn into bite-size pieces

½ cup feta cheese, crumbled

Cook's Note:

Tangy feta cheese hails from Greece, where it was traditionally made from goat's milk. It makes a zesty addition to salads and cooked dishes.
2 tablespoons = 4 fat grams

FOR THE CINNAMON PLUM SAUCE:

2 tablespoons plum wine

½ cinnamon stick

¼ cup water

½ cup thinly sliced plums

3 tablespoons seasoned rice vinegar

Pinch red chili flakes

1 teaspoon honey

FOR THE SALAD:

4 4-ounce Ahi tuna steaks

2 tablespoons olive oil

½ teaspoon salt

½ teaspoon black pepper

2 teaspoons canola oil

1½ cups peeled and thinly sliced carrots

1½ cups thinly sliced red bell pepper

1½ cups thinly sliced red onion

3 scallions, sliced on the bias

1 cup asparagus tips

8 cups mixed salad greens

4 teaspoons toasted sesame seeds

Created by Frank Cañez

Ahi Tuna Salad with Cinnamon Plum Sauce

1. In a small sauté pan, combine plum wine with cinnamon stick and water and bring to a boil over medium heat. Reduce heat, add plums and cook for 5 to 10 minutes, or until plums are soft. Add a bit more water to prevent sticking, if necessary. Remove plums and place in a small bowl. Add rice vinegar, chili flakes and honey to sauce and simmer until reduced by a third. Refrigerate sauce and plums.

2. Coat tuna steaks with olive oil. Season with salt and pepper. Set aside.

3. Preheat a wok or sauté pan. Lightly coat with 2 teaspoons canola oil and stir-fry vegetables, adding them in the order given, stirring each new addition until tender-crisp. Remove from pan and cool.

4. In same wok or sauté pan, cook tuna steaks over medium heat to desired doneness, about 3 to 5 minutes on each side.

5. Divide salad greens among 4 large bowls. Arrange 1½ cups stir-fry vegetables over salad greens. Slice tuna steaks and fan across vegetables. Drizzle each salad with 3 tablespoons cinnamon plum sauce. Garnish with cooked plums and 1 teaspoon sesame seeds.

MAKES 4 SERVINGS
EACH SERVING CONTAINS APPROXIMATELY:
380 calories | 38 gm. carbohydrate
10 gm. fat | 82 mg. cholesterol
34 gm. protein | 568 mg. sodium | 10 gm. fiber

Ahi Tuna Salad with Cinnamon Plum Sauce

Ingredients

FOR THE HONEY MUSTARD VINAIGRETTE:

½ cup balsamic vinegar

2 tablespoons dried cranberries

8 dried apricots, thinly sliced

2 teaspoons Dijon mustard

2 teaspoons honey

1 tablespoon olive oil

FOR THE SALAD:

1 pound salmon fillet, cut into 4 equal portions

½ teaspoon salt

¼ teaspoon black pepper

8 cups fresh spinach, washed, well-drained and torn into bite-size pieces

2 cups thinly sliced yellow squash

2 cups thinly sliced red bell pepper

3 tablespoons toasted chopped pecans

Created by Steve Matson

Roasted Salmon Salad with Honey Mustard Vinaigrette

 30 MIN

1. Preheat oven to 425°. Lightly coat a baking sheet with canola oil.

2. In a small saucepan, combine balsamic vinegar, cranberries and apricots. Bring to a boil and simmer for 5 minutes. Strain and reserve liquid and fruit. Combine liquid with mustard, honey and oil.

3. Season salmon fillets with salt and pepper. Place on baking sheet and bake for 5 minutes or until just cooked through.

4. Place 2 cups spinach on plate. Top with ½ cup each squash and red bell pepper. Place salmon fillet on salad and sprinkle with 2 teaspoons pecans. Top with 2 tablespoons dressing and 1 tablespoon reserved fruit.

MAKES 4 SERVINGS
EACH SERVING CONTAINS APPROXIMATELY:
335 calories | 27 gm. carbohydrate
15 gm. fat | 60 mg. cholesterol
27 gm. protein | 510 mg. sodium | 9 gm. fiber

Cook's Note:

The cranberries and apricots add zing to a traditional honey mustard vinaigrette.

Grilled Tuna on Tropical Salad

1. Combine pineapple juice concentrate and lime juice in blender container. While machine is running, add canola oil in a steady stream until smooth and white. Add peppercorns and salt. Remove from blender and whisk in shallots, scallion, ginger and coconut.

2. Prepare hot coals for grilling.

3. In a large bowl, combine jicama, red apple, onion and bell pepper in a bowl. Toss with dressing. Arrange 2 cups romaine lettuce on a large plate and top with 1 cup salad.

4. Grill pineapple rings until slightly brown. Remove from grill and set aside.

5. For rare tuna, grill or broil fish on each side for 1½ to 2 minutes. Slice diagonally and arrange over top of salad. Garnish with grilled pineapple rings.

MAKES 4 SERVINGS
EACH SERVING CONTAINS APPROXIMATELY:
395 calories | 39 gm. carbohydrate
15 gm. fat | 49 mg. cholesterol
29 gm. protein | 642 mg. sodium | 7 gm. fiber

Cook's Note:

Jicama (HE-kah-mah) – a turnip-shaped, brown-skinned root vegetable – is popular in Mexico and the Southwest, where its white flesh is valued for its clean, slightly sweet flavor and crisp texture. For an easy appetizer or informal salad, slice jicama and sprinkle with fresh lemon or lime juice and a little chili powder or cayenne. Select jicamas that have no soft or wrinkled spots.

Ingredients

FOR THE DRESSING:

2 tablespoons pineapple juice concentrate

2 tablespoons fresh lime juice

¼ cup canola oil

1 teaspoon peppercorns, coarsely ground

1 teaspoon salt

1 tablespoon minced shallots

1 scallion, white part only, finely chopped

½ teaspoon peeled and grated fresh ginger

1 tablespoon unsweetened coconut flakes

4 fresh pineapple rings, ½-inch slices

FOR THE SALAD:

1 large jicama, peeled and julienne

2 red apples, cored and thinly sliced

1 red onion, chopped

1 red bell pepper, chopped

1 large head romaine lettuce

1 pound fresh tuna fillet, cut into 4 equal portions

Created by Maggie Flowers

Cashew Chicken Salad with Baked Wontons

FOR THE DRESSING:

- 1 tablespoon minced fresh ginger
- ½ teaspoon minced fresh garlic
- 2 teaspoons chopped fresh cilantro
- 1 tablespoon minced scallions
- 2 tablespoons minced shallots
- 3 tablespoons fresh lime juice
- 1½ tablespoons rice vinegar
- 2 tablespoons water
- 2 tablespoons low-sodium tamari sauce
- 2½ teaspoons sugar
- 1 tablespoon cashew butter
- 6 tablespoons minced cashews

FOR THE SALAD:

- 4 skinless chicken breasts, boned and defatted
- 8 eggroll wrappers (or skins)
- 2 cups shredded Napa cabbage
- 1 cup chopped bok choy
- ¼ cup chopped daikon radish
- ½ cup sliced red onion
- 1 cup thinly sliced carrots
- 1 cup broccoli florets
- ½ cup snow peas

1. Preheat oven to 350°.

2. In a medium bowl, whisk together all ingredients for dressing. Set aside.

3. Place chicken breasts in baking pan. Cover and cook in oven for 15 minutes or until juices run clear when pierced with a fork. Cool and slice.

4. While the chicken bakes, lightly coat a baking sheet with canola oil. Cut eggroll wrappers in half and distribute over baking sheet. Bake for 5 to 10 minutes or until light brown. Cool.

5. Place vegetables in a large bowl. Add dressing, toss lightly and divide into 4 equal portions. Top each salad with a sliced chicken breast and garnish with 4 baked wonton halves.

MAKES 4 SERVINGS
EACH SERVING CONTAINS APPROXIMATELY:
415 calories | 43 gm. carbohydrate
11 gm. fat | 76 mg. cholesterol
37 gm. protein | 673 mg. sodium | 7 gm. fiber

Nutrition Note:

Cashew butter provides a rich nutty flavor to the dressing and has a good percentage of healthy monounsaturated fat.

Created by Scott Uehlein

Cashew Chicken Salad with Baked Wontons

FOR THE SPICY BUTTERMILK DRESSING:

½ cup buttermilk

1½ tablespoons nonfat yogurt

1 teaspoon garlic powder

¼ teaspoon dry mustard

½ teaspoon chopped fresh dill

½ teaspoon black pepper

2 tablespoons Sweet Garlic Paste (see recipe)

2 tablespoons fresh lemon juice

¼ teaspoon cayenne pepper

FOR THE FAJITAS:

¾ teaspoon chili powder

¼ teaspoon ground cumin

½ teaspoon garlic powder

½ teaspoon black pepper

½ teaspoon salt

4 skinless chicken breast halves, boned and defatted

4 teaspoons olive oil

FOR THE SALAD:

4 cups mixed salad greens

2 cups thinly sliced red onion

2 medium tomatoes, cut into wedges

½ cup chopped scallions

¼ cup sliced kalamata olives

2 cups thinly sliced red bell peppers

Created by Frank Cañez

Chicken Fajita Salad

1. In a blender container, combine all ingredients for dressing and puree until smooth.

2. In a small bowl, combine chili powder, cumin, garlic powder, pepper and salt. Cut chicken breast meat into 1-inch strips. Lay strips flat on a plate and season with spice mix.

3. Heat a large sauté pan over medium heat and add olive oil. Cook chicken in batches, about 3 to 5 minutes to ensure nice browning. When cooked through, remove from heat and allow to cool completely. Refrigerate.

4. In a large bowl, combine mixed greens, red onion, tomato wedges, scallions, olives and red bell peppers. Toss to combine.

5. Divide salad into 4 equal portions and place on large plates. Top with 4 ounces chicken strips and drizzle with 3 tablespoons dressing.

MAKES 4 SERVINGS
EACH SERVING CONTAINS APPROXIMATELY:
320 calories | 23 gm. carbohydrate
9 gm. fat | 84 mg. cholesterol
38 gm. protein | 466 mg. sodium | 6 gm. fiber

Caesar Salad

1. In a blender container, puree silken tofu on medium until smooth.

2. Add lemon juice and water and continue to blend.

3. Add remaining dressing ingredients and continue to puree until smooth. Place in airtight container and refrigerate.

4. Preheat oven to 400°. Lightly spray a baking sheet with olive oil.

5. In a small bowl, combine water with spices. Using a pastry brush lightly coat one side of bread slices with spice mix. Cut bread into 1-inch pieces and spread on baking sheet.

6. Bake in oven for 10 to 15 minutes or until bread cubes are crisp and dry.

7. In a large bowl, combine romaine lettuce with dressing and toss lightly. Divide into 4 equal portions and place on large plates. Top each salad with ¼ of croutons and 1 tablespoon freshly grated Parmesan cheese.

MAKES 4 SALADS
EACH SALAD CONTAINS APPROXIMATELY:
120 calories | 14 gm. carbohydrate
4 gm. fat | 6 mg. cholesterol
10 gm. protein | 442 mg. sodium | 5 gm. fiber

Nutrition Note:

Brewer's yeast as another name for nutritional, non-leavening yeast – and yes, it is used in making beer. Besides adding a slightly nutty flavor, it is a good source of B vitamins and trace minerals, including chromium and selenium.

Ingredients

FOR THE DRESSING:

6 ounces silken firm organic tofu, about ¾ cup

⅓ cup fresh lemon juice

½ cup water

1 teaspoon minced fresh garlic

2 tablespoons capers, drained

¼ cup nutritional yeast

2 teaspoons Dijon mustard

Pinch black pepper

Pinch salt (optional)

FOR THE CROUTONS:

2 teaspoons water

1 teaspoon ground cumin

1 teaspoon chili powder

1 teaspoon garlic powder

1 teaspoon ground oregano

2 slices whole-wheat or multi-grain bread

FOR THE SALAD:

1½ heads romaine lettuce, cut into bite-size pieces

1 cup dressing

4 tablespoons freshly grated Parmesan cheese

Created by Frank Cañez

Asian Marinated Duck Salad

½ cup fresh lime juice

½ cup low-sodium tamari sauce

1 cup water

2 tablespoons honey

2 teaspoons minced fresh garlic

1 teaspoon minced fresh ginger

1 teaspoon chopped scallions

½ minced fresh jalapeño pepper, seeds and strings removed

1 teaspoon red chili flakes

FOR THE SALAD:

½ pound boneless duck breast

1 tablespoon cornstarch

1 tablespoon water

1½ cups sliced mushrooms

4 cups shredded Napa cabbage

1 cup snow peas

¼ cup chopped scallions

1 cup sliced canned water chestnuts

½ cup enoki mushrooms

1 cup roasted red bell peppers

Pinch red chili flakes

1. Combine all marinade ingredients in a small bowl and mix well. Divide into 2 equal parts.

2. Place duck in a shallow glass baking dish and pour half of marinade over top. Cover and marinate in refrigerator for 2 to 4 hours.

3. To make sauce from other half of marinade, pour into a saucepan and bring to a boil. In a small bowl, combine cornstarch and water to make a paste. Add to sauce and cook until thickened, about 1 minute. Set aside to cool.

4. Prepare hot coals for grilling or preheat broiler. Remove duck from marinade and grill or broil until cooked through, about 3 to 5 minutes on each side. Discard marinade. Cut duck into ¼-inch strips.

5. In a large bowl, combine mushrooms, cabbage, snow peas, scallions, water chestnuts, enoki mushrooms and red peppers. Pour cooked sauce over vegetables and toss lightly.

6. Place 2 cups of vegetable mixture in a bowl and 2 ounces of duck breast. Garnish with red pepper flakes, if desired.

MAKES 4 SERVINGS

EACH SERVING CONTAINS APPROXIMATELY:
195 calories | 26 gm. carbohydrate
3 gm. fat | 89 mg. cholesterol
18 gm. protein | 854 mg. sodium | 5 gm. fiber

Cook's Note:

For an eye-catching presentation, use the roasted red peppers as a garnish rather than tossing them with the rest of the vegetables.

Asian markets and some supermarkets carry fresh enoki mushrooms, whose crisp delicacy and unusual shape add interest to any salad.

Created by Barry Correia

Asian Marinated Duck Salad

FOR THE SAUCE:

¾ cup water

1½ tablespoons peeled and minced fresh ginger

1½ teaspoons minced fresh garlic

1½ teaspoons minced lemon grass

1 tablespoon low-sodium tamari sauce

1 teaspoon wasabi powder

1 tablespoon rice vinegar

1 tablespoon fresh lemon juice

FOR THE PINEAPPLE GINGER DRESSING:

½ cup apple juice

¼ cup diced pineapple

1 tablespoon peeled and minced fresh ginger

1½ tablespoons rice vinegar

1 tablespoon brown sugar

1 teaspoon cornstarch

1½ tablespoons water

¼ teaspoon canned chipotle pepper, minced

FOR THE STIR-FRY:

1½ tablespoons canola oil

8 ounces shrimp, peeled and deveined

8 ounces scallops

¾ cup peeled and julienne carrots

¾ cup chopped red bell pepper

¾ cup chopped yellow bell pepper

¾ cup thinly sliced red onion

¾ cup peeled and julienne jicama

2 cups chopped Napa cabbage

½ cup chopped scallions

1 large head romaine lettuce, torn in bite-size pieces

Created by Frank Cañez

Firecracker Salad

1. In a medium sauté pan, combine all ingredients for sauce. Bring to a boil and cook until sauce reduces by half. Remove from heat and set aside.

2. In large sauté pan, combine apple juice, pineapple and ginger. Simmer for 10 minutes. Add rice vinegar and brown sugar and cook until sugar dissolves. In a small bowl, combine cornstarch and water to make a paste. Add to dressing and simmer until thickened. Add chipotle pepper. Remove from heat and set aside.

3. Heat wok to high and add canola oil. Stir-fry scallops and shrimp until almost cooked through. Remove from wok. Add vegetables in the order given and stir-fry each briefly, until tender-crisp, before adding the next vegetable. Add sauce and shellfish and stir to coat.

4. Place 4 ounces romaine lettuce on plate. Top with 1 cup stir-fry and drizzle with 2 tablespoons dressing.

MAKES 4 SERVINGS
EACH SERVING CONTAINS APPROXIMATELY:
380 calories | 36 gm. carbohydrate
11 gm. fat | 157 mg. cholesterol
37 gm. protein | 342 mg. sodium | 9 gm. fiber

Firecracker Salad

Ingredients

¼ cup low-sodium tamari sauce

¼ cup Vegetable Stock (see recipe)

½ teaspoon Tabasco sauce

1 tablespoon minced fresh garlic

1 tablespoon peeled and minced fresh ginger

¼ cup sesame oil

2 tablespoons sesame seeds

6 cups cooked rice noodles

4 tablespoons chopped scallions

3 cups broccoli florets

2 cups peeled and sliced carrots

2 cups snow peas

Thai Sesame Noodle Salad

30 MIN

1. Combine tamari sauce, vegetable stock, Tabasco sauce, garlic and ginger in a small bowl. Stir until mixed well.

2. Place sesame oil in a small saucepan. Heat to medium, and add sesame seeds and toast until golden brown. Add tamari mixture to seeds and cover. Let sit 5 minutes.

3. Place noodles and tamari mixture in a large bowl and mix well. Garnish with scallions.

4. Steam broccoli, carrots and snow peas to desired doneness.

5. Serve 1½ cups of noodles with 1 cup vegetables.

MAKES 6 SERVINGS
EACH SERVING CONTAINS APPROXIMATELY:
345 calories | 47 gm. carbohydrate
12 gm. fat | 0 mg. cholesterol
12 gm. protein | 413 mg. sodium | 5 gm. fiber

Cook's Note:

This recipe may be served hot or cold. If served warm, toss the warm rice noodles with the tamari/sesame seed mixture and let sit for 5 minutes.

Rice flour noodles are usually thin Chinese noodles resembling long, translucent white hairs. They may need to be pre-soaked before using – check package directions. Look for "rice sticks" if you want a thicker noodle. For amazing texture, try ethereal, slippery "cellophane noodles" made from mung-bean starch. Shop Asian markets for best selection.

Created by Steve Betti

Roasted Butternut Squash, Apple and Pecan Salad

 30 MIN

Created by Steve Matson

Ingredients

- 2 pounds peeled butternut squash, deseeded and cubed
- 2 teaspoons canola oil
- 1 tablespoon pumpkin pie spice mix
- ¾ cup red wine vinegar
- ½ cup maple syrup
- 5 Granny Smith apples, cored and cubed
- ½ cup pecans, chopped

1. Preheat oven to 400°. Mix squash with oil in a bowl. Sprinkle in the spice mix and toss to coat. Spread squash on an ungreased baking sheet and bake for 15 minutes, or until golden.

2. In a small bowl, combine vinegar and maple syrup, pour over squash and bake for 5 more minutes.

3. Place apples and pecans in a large bowl and add hot squash mixture. Toss lightly and allow to cool before serving.

MAKES 10 SERVINGS
EACH ½ CUP SERVING CONTAINS APPROXIMATELY:
115 calories | 17 gm. carbohydrate
5 gm. fat | 0 mg. cholesterol
1 gm. protein | 4 mg. sodium | 2 gm. fiber

Cook's Note:

Delicious, dense-textured, vitamin-packed butternut squash is the tastiest of all the winter squash – it's the one that looks something like a huge, buff-colored pear. Peeling it takes determination and a sharp, stout knife, but the results are more than worth the work. (Using a cleaver, hack off the stem and then cut the long part off the bulbous base before you start peeling – you'll want to attack to the two shapes separately.)

Ingredients

FOR THE ROASTED TOMATOES:

6 ounces cherry tomatoes, about
    12 tomatoes

¼ teaspoon olive oil

¼ teaspoon garlic powder

FOR THE DRESSING:

¼ cup lemon juice

2 teaspoons olive oil

¼ teaspoon salt

¼ teaspoon black pepper

FOR THE SALAD:

4 cups fresh arugula

12 endive leaves

4 tablespoons freshly grated
    Parmesan cheese

Arugula Salad with Roasted Tomatoes

 30 MIN

1. Preheat oven to 350°. Lightly coat a baking sheet with canola oil. Rub tomatoes with olive oil and sprinkle with garlic powder. Roast in oven for 10 minutes or until just beginning to brown. Cool slightly.

2. In a small bowl, combine lemon juice, olive oil, salt and pepper. Place arugula in large bowl, add dressing and toss lightly.

3. Arrange 1 cup greens with 3 endive leaves on each plate; top with roasted cherry tomatoes. Sprinkle each salad with 1 tablespoon Parmesan cheese.

MAKES 4 SERVINGS
EACH SERVING CONTAINS APPROXIMATELY:
85 calories | 9 gm. carbohydrate
5 gm. fat | 5 mg. cholesterol
5 gm. protein | 195 mg. sodium | 2 gm. fiber

Cook's Note:

Arugula, also known as "Italian cress," is an anti-oxidant-rich green with a peppery mustard flavor.

Created by Rebecca Poage

Arugula Salad with Roasted Tomatoes

2 Bartlett pears, cored and cut in half

4 cups fresh baby spinach, washed

4 teaspoons toasted chopped pecans

½ cup Rosemary Vinaigrette dressing (see recipe)

1 ounce blue cheese, crumbled

Spinach and Pear Salad

30 MIN

Blue cheese, pears and spinach unite in a harmonious and elegant dish. Our chef's preferred blue for this recipe is Gorgonzola.

1. Slice pears and place in steamer basket over boiling water for about 3 minutes, or until soft.

2. In a large bowl, combine spinach, pecans and dressing.

3. Divide into 4 equal portions and top each with ¼ of the crumbled blue cheese and sliced pears.

MAKES 4 SERVINGS
EACH SERVING CONTAINS APPROXIMATELY:
70 calories | 7 gm. carbohydrate
4 gm. fat | 5 mg. cholesterol
3 gm. protein | 267 mg. sodium | 2 gm. fiber

Cook's Note:

Try using seasonal pears without steaming for a crisper salad.

Created by Rebecca Poage

Spinach and Pear Salad

FOR THE PINEAPPLE VINAIGRETTE:

¼ cup frozen pineapple juice concentrate

3 tablespoons champagne vinegar

1 tablespoon olive oil

¼ teaspoon salt

Pinch black pepper

1½ teaspoons chopped fresh mint

FOR THE TORTILLA CHIPS:

1 small flour tortilla, about 6 inches in diameter

Pinch garlic powder

Pinch chili powder

Pinch ground cumin

Pinch salt

FOR THE SALAD:

4 ounces spinach, thinly sliced, about 2 cups

4 ounces romaine lettuce, thinly sliced, about 2 cups

¼ cup thinly sliced red onion

1 small Roma tomato, thinly sliced

½ red bell pepper, roasted and thinly sliced

½ yellow bell pepper, roasted and thinly sliced

½ avocado, mashed

Created by James Boyer

Southwest Roasted Pepper and Avocado Salad with Pineapple Vinaigrette

1. In a blender container, combine all ingredients for pineapple vinaigrette and mix well.

2. Preheat oven to 350°. Slice tortilla into 8 bite-size chips. Place chips on ungreased baking sheet and sprinkle with seasonings. Bake for 3 to 5 minutes or until chips are golden brown.

3. In a large bowl, combine spinach, romaine lettuce, onion and tomato. Add pineapple vinaigrette and mix well.

4. Divide salad into 4 portions and place on salad plates. Arrange 1 tablespoon each of roasted red and yellow peppers over greens and top with 1 tablespoon mashed avocado.

5. Garnish with 2 tortilla chips.

MAKES 4 SERVINGS
EACH SERVING CONTAINS APPROXIMATELY:
115 calories | 17 gm. carbohydrate
5 gm. fat | 0 mg. cholesterol
3 gm. protein | 261 mg. sodium | 3 gm. fiber

Southwest Roasted Pepper and Avocado Salad with Pineapple Vinaigrette

Ingredients

1 can albacore tuna in water,
drained, about 6 ounces

2 tablespoons diced red bell
pepper

2 tablespoons diced yellow bell
pepper

2 tablespoons sweet pickle relish

2 tablespoons diced celery

2 tablespoons canola oil
mayonnaise

½ teaspoon Dijon mustard

Pinch salt

Pinch black pepper

Tuna Salad

Our lighter take on a beloved standard.

Combine all ingredients in a medium
bowl and mix well. Serve immediately or
refrigerate, covered, for up to 2 days.

MAKES 4 SERVINGS
EACH ¼ CUP SERVING CONTAINS APPROXIMATELY:
95 calories | 4 gm. carbohydrate
6 gm. fat | 4 mg. cholesterol
12 gm. protein | 246 mg. sodium | Trace fiber

Ingredients

FOR THE DRESSING:

3 tablespoons nonfat sour cream

3 tablespoons canola oil
mayonnaise

3 tablespoons white wine vinegar

2 tablespoons Dijon mustard

2½ teaspoons sugar

1 teaspoon caraway seed

Pinch salt

¼ teaspoon black pepper

FOR THE COLESLAW:

2 cups shredded green cabbage

½ cup shredded red cabbage

½ cup peeled and grated carrot

⅓ cup minced red onion

½ cup chopped apple

½ cup shredded jicama

Chuckwagon Coleslaw

1. Combine nonfat sour cream, canola oil
   mayonnaise, vinegar, mustard, sugar,
   caraway seed, salt and pepper in a
   small bowl. Mix well.

2. Toss together green cabbage, red
   cabbage, carrot, onion, apple and
   jicama in a large bowl. Add dressing
   and toss until thoroughly mixed.
   Chill until ready to serve.

MAKES 12 SERVINGS
EACH ⅓ CUP SERVING CONTAINS APPROXIMATELY:
60 calories | 6 gm. carbohydrate
4 gm. fat | 0 mg. cholesterol
Trace protein | 112 mg. sodium | 1 gm. fiber

Asian Cabbage Salad

1. In a large bowl, combine bok choy, cabbages, onion and cucumber.

2. In a blender container, combine tamari, sesame oil, rice vinegar, garlic, chili flakes and lime juice. Puree until smooth.

3. Pour sauce over vegetables and mix well.

MAKES 4 SERVINGS

EACH ¾ CUP SERVING CONTAINS APPROXIMATELY:
80 calories | 9 gm. carbohydrate
4 gm. fat | 0 mg. cholesterol
2 gm. protein | 664 mg. sodium | 2 gm. fiber

Ingredients

FOR THE SALAD:

1 cup shredded bok choy
½ cup shredded savoy cabbage
1 cup shredded Napa cabbage
¼ cup thinly sliced onion
½ cup peeled julienne cucumber

FOR THE DRESSING:

1 tablespoon low-sodium tamari sauce
2 tablespoons sesame oil
4 tablespoons seasoned rice vinegar
¼ teaspoon minced fresh garlic
Pinch red chili flakes
¼ teaspoon fresh lime juice

Created by Barry Correia

Tabbouleh Salad

Tabbouleh is a popular Middle Eastern dish, often served cold and accompanied by crisp bread such as lavosh or pita. The fresh vegetables, mint and lemon juice make it a uniquely refreshing salad for a hot day.

1. Place bulgur wheat in a small bowl, add hot water, cover and let soak for 20 minutes.

2. Combine bulgur with remaining ingredients and mix well.

MAKES 8 SERVINGS

EACH ⅓ CUP SERVING CONTAINS APPROXIMATELY:
75 calories | 8 gm. carbohydrate
4 gm. fat | 0 mg. cholesterol
2 gm. protein | 126 mg. sodium | 2 gm. fiber

Ingredients

½ cup bulgur wheat
1 cup hot water
½ bunch chopped fresh parsley
¼ cup chopped fresh peppermint
1 cup diced tomato
¼ cup diced scallions
¼ cup chopped red onion
3 tablespoons peeled, chopped cucumber
2 tablespoons olive oil
3 tablespoons fresh lemon juice
½ teaspoon salt
½ teaspoon black pepper

3 cups boiling water

1 package hijiki, about 2 ounces

FOR THE DRESSING:

1 tablespoon sesame oil

3 tablespoons seasoned rice vinegar

2 tablespoons water

1½ teaspoons crushed red pepper flakes

1½ tablespoons low-sodium tamari sauce

12 cups shredded Napa cabbage

4 tablespoons sliced almonds, toasted

Hijiki and Napa Cabbage Salad

Sea meets shore and East meets West in an intriguing combination of flavors and textures.

1. In a medium bowl, pour boiling water over the hijiki to soften. Let soak for 15 minutes, then drain well.

2. In a small bowl, combine oil, vinegar, water, crushed red pepper, and tamari sauce. Mix well.

3. In a large bowl, toss cabbage and hijiki with dressing.

4. Portion 2 cups salad on each plate and sprinkle with 2 teaspoons almonds.

MAKES 6 SERVINGS
EACH 2 CUP SERVING CONTAINS APPROXIMATELY:
120 calories | 12 gm. carbohydrate
6 gm. fat | 0 mg. cholesterol
4 gm. protein | 188 mg. sodium | 4 gm. fiber

Cook's Note:

Hijiki is Japanese seaweed that comes as dry, narrow black ribbons several inches long. It is the most mineral-rich of the commercial seaweeds and has a slight anise flavor. Look for packaged hijiki in Asian and natural food stores.

Hijiki and Napa Cabbage Salad

Ingredients

2 tablespoons canola or olive oil

6 tablespoons balsamic vinegar

1½ cups Vegetable Stock (see recipe)

2 tablespoons chopped shallots

2 tablespoons Dijon mustard

1½ tablespoons white grape juice

1 teaspoon whole grain mustard

½ teaspoon minced fresh garlic

1½ tablespoons low-sodium tamari sauce

Pinch black pepper

1 tablespoon rice vinegar

1 tablespoon cornstarch

1 tablespoon water

Balsamic Dijon Dressing

For a vinaigrette that works equally well as a salad dressing or a marinade, proceed through step 1. If you'd like a sauce for chicken or fish, continue through step 3.

1. Combine all ingredients except cornstarch and water in a medium saucepan or bowl. Mix well with a whisk.

2. Bring sauce to a boil. In a small bowl or cup, mix cornstarch with water to make a thin paste. Add to sauce mixture and cook, stirring, until slightly thickened, about 2 to 3 minutes. Remove from heat and cool. The sauce should not be too thick when hot, as it will thicken as it cools.

3. Allow to cool. Pour into a jar, cover tightly and refrigerate up to 2 weeks.

MAKES 10 SERVINGS
EACH 2 TABLESPOON SERVING CONTAINS APPROXIMATELY:
35 calories | 3 gm. carbohydrate
2 gm. fat | 0 mg. cholesterol
Trace protein | 209 mg. sodium | Trace fiber

Ingredients

1½ cups fresh or frozen raspberries

¼ teaspoon ground thyme

¼ teaspoon black pepper

3 tablespoons raspberry vinegar

¼ cup water

2 teaspoons canola oil

1½ teaspoons low-sodium tamari sauce

1 tablespoon sugar

Raspberry Vinaigrette

30 MIN

1. Combine all ingredients in a blender container and puree until smooth. Pour into a jar.

2. Cover tightly and refrigerate up to 1 week.

MAKES 10 SERVINGS
EACH 2 TABLESPOON SERVING CONTAINS APPROXIMATELY:
30 calories | 5 gm. carbohydrate
1 gm. fat | 0 mg. cholesterol
Trace protein | 38 mg. sodium | Trace fiber

Cook's Note:

Be adventurous – substitute blackberries or boysenberries for the raspberries, or try other flavored vinegars.

Dressings

Ingredients

1 cup yogurt cheese

⅓ cup canola oil mayonnaise

2½ tablespoons sugar

½ teaspoon minced fresh garlic

1 tablespoon minced onion

2½ teaspoons dried parsley

¾ teaspoon dried basil

½ teaspoon cream of tartar

¼ teaspoon black pepper

1¼ teaspoons salt

2 tablespoons buttermilk

3 tablespoons 2% milk

Created by Justin Morrow

Ranch Dressing

1. Combine all ingredients in a medium bowl and beat with a wire whisk to blend. Pour into a jar.

2. Cover tightly and refrigerate up to 1 week.

MAKES 16 SERVINGS
EACH 2 TABLESPOON SERVING CONTAINS
APPROXIMATELY:
60 calories | 4 gm. carbohydrate
5 gm. fat | 6 mg. cholesterol
1 gm. protein | 208 mg. sodium | Trace fiber

Ingredients

¼ cup canola oil mayonnaise

⅔ cup nonfat sour cream

1 tablespoon minced shallots

¾ cup chili sauce

⅓ cup sweet pickle relish

Pinch salt

Pinch black pepper

⅓ cup 2% milk

Created by Justin Morrow

Thousand Island Dressing

A perennial favorite with children, often used as a sandwich spread.

1. Combine all ingredients in a medium bowl and mix well. Pour into a jar.

2. Cover tightly and refrigerate up to 1 week.

MAKES 16 SERVINGS
EACH 2 TABLESPOON SERVING CONTAINS
APPROXIMATELY:
55 calories | 6 gm. carbohydrate
3 gm. fat | 4 mg. cholesterol
1 gm. protein | 188 mg. sodium | Trace fiber

 30 MIN

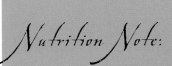

Nutrition Note:

We use small amounts of whole-fat mayonnaise in many dressings. We recommend that you choose a brand high in monounsaturated oil such as canola and olive oils. The healthiest prepared mayonnaise is also free of "mystery chemicals" – preservatives, additives and stabilizers such as guar gum.

Grapefruit and Sage Dressing

 30 MIN

This unusual-sounding combination is a low-fat favorite at our salad bars.

1. In a small saucepan, combine vegetable stock and mustard. Beat with a wire whip. Continue to beat while adding canola oil. Place on stove over medium heat and bring to a boil.

2. In a small bowl or cup, combine cornstarch and water to make a thin paste. Add the cornstarch mixture, while stirring constantly, to the simmering vegetable stock mixture; cook until thickened. Remove from heat and cool.

3. In a blender container, combine roasted garlic, orange juice, grapefruit juice, salt, pepper, shallots and sage. Puree until smooth. Add to cooled vegetable stock mixture and mix by hand using a wire whip. Pour into a jar.

4. Cover tightly and refrigerate up to 2 weeks.

MAKES 16 SERVINGS
EACH 2 TABLESPOON SERVING CONTAINS
APPROXIMATELY:
15 calories | 2 gm. carbohydrate
Trace fat | 0 mg. cholesterol
Trace protein | 96 mg. sodium | Trace fiber

Ingredients

- ⅔ cup Vegetable Stock (see recipe)
- 2 teaspoons Dijon mustard
- 1 tablespoon canola oil
- 2 teaspoons cornstarch
- 2 teaspoons water
- 3 cloves roasted garlic
- ½ cup orange juice
- ½ cup grapefruit juice
- ½ teaspoon salt
- ¼ teaspoon black pepper
- 1½ tablespoons diced shallots
- ½ teaspoon chopped fresh sage

Created by Rebecca Poage

Honey Mustard Tarragon Dressing

 30 MIN

Ingredients

2¼ teaspoons dry mustard

¼ cup honey

1 tablespoon diced shallots

½ cup pineapple juice concentrate

¾ teaspoon garlic powder

2 teaspoons ground tarragon

1 tablespoon canola oil

½ cup firm silken organic tofu

1. Combine all ingredients in a blender container and blend until smooth. Pour into a jar.

2. Cover tightly and refrigerate up to 1 week.

MAKES 12 SERVINGS
EACH 2 TABLESPOON SERVING CONTAINS
APPROXIMATELY:
55 calories | 10 gm. carbohydrate
2 gm. fat | 0 mg. cholesterol
1 gm. protein | 39 mg. sodium | Trace fiber

Created by Steve Betti

Yogurt Mayonnaise

30 MIN

Ingredients

¾ cup olive oil

1 tablespoon dry mustard

1 tablespoon sugar

1 teaspoon salt

¼ teaspoon Dijon mustard

3¼ cups yogurt cheese

Use this more nutritious, lower fat alternative in place of the calorie-laden classic.

1. Combine all ingredients in a large bowl and mix gently by hand until just combined.

2. Do not over-mix! (Mayonnaise will separate.) Pour into a jar.

3. Cover tightly and refrigerate up to 1 week.

MAKES 1 QUART
EACH 2 TABLESPOON SERVING CONTAINS
APPROXIMATELY:
55 calories | 2 gm. carbohydrate
5 gm. fat | Trace cholesterol
1 gm. protein | 121 mg. sodium | Trace fiber

Created by Scott Uehlein

Blue Cheese Dressing

 30 MIN

Equally delicious over salad greens or a steaming baked potato – and a natural with crisp slices of apple or pear.

1. In a medium bowl, combine all ingredients except for cheese and mix well. Add cheese and gently stir to combine. Pour into a jar.

2. Cover tightly and refrigerate up to 1 week.

MAKES 16 SERVINGS
EACH 2 TABLESPOON SERVING CONTAINS
APPROXIMATELY:
65 calories | 3 gm. carbohydrate
5 gm. fat | 10 mg. cholesterol
2 gm. protein | 206 mg. sodium | 0 gm. fiber

Ingredients

⅔ cup buttermilk

⅓ cup canola oil mayonnaise

½ cup nonfat sour cream

1½ tablespoons Worcestershire sauce

1¼ teaspoons dry mustard

1¼ teaspoons garlic powder

1¼ teaspoons onion powder

1½ tablespoons white vinegar

¼ teaspoon black pepper

½ teaspoon salt

1 tablespoon white wine

½ cup crumbled blue cheese

Cook's Note:

Roquefort is the best known of the family of savory cheeses that includes Gorgonzola, from Italy, and Stilton, from England. Their powerful flavors and unique colors come from special strains of mold and become stronger with age.

Created by Scott Uehlein

Rosemary Vinaigrette

Ingredients

- ⅔ cup red wine vinegar
- ⅔ cup champagne vinegar
- ½ cup Vegetable Stock (see recipe)
- 1 tablespoon minced shallots
- 2 teaspoons black pepper
- 4 teaspoons white miso paste
- 1 tablespoon chopped fresh oregano
- 1 tablespoon chopped fresh rosemary

1. In a blender container, combine all ingredients except for oregano and rosemary and blend until smooth. Add herbs and mix by hand. Pour into a jar.

2. Cover tightly and refrigerate for up to 2 weeks.

MAKES 16 SERVINGS

EACH 2 TABLESPOON SERVING CONTAINS APPROXIMATELY:
10 calories | 2 gm. carbohydrate
Trace fat | 0 mg. cholesterol
Trace protein | 292 mg. sodium | Trace fiber

Lemon Miso Dressing

30 MIN

Ingredients

- 1 tablespoon dry mustard
- 3 tablespoons water, divided
- 3 tablespoons white miso paste
- ½ cup fresh lemon juice
- ¾ cup unsweetened apple juice
- ¼ cup seasoned rice vinegar
- 1½ teaspoons peeled and minced fresh ginger
- 2 teaspoons minced fresh garlic
- 1 teaspoon grated lemon peel
- 1 tablespoon chopped fresh parsley

1. In a small bowl, mix dry mustard with 1 tablespoon water until mixture forms a smooth paste.

2. In a separate bowl, mix miso paste with remaining 2 tablespoons water. Set aside.

3. In a blender container, combine lemon juice, apple juice and rice vinegar. Add mustard paste and ginger. Blend on low for 10 seconds. Add garlic, lemon peel, parsley and miso paste. Blend high speed for 30 seconds, or until smooth. Pour into a jar.

4. Cover tightly and refrigerate for up to 1 week.

MAKES 16 SERVINGS

EACH 2 TABLESPOON SERVING CONTAINS APPROXIMATELY:
20 calories | 4 gm. carbohydrate
Trace fat | 0 mg. cholesterol
Trace protein | 100 mg. sodium | Trace fiber

Created by Frank Cañez

Cook's Note:

White miso is one of the milder types of fermented bean paste.

Vegetarian Entrées

MORE GREAT TASTES

On beyond veggie burgers! Actually, we love veggie burgers, but the vegetable realm is a true land of possibility.

Our selection of vegetarian entrées, incorporating flavors and foods from all around the world, illustrates the potential of plant-based protein sources for the creative cook. Our vegetarian main dishes contain ten or more grams of protein per serving – that's the Ranch standard.

In developing your own vegetarian repertoire, keep soy beans and soy products in mind: tofu, tempeh and edamame (green soy beans in the pod) are chock-full of protein and so mild in flavor that they pair up successfully with just about any other food. And don't forget about other beans: While soy beans are richest in amino acids, all beans contain protein, fiber and vitamins.

Vegetable Napoleon with Dry Ricotta Cheese

Ingredients

¾ cup low-fat ricotta cheese

1. Place ricotta cheese in a strainer lined with cheesecloth over a small bowl. Cover. Let liquid drain from cheese overnight in the refrigerator. Refrigerate dry ricotta until ready to use.

2. Preheat oven to 350°. Lightly coat four large (12 oz.) ovenproof individual baking dishes with canola oil.

3. Combine all ingredients for dressing in a small bowl and mix well.

4. Season orzo with salt. Place ½ cup orzo in each baking dish. Layer all ingredients, except for mozzarella cheese, in order they are listed, with the dry ricotta going between the squash and tomatoes. Reserve 4 teaspoons of dry ricotta. Mix dressing with wire whip. Place 3 tablespoons dressing over vegetables.

5. In a small bowl, mix ricotta with mozzarella cheese. Spread cheese mixture on top of vegetables. Bake for 20 to 25 minutes or until vegetables are tender and cheese is melted.

MAKES 4 SERVINGS

EACH SERVING CONTAINS APPROXIMATELY:
335 calories | 51 gm. carbohydrate
9 gm. fat | 17 mg. cholesterol
14 gm. protein | 503 mg. sodium | 3 gm. fiber

FOR THE DRESSING:

2 tablespoons minced shallots

1 tablespoon minced fresh garlic

1 teaspoon finely minced fresh oregano

1 tablespoon finely minced fresh basil

½ teaspoon salt

½ teaspoon black pepper

¼ cup finely minced fresh spinach

2 tablespoons red wine vinegar

2 teaspoons olive oil

1¾ teaspoons canola oil

1 tablespoon freshly grated Parmesan cheese

FOR THE NAPOLEON:

2 cups cooked orzo pasta

¼ teaspoon salt

1 medium zucchini squash, thinly sliced

½ cup thinly sliced fennel

4 tablespoons chopped fresh parsley

1 medium yellow squash, thinly sliced

2 medium tomatoes, thinly sliced

1 large red onion, thinly sliced

½ cup shredded mozzarella cheese

Created by Scott Uehlein

Cook's Note:

This beautiful layered casserole calls for a number of interesting ingredients – a "Green Goddess" type dressing, dry ricotta and orzo, a rice-shaped pasta. This is a fun dish to make with a young helper, or on a relaxed Sunday afternoon with the radio on.

Moroccan Vegetable Stew with Harissa Paste

FOR THE STEW:

2 tablespoons olive oil

1½ cups chopped onion

1 tablespoon minced fresh garlic

1 teaspoon turmeric

1 cup peeled and diced Roma tomatoes

5 cups Vegetable Stock (see recipe)

2 cups peeled and cubed turnips

1½ cups peeled and sliced carrots

1 parsley bouquet garni

1½ cups peeled and cubed butternut squash

2 cups chopped cabbage

1 cup canned garbanzo beans, drained and rinsed

1 cinnamon stick

1 teaspoon salt

1 teaspoon pepper

2⅔ cups couscous

3 cups boiling water

¼ teaspoon salt

1 teaspoon Harissa Paste (see recipe)

FOR THE HARISSA PASTE:

½ cup dried red chili peppers

1 tablespoon olive oil

Pinch ground cumin

Pinch ground coriander

Pinch caraway seed

1 teaspoon minced fresh garlic

Pinch salt

Created by Touria Semingson

STEW:

1. Heat oil in a large saucepan. Add onions and cook for 2 to 3 minutes over medium heat until translucent. Add garlic, turmeric and tomato and cook for 2 more minutes.

2. Add half of stock and bring to a boil. Simmer 5 minutes. Add turnips, carrots and parsley bouquet (wrap parsley sprigs in cheesecloth and tie with a bit of kitchen twine). Bring back to a simmer and cook for 15 minutes. Add squash and cabbage and cook for another 15 minutes. Add garbanzo beans, cinnamon stick and salt and pepper and remaining stock. Bring back to simmer and cook 10 to 15 more minutes.

3. Place uncooked couscous in a large bowl. Pour in boiling water and salt and stir briefly. Cover bowl with lid or plastic wrap to trap steam. Let sit for 10 minutes. Remove cover and fluff with a fork.

4. In a small bowl, combine ½ cup broth from stew with 1 teaspoon harissa paste. Serve ½ cup couscous with 1¼ cups vegetable stew and top with 2 tablespoons harissa broth (optional).

MAKES 8 SERVINGS
EACH SERVING CONTAINS APPROXIMATELY:
350 calories | 66 gm. carbohydrate
5 gm. fat | 0 mg. cholesterol
11 gm. protein | 452 mg. sodium | 8 gm. fiber

HARISSA PASTE:

1. In a small bowl, pre-soak dried chiles in hot water for 5 minutes. Drain and chop chiles into a fine pulp and combine with olive oil in a small bowl. Add seasonings and salt. Mix well.

2. May be stored in refrigerator in a covered container for several weeks.

MAKES 8 SERVINGS
EACH 1 TABLESPOON SERVING CONTAINS APPROXIMATELY:
45 calories | 4 gm. carbohydrate
3 gm. fat | 0 mg. cholesterol
Trace protein | 279 mg. sodium | Trace fiber

Moroccan Vegetable Stew with Harissa Paste

Ingredients

- 2 pounds sweet potatoes, about 4 cups cooked and pureed
- 2 cups peeled and diced carrots
- 3 cups peeled and diced butternut squash
- 1 cup peeled and diced parsnips
- 1½ cups peeled and diced turnips
- 1½ cups quartered mushrooms
- ½ cup diced onions
- ½ cup diced celery
- 3 tablespoons olive oil
- ½ teaspoon ground or grated nutmeg
- 1 teaspoon chopped fresh rosemary
- 2 teaspoons salt
- ½ teaspoon black pepper
- ¾ cup Vegetable Stock (see recipe)
- ¾ cup apple cider
- 3 teaspoons brown sugar
- ½ teaspoon peeled and grated fresh ginger
- 2 teaspoons maple syrup

Created by Dave Joyner

Autumn Vegetable Shepherd's Pie

All the goodness of the harvest is packed into this satisfying vegetarian adaptation of a hefty classic.

1. Preheat oven to 400°. Wrap sweet potatoes in aluminum foil and bake for 1 hour or until soft in the center when pierced with a fork. Remove from oven and set aside.

2. In a large sauté pan, sauté carrots, squash, parsnips, turnips, mushrooms, onions and celery in olive oil, until onions are translucent. Add nutmeg, rosemary, salt and pepper. Continue cooking over medium heat for 5 minutes.

3. Add vegetable stock, apple cider and brown sugar to the vegetables. Bring to a boil, then reduce heat and simmer until vegetables are cooked through, about 25 minutes.

4. Unwrap and peel the sweet potatoes. Transfer to a food processor and puree with ginger and maple syrup.

5. Place vegetable mixture on the bottom of an 1½-quart casserole dish and spread sweet potato mixture top. Bake at 350° for 15 minutes.

MAKES 5 SERVINGS
EACH SERVING CONTAINS APPROXIMATELY:
350 calories | 70 gm. carbohydrate
8 gm. fat | 0 mg. cholesterol
7 gm. protein | 486 mg. sodium | 10 gm. fiber

Cook's Note:

Add 4 ounces of tempeh to enhance the protein in this recipe.

Squash Casserole

1. Preheat oven to 350°. Lightly coat a baking sheet with olive oil.

2. Spread turnips and butternut squash on baking sheet and roast in oven until edges are golden brown, about 20 minutes.

3. In a large sauté pan, over medium heat, sauté onions in 1 tablespoon olive oil until golden brown, about 5 minutes. Add garlic and sauté about 30 seconds. Add eggplant, zucchini, yellow squash, peppers, tomatoes and scallions and cook over medium heat until soft, about 5 minutes. Add bay leaf, black pepper and salt. Remove vegetables from oven and add to sauté pan. Cook for 5 more minutes. Remove from heat, take out bay leaf and stir in fresh herbs.

4. Spread ⅓ cup of cooked rice in bottom of lightly oiled 12-ounce individual casserole dishes. Divide vegetable mixture into 6 equal portions and distribute over the rice. Top each with ⅓ cup breadcrumbs and 2 tablespoons Parmesan cheese. Warm in oven for 10 minutes, or until cheese is melted.

MAKES 6 SERVINGS
EACH SERVING CONTAINS APPROXIMATELY:
335 calories | 62 gm. carbohydrate
6 gm. fat | 5 mg. cholesterol |
11 gm. protein | 145 mg. sodium | 7 gm. fiber

Ingredients

- 2 cups peeled and diced turnips
- 2 cups peeled and diced butternut squash
- 2 cups julienne onions
- 1 tablespoon minced fresh garlic
- 1 tablespoon olive oil
- 2½ cups peeled and diced eggplant
- 2 cups diced zucchini
- 2 cups diced yellow squash
- 2 cups julienne red bell peppers
- 1½ cups diced Roma tomatoes
- 1 tablespoon chopped scallions
- ½ bay leaf
- ½ teaspoon black pepper
- ½ teaspoon salt
- 1 tablespoon chopped fresh basil
- 1 tablespoon chopped fresh oregano
- 1 tablespoon chopped fresh parsley
- 2 cups cooked brown rice
- 2 cups bread crumbs
- ¾ cup grated Parmesan cheese

4 large yellow bell peppers

2 teaspoons olive oil

½ cup diced red onion

1 teaspoon minced fresh garlic

½ cup diced zucchini

½ cup diced fennel

½ cup diced yellow squash

½ cup peeled and diced eggplant

⅓ cup finely chopped pine nuts

⅓ cup raisins

1 teaspoon salt

¼ teaspoon black pepper

⅔ cup Panko breadcrumbs

1 cup Classic Marinara Sauce (see recipe)

Stuffed Yellow Bell Pepper

1. Preheat oven to 375°. Lightly coat a baking sheet with canola oil. Place whole peppers on baking sheet pan and roast for 15 to 20 minutes or until skin is brown. Transfer from oven and quickly dip in ice cold water. Peel skins, careful not to remove stem. Using a sharp knife, make a slit, starting at the base of the stem, lengthwise down one side. Carefully scoop out seeds and membrane. Set aside.

2. In a large sauté pan, sauté onions and garlic in olive oil until onions are translucent. Add zucchini, fennel, yellow squash and eggplant. Add nuts, raisins, salt and pepper. Transfer to a food processor and chop slightly. Stuff each roasted pepper with ½ cup mixture. Lightly spray with olive oil and roll in Panko breadcrumbs. Place on sheet pan.

3. Increase oven temperature to 400° and bake stuffed peppers for 15 minutes, turning every 5 minutes, until golden brown. Serve with ¼ cup Marinara Sauce.

MAKES 4 SERVINGS

EACH 1 PEPPER SERVING CONTAINS APPROXIMATELY:
305 calories | 47 gm. carbohydrate
14 gm. fat | 0 mg. cholesterol
10 gm. protein | 679 mg. sodium | 6 gm. fiber

Cook's Note:

Panko breadcrumbs are available at Asian markets.

Created by Scott Uehlein

Stuffed Yellow Bell Pepper

FOR THE MARINATED EGGPLANT:

1½ cups peeled and diced eggplant

2 tablespoons olive oil

2½ teaspoons paprika

Pinch freshly cracked black pepper

¼ teaspoon ground sage

¼ teaspoon nonsalt vegetable seasoning (such as Mrs. Dash®)

Pinch cayenne pepper

FOR THE JAMBALAYA:

½ cup diced onions

½ cup diced celery

1 tablespoon olive oil

1 clove minced fresh garlic

1½ cups diced tomatoes

¾ cup sliced red bell pepper

1 cup diced zucchini

¼ teaspoon paprika

¼ teaspoon ground thyme

1¼ teaspoons salt

Pinch saffron

2 cups cooked brown rice

3 cups blackeyed peas, boiled and drained

Created by Steve Betti

Vegetarian Jambalaya

1. Preheat oven to 350°. Lightly coat a baking sheet with a small amount of olive oil.

2. In a large bowl, combine eggplant, olive oil, paprika, black pepper, sage, vegetable seasoning, and cayenne pepper. Mix well. Spread seasoned eggplant mixture evenly over the baking sheet, and roast for 20 minutes. Remove from oven and cool.

3. In a large sauté pan, sauté onions and celery until translucent in olive oil. Add garlic, tomatoes, red bell pepper, and zucchini and simmer for 7 to 10 minutes. Stir in paprika, cayenne, thyme, salt and saffron and simmer for an additional 10 minutes.

4. Stir eggplant mixture and rice into sautéed vegetables. Mix gently. Serve ¾ cup vegetable/eggplant/rice mixture in a soup bowl with ½ cup of warm blackeyed peas on top.

MAKES 6 SERVINGS
EACH SERVING CONTAINS APPROXIMATELY:
300 calories | 48 gm. carbohydrate
9 gm. fat | 0 mg. cholesterol
11 gm. protein | 488 mg. sodium | 10 gm. fiber

Vegetarian Jambalaya

1½ cups chopped asparagus spears

4 cups sliced shiitake mushrooms

2 medium yellow onions, sliced

1 sliced red bell pepper

1 sliced yellow bell pepper

2 tablespoons olive oil

1 teaspoon salt

½ teaspoon black pepper

1½ tablespoons minced fresh garlic

¾ cup chèvre cheese

¼ cup grated Parmesan cheese

2 tablespoons chopped fresh basil

16 6" x 6" pasta sheets

3 cups Classic Marinara Sauce (see recipe)

Roasted Vegetable Manicotti

1. Preheat oven to 400°.

2. Mix together all vegetables, oil, salt, pepper and garlic. Spread out on a sheet pan and roast for 15 minutes or until lightly browned. Cool. Place roasted vegetables in a medium bowl and mix in cheeses and basil.

3. Cook pasta sheets in boiling water until al dente, about 7 to 10 minutes.

4. Place ⅓ cup of vegetable mix on pasta sheet and roll. Repeat to make 16 manicotti.

5. Spread a small amount of Marinara Sauce on the bottom of a lightly oiled 9" x 13" baking pan. Arrange manicotti on layer of sauce, top with remaining sauce, cover with foil and bake for 30 minutes.

MAKES 8 SERVINGS
EACH 2 MANICOTTI SERVING CONTAINS APPROXIMATELY:
355 calories | 49 gm. carbohydrate
10 gm. fat | 33 mg. cholesterol
17 gm. protein | 583 mg. sodium | 5 gm. fiber

Cook's Note:

Check your grocer's freezer for ultra-convenient pre-cooked pasta sheets.

Created by Steve Matson

Lemon Grass-Marinated Tofu

1. In a shallow glass baking dish, combine marinade ingredients.

2. Lay tofu slices in marinade and turn. Cover and allow to marinate 2 to 3 hours or overnight.

MAKES 8 SERVINGS

EACH 2 OUNCE SERVING CONTAINS APPROXIMATELY:
80 calories | 2 gm. carbohydrate
6 gm. fat | 0 mg. cholesterol
7 gm. protein | 139 mg. sodium | Trace fiber

Ingredients

FOR THE MARINADE:

¼ cup low-sodium tamari sauce

¼ cup Vegetable Stock (see recipe)

2 tablespoons chopped scallions

2 teaspoons finely chopped lemon grass

1 teaspoon minced fresh garlic

1 tablespoon dark sesame oil

Pinch black pepper

1 teaspoon brown sugar

16 ounces firm organic tofu, cut into 8 slices

Marinated Tofu with Mongolian BBQ Sauce

1. Prepare Mongolian BBQ sauce.

2. Lay tofu slices flat in a shallow glass baking dish.

3. Add sauce, cover and marinate 2 to 3 hours or overnight.

MAKES 8 SERVINGS

EACH 2 OUNCE SERVING CONTAINS APPROXIMATELY:
70 calories | 2 gm. carbohydrate
4 gm. fat | 0 mg. cholesterol
7 gm. protein | 96 mg. sodium | Trace fiber

Ingredients

1 cup Mongolian BBQ sauce (see recipe)

16 ounces firm organic tofu, cut into 8 slices

Created by Scott Uehlein

Sweet Potato Cakes with Jicama Slaw

2 tablespoons peeled fresh mango

½ cup fresh lime juice

¼ cup concentrated pineapple juice

½ teaspoon salt

2 teaspoons sugar

FOR THE JICAMA SLAW:

2 medium jicama, peeled and julienne

⅓ cup diced red bell pepper

¼ cup chopped scallions

FOR THE SWEET POTATO CAKES:

1 pound sweet potatoes, cleaned and pierced with a fork

⅓ cup minced red bell pepper

⅓ cup minced yellow bell pepper

⅓ cup minced red onion

2 tablespoons chopped fresh cilantro

¾ teaspoon black pepper

1 teaspoon ground coriander

1 teaspoon ground cumin

2½ teaspoons sugar

¾ teaspoon salt

1 tablespoon fresh lime juice

1 cup dry breadcrumbs

1 cup toasted and chopped pecans

Created by Scott Uehlein

1. Puree mango in a blender with lime juice, pineapple juice, salt and sugar.

2. In a large bowl, combine jicama, red bell pepper and chopped scallions. Toss.

3. Pour dressing over vegetables and toss again.

4. Preheat oven to 375°. Cut off ends of sweet potatoes and wrap in foil. Bake for 45 minutes or until soft. Let cool. Peel off skin and mash with a potato masher to a smooth consistency.

5. In a large bowl, combine sweet potatoes, peppers, onion, cilantro, spices and lime juice. Add ½ cup of breadcrumbs and mix well. Cover and place in refrigerator overnight.

6. In a shallow bowl, combine remaining breadcrumbs with pecans. Form ¼ cup of the mixture at a time into balls. Dredge in breadcrumb/pecan mixture and flatten.

7. Heat a large nonstick sauté pan and lightly spray with canola oil. Sauté sweet potato cakes until golden brown on each side. Serve 3 patties with ½ cup jicama slaw.

MAKES 6 SERVINGS
EACH SERVING CONTAINS APPROXIMATELY:
380 calories | 56 gm. carbohydrate
15 gm. fat | 0 mg. cholesterol
10 gm. protein | 429 mg. sodium | 7 gm. fiber

Sweet Potato Cakes with Jicama Slaw

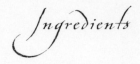
Ingredients

10 ounces sliced firm organic tofu

FOR THE SAUCE:

2 tablespoons low-sodium tamari sauce

2 tablespoons brown sugar

Pinch red chili flakes

2 teaspoons sesame tahini

FOR THE STIR-FRY:

1½ tablespoons olive oil

1 tablespoon minced fresh garlic

1 tablespoon peeled and minced fresh ginger

1 cup sliced scallions

1 cup sliced jicama

1 medium red bell pepper, large dice

2 cups broccoli florets, blanched

1½ cups sliced mushrooms

2 cups cooked chuka soba or buckwheat soba noodles

Caramelized Vegetable and Tofu Stir-fry

1. Heat a wok or large sauté pan over medium high heat and lightly oil. Cook tofu until golden brown on each side. Remove from pan and cut into cubes.

2. In a small saucepan, combine tamari sauce, brown sugar, chili flakes and tahini. Simmer until sugar is melted and mixture becomes a syrup, about 5 minutes. Set aside.

3. Add olive oil to wok and when hot, add garlic and ginger. Stir-fry briefly. Add remaining vegetables in order and stir-fry each one for about 30 seconds. Add tofu and continue to stir-fry until vegetables are tender, but crisp. Add tahini sauce and stir-fry until vegetables are coated.

4. Divide stir-fry into 4 equal portions and serve each portion over ½ cup cooked noodles.

MAKES 4 SERVINGS

EACH SERVING CONTAINS APPROXIMATELY:
325 calories | 44 gm. carbohydrate
12 gm. fat | 0 mg. cholesterol
19 gm. protein | 429 mg. sodium | 7 gm. fiber

Created by Maggie Flowers

Caramelized Vegetable and Tofu Stir-fry

FOR THE TOFU:

¼ cup low-sodium tamari sauce

¼ cup honey

2 tablespoons sherry

1 teaspoon five-spice powder

2 teaspoons peeled and minced fresh ginger

16 ounces firm organic tofu, cut into six ½-inch pieces

1 tablespoon canola oil

FOR THE MU SHU VEGETABLES:

6 Wild Rice Crepes (see recipe)

1½ cups thinly sliced carrots

1 cup chopped scallions

1 cup sliced red onion

3 cups shredded Napa cabbage

1 cup bean sprouts

¼ teaspoon salt

¼ teaspoon black pepper

6 tablespoons hoisin sauce

Created by Steve Matson/Scott Uehlein

Mu Shu Vegetables and Twice-Cooked Tofu with Wild Rice Crepes

Mu shu, a favorite in Chinese restaurants, comes home. Five-spice powder and bottled hoisin sauce are available in most supermarkets.

1. Combine tamari, honey, sherry, five-spice powder and ginger in a large bowl and mix well. Add tofu and marinate covered for several hours or overnight in refrigerator.

2. Remove tofu from marinade and cut each piece in half. Reserve marinade. Heat 1 tablespoon canola oil in a large sauté pan over medium. Sauté tofu until golden brown on each side. Return to marinade while cooking vegetables.

3. Prepare rice crepes and set aside.

4. Lightly spray a wok or large sauté with canola oil. Stir-fry carrots, scallions, onions, cabbage and bean sprouts until tender, but still crisp. Season with salt and pepper. Remove tofu from marinade and sauté again briefly to warm.

5. Spread 1 tablespoon hoisin sauce over each rice crepe. Top with ¾ cup stir-fry vegetables and 2 pieces tofu. Fold in half.

MAKES 6 SERVINGS

EACH SERVING CONTAINS APPROXIMATELY:
325 calories | 43 gm. carbohydrate
13 gm. fat | 0 mg. cholesterol
13 gm. protein | 681 mg. sodium | 5 gm. fiber

Cook's Note:

Unfortunately, rice crepes don't keep well. It is best to make them just prior to serving.

Mu Shu Vegetables and Twice-Cooked Tofu with Wild Rice Crepes

Ingredients

½ cup rice flour

2½ tablespoons cornstarch

2½ tablespoons potato flour

½ teaspoon salt

1½ tablespoons canola oil

⅓ cup water

½ cup cooked wild rice

Wild Rice Crepes

1. Mix all ingredients in a large bowl and allow to rest for 30 minutes. Batter should be the consistency of heavy cream.

2. Heat a crepe pan or large sauté pan over medium heat and lightly spray with canola oil. Ladle ¼ cup batter into pan and turn pan to quickly distribute to edges. Cook until edges begin to turn golden brown. Loosen edges and flip crepe. Cook on the other side for 10 to 20 seconds.

3. If making crepes ahead of time, layer with parchment paper or paper towels.

MAKES 6 CREPES

EACH CREPE CONTAINS APPROXIMATELY:
120 calories | 20 gm. carbohydrate
3 gm. fat | 0 mg. cholesterol
2 gm. protein | 237 mg. sodium | Trace fiber

Cook's Note:

Wild rice is actually a long-grain marshgrass native to the Great Lakes area. Known for its unique nutty flavor and chewy texture, it is a source of folic acid and other B vitamins.

Created by Steve Matson/Scott Uehlein

Vegetarian Chili with Tempeh

1. Lightly coat a large saucepan with olive oil. Add onions and chili powder and sauté over medium heat until onions are translucent. Add the garlic and sauté for about 30 seconds. Mix in all dry herbs and peppers and sauté 30 more seconds.

2. Add tomato sauce, tomatoes, tempeh, chipotle pepper, cilantro and molasses and mix thoroughly.

3. Pour in vegetable stock and let simmer for 30 minutes. Add beans into saucepan, stir and cook for an additional 30 minutes.

MAKES 6 SERVINGS
EACH 1 CUP SERVING CONTAINS APPROXIMATELY:
180 calories | 34 gm. carbohydrate
2 gm. fat | 0 mg. cholesterol
10 gm. protein | 537 mg. sodium | 7 gm. fiber

Cook's Note:

Adzuki and Anasazi beans are small, sweet beans that we love in this recipe. They are, however, difficult to find canned. Feel free to experiment by substituting any beans you particularly like or that you happen to have on hand.

Ingredients

2½ cups finely diced onions

2 tablespoons chili powder

2 teaspoons minced fresh garlic

½ cup diced red bell peppers

½ cup diced yellow bell peppers

¾ cup tempeh, small diced

1½ teaspoons ground cumin

1 tablespoon dried basil

1 teaspoon dried ground thyme

1¾ cups canned tomato sauce

2¼ cups tomatoes, diced

¾ teaspoon minced chipotle pepper

1½ teaspoons chopped fresh cilantro

1 tablespoon blackstrap molasses

2¾ cups Vegetable Stock (see recipe)

½ cup canned adzuki beans, drained and rinsed

½ cup canned anasazi beans, drained and rinsed

¼ cup canned kidney beans, drained and rinsed

Created by Steve Betti

Ingredients

FOR THE BAKED MUSHROOMS:

4 teaspoons olive oil

I large onion, diced

2 tablespoons minced fresh garlic

½ cup thinly sliced fennel

2 cups Vegetable Stock (see recipe)

½ pound portobello mushrooms, diced

½ pound button mushrooms, quartered

½ pound shiitake mushrooms, diced

½ pound oyster mushrooms, diced

1⅓ cups Madeira wine

½ teaspoon salt

½ teaspoon pepper

2 teaspoons chopped fresh thyme

PECAN PASTRY CRUST:

½ cup pecan halves, about 2 ounces

2 tablespoons whole-wheat flour

½ cup all-purpose flour

½ teaspoon salt

2 to 3 tablespoons cold water

Created by Scott Uehlein

Baked Wild Mushrooms Madeira with Pecan Pastry Crust

1. In a large saucepan, sauté onions in oil until translucent. Add garlic and fennel and sauté briefly. Add vegetable stock and bring to a boil. Add mushrooms and cook until stock is reduced by half. Add wine and simmer for 5 minutes. Add salt, pepper and thyme and simmer for 2 more minutes. Portion into 4 12-ounce individual casserole dishes and set aside.

2. Preheat oven to 350°.

3. In a blender container, puree pecans to a buttery consistency.

4. In a medium bowl, combine flours and salt. Add pecan butter and cut into flour using a pastry cutter until the butter is the size of peas. Add cold water, 1 tablespoon at a time until soft dough forms.

5. Divide dough into 4 equal balls and roll each into a circle large enough to cover individual (12 oz.) casserole. Place crust over mushrooms and bake for 20 to 30 minutes or until crust is golden brown and mushrooms are bubbling.

MAKES 4 SERVINGS
EACH SERVING CONTAINS APPROXIMATELY:
360 calories | 41 gm. carbohydrate
14 gm. fat | 0 mg. cholesterol
10 gm. protein | 629 mg. sodium | 7 gm. fiber

Cook's Note:

You can use ½ ounce kataifi (shredded phyllo dough) in lieu of pastry crust.

Baked Wild Mushrooms Madeira with Pecan Pastry Crust

Fish & Seafood

MORE GREAT TASTES

The seas are richer in some fish than others, and environmental concerns may influence your choice of the fish you eat most often. An indispensable resource for fish lovers is the National Audubon Society's charming and informative *Seafood Lover's Almanac.*

Fish, especially the oily, cold-water varieties such as salmon, are superb sources of protein and inflammation-fighting omega-3 fatty acids . Unless you have a sensitivity to seafood, you would be well-advised to eat 3 to 4 servings of fish a week.

A word about freshness and safety: There's no other type of food in which freshness is so critical. Know your fishmonger, find out when the fish comes in and buy on those days. Really fresh seafood smells faintly like fish, but sweet – it should not be rank or have a "fishy" ammonia-like tang. Wash surfaces and hands with soapy water and, of, course, keep raw seafood refrigerated.

Sea Bass with Sweet Mushroom Sauce

1. Preheat oven to 400°.

2. Wrap mushroom, pepper, pineapple and garlic in aluminum foil. Place in oven for 30 minutes, or until vegetables are golden brown. Allow to cool.

3. In a medium sauté pan, sauté onion in olive oil until translucent. Add wine and cook briefly. Add lemon juice and clam juice. Simmer 5 minutes.

4. In a small bowl or cup, mix cornstarch with 1 teaspoon water to make a thin paste. Set aside.

5. Combine cream, milk, butter and salt in a medium saucepan. Bring to a boil and whisk in cornstarch mixture, with a wire whip. Simmer 1 to 2 minutes or until thickened. Cool slightly.

6. Transfer cream mixture to a blender container and add onion mixture and roasted vegetables. Puree until smooth. Remove from blender and stir in chopped fresh herbs.

7. Preheat grill or broiler and cook fish 3 to 5 minutes on each side or until cooked through. Serve 1 fish fillet with ¼ cup sauce.

MAKES 4 SERVINGS
EACH SERVING CONTAINS APPROXIMATELY:
155 calories | 5 gm. carbohydrate
5 gm. fat | 49 mg. cholesterol
22 gm. protein | 278 mg. sodium | Trace fiber

MEAL SUGGESTION:
Orzo pasta and broccoli florets

Ingredients

FOR THE SWEET MUSHROOM SAUCE:

¼ cup chopped portobello mushroom cap

2 tablespoons chopped red bell pepper

2 tablespoons diced fresh pineapple

1 clove minced fresh garlic

¼ cup diced onion

1 teaspoon olive oil

2 teaspoons white port wine

1 teaspoon fresh lemon juice

¼ cup clam juice

1 teaspoon cornstarch

2 teaspoons heavy cream

½ cup skim milk

½ teaspoon butter

½ teaspoon salt (optional)

2 teaspoons chopped fresh cilantro

2 teaspoons chopped fresh dill

4 4-ounce sea bass fillets

Cook's Note:

To prevent sauce from becoming too dark, remove the gills from the underside of the portobello mushroom before chopping.

Created by Jeff Prew

Potato-Crusted Salmon with Dijon Shallot Sauce

FOR THE DIJON SHALLOT SAUCE:

2 tablespoons minced shallots

1 teaspoon butter

1 tablespoon all-purpose flour

½ cup 2% milk

½ bay leaf

2 tablespoons white wine

½ teaspoon Dijon mustard

FOR THE SALMON:

3 medium potatoes, washed, peeled and grated, about 1 pound

1 tablespoon fresh lemon juice

4 4-ounce salmon fillets

1. In a medium saucepan, sauté shallots in butter over medium low heat until translucent, about 1 minute. Add flour and mix to form a roux. Cook 1 to 2 minutes, stirring constantly, or until mixture turns light brown.

2. Slowly pour in milk and whisk with a wire whip until mixture comes to a boil and thickens. Add bay leaf and wine. Reduce heat to low and simmer 5 minutes. Remove from heat and add mustard.

3. Place shredded potatoes in colander and rinse several times in cold water until water is clear and starch is removed. Transfer to a large bowl and add lemon juice.

4. Preheat oven to 350°. Lightly coat an ovenproof sauté pan with canola oil.

5. Pack ½ cup potato on each salmon fillet and sear, potato-side-down, in sauté pan until golden brown. Transfer to oven and bake for 8 to 10 minutes, or until salmon flakes easily.

6. Serve 1 salmon fillet with 1 tablespoon of sauce.

MAKES 4 SERVINGS
EACH SERVING CONTAINS APPROXIMATELY:
320 calories | 23 gm. carbohydrate
10 gm. fat | 83 mg. cholesterol
33 gm. protein | 108 mg. sodium | Trace fiber

MEAL SUGGESTION:
Roasted patty-pan squash

Cook's Note:

A roux is a gently browned mixture of flour and fat used to thicken and flavor soups and sauces.

Created by Steve Betti

Potato-Crusted Salmon with Dijon Shallot Sauce

Ingredients

FOR THE YELLOW BELL PEPPER COULIS:

2 small yellow bell peppers, seeded and quartered

½ cup diced onions

2 cloves minced fresh garlic

1 tablespoon chopped fresh cilantro

½ teaspoon chili powder

⅔ cup Chicken Stock (see recipe)

2 teaspoons fresh lemon juice

2 teaspoons sugar

¼ teaspoon black pepper

Pinch salt (optional)

FOR THE SEA BASS:

4 yellow corn tortillas

4 4-ounce sea bass fillets

¼ cup Sweet Garlic Paste (see recipe)

Created by Frank Cañez

Tortilla-Crusted Sea Bass with Yellow Bell Pepper Coulis

1. Preheat oven to 400°. Lightly coat a baking sheet with olive oil.

2. Lay peppers skin-side up on greased baking sheet and roast in oven 10 to 15 minutes or until skins have blackened. Remove from oven and rinse under cold water to peel away skins.

3. Lightly coat a sauté pan with a small amount of canola oil. Sauté onions and garlic over medium-low heat until garlic begins to turn golden brown. Add peppers, cilantro and chili powder. Sauté 1 minute and add stock. Bring to a boil. Add lemon juice and sugar. Cook, stirring occasionally until all ingredients are soft, about 5 minutes.

4. Allow to cool slightly. Place in blender container and puree until smooth. Season with pepper and salt.

5. Place tortillas on baking sheet. Bake in oven until very crisp, about 5 to 10 minutes. (Leave oven on.) Cool. Crush tortillas between layers of wax paper using a rolling pin.

6. Brush garlic paste over fish and roll in crushed tortilla mixture. Transfer fish to a baking dish which has been lightly coated with canola oil. Bake in oven for 10 to 12 minutes, or until just cooked through. Serve each fillet with ¼ cup coulis.

MAKES 4 SERVINGS
EACH SERVING CONTAINS APPROXIMATELY:
255 calories | 23 gm. carbohydrate
5 gm. fat | 75 mg. cholesterol
37 gm. protein | 176 mg. sodium | 4 gm. fiber

MEAL SUGGESTION:
Lime Cilantro Potatoes and chayote squash

Tuna with Horseradish Ginger Sake Sauce

1. Mix sesame seeds and cracked black pepper in a small bowl. Spread mixture on a large plate and roll sides of tuna fillets in mixture until they are coated. Refrigerate, covered.

2. Prepare hot coals for grilling or preheat broiler.

3. In a small saucepan, sauté shallots and ginger in sesame oil over medium low heat until shallots are translucent. Add vegetable stock, tamari, honey and sake and bring to a quick boil.

4. In a small bowl or cup, combine wasabi powder and cornstarch with 1 tablespoon water to make a paste. Stir mixture into simmering sauce and cook until thickened, about 1 minute. Add scallions, lemon grass and red chili flakes and mix well. Set aside.

5. Grill or broil tuna until cooked through, about 3 to 5 minutes per side. Serve 1 tuna fillet with 2 tablespoons sauce.

MAKES 4 SERVINGS
EACH SERVING CONTAINS APPROXIMATELY:
155 calories | 4 gm. carbohydrate
2 gm. fat | 49 mg. cholesterol
27 gm. protein | 324 mg. sodium | Trace fiber

MEAL SUGGESTION:
Buckwheat soba noodles and stir-fry bok choy

Ingredients

FOR THE TUNA:

1 tablespoon sesame seeds

1 teaspoon cracked black pepper

4 4-ounce tuna fillets

FOR THE HORSERADISH GINGER SAKE SAUCE:

1 tablespoon minced shallots

½ tablespoon peeled and minced fresh ginger

½ teaspoon sesame oil

6 tablespoons Vegetable Stock (see recipe)

1½ tablespoons low-sodium tamari sauce

1½ teaspoons honey

2 tablespoons sake

2 teaspoons wasabi powder

1½ teaspoons cornstarch

1 tablespoon chopped scallions

2 teaspoons chopped lemon grass

1 teaspoon crushed red chili flakes

Created by Barry Correia

Ingredients

FOR THE ORANGE BASIL RELISH:

1¼ cups orange segments

3 tablespoons basil chiffonade

1 cup finely diced red onion

1 minced jalapeño pepper, seeds and veins removed

1 tablespoon olive oil

¼ cup red wine vinegar

1 teaspoon salt

½ teaspoon black pepper

FOR THE SALMON:

2 cups orange juice

1 tablespoon grated orange peel

1 cup white wine

6 4-ounce salmon fillets

Poached Salmon with Orange Basil Relish

30 MIN

Poaching is a gentle way to cook: it requires lower temperatures and less manipulation than most other methods. Salmon, which can become dry if not cooked carefully, is lovely poached. (The general rule for poaching fish is 10 minutes for every inch of thickness.)

1. In a medium bowl, combine all ingredients for relish and mix well. Set aside.

2. Combine orange juice, orange peel and white wine in a large saucepan. Bring to a boil and reduce heat to medium-low. As liquid is simmering, gently lower salmon fillets into poaching liquid with a slotted spoon one at a time. Allow liquid to return a simmer, cover and remove pan from heat. Let sit for 10 minutes. Check salmon for doneness and remove from liquid with slotted spoon.

3. Serve 1 salmon fillet with ¼ cup relish.

MAKES 6 SERVINGS

EACH SERVING CONTAINS APPROXIMATELY:
275 calories | 19 gm. carbohydrate
10 gm. fat | 60 mg. cholesterol
23 gm. protein | 448 mg. sodium | 3 gm. fiber

MEAL SUGGESTION:
Roasted potatoes and steamed asparagus

Cook's Note:

Chiffonade basil is gorgeous, more consistent than chopped basil – and it's a snap. Wash fresh basil and let dry. Pull off a half-dozen leaves and roughly stack, then roll up into a loose little cigar-shape. Cut across the cylinder with fast, close strokes. Voilà!

When cleaning and chopping jalapeños and other hot peppers, be careful not to touch your eyes or nose – and wash your hands with soap after you've finished.

Created by Steve Matson

Poached Salmon with Orange Basil Relish

FOR THE GREMOLATA:

- 2 tablespoons minced fresh parsley
- 1 tablespoon minced fresh oregano
- 1 teaspoon minced fresh garlic
- ½ teaspoon minced lemon peel

FOR THE TUNA:

- 1 pound tuna steaks, cut into 4 equal portions
- 4 teaspoons olive oil
- ½ teaspoon salt
- ¼ teaspoon black pepper
- 1 tablespoon lemon juice

Grilled Tuna Gremolata

 30 MIN

Gremolata is a tangy Italian garnish traditionally served with osso bucco. This is a fun use for it.

1. Prepare hot coals for grilling or preheat broiler.

2. Combine all ingredients for gremolata and mix well. Set aside.

3. Brush each tuna fillet with 1 teaspoon olive oil. Lightly season with salt and pepper and drizzle with lemon juice.

4. Grill or broil for 3 to 5 minutes on each side or to desired doneness.

5. Serve 2 teaspoons gremolata over each fillet.

MAKES 4 SERVINGS
EACH SERVING CONTAINS APPROXIMATELY:
160 calories | Trace carbohydrate
6 gm. fat | 49 mg. cholesterol
26 gm. protein | 334 mg. sodium | Trace fiber

MEAL SUGGESTION:
Tuscan Beans

Created by Steve Matson

Halibut with Avocado Sauce

30 MIN

1. Combine avocado, sour cream, lime juice, hot sauce, cumin and white wine in a blender container and puree.

2. Preheat grill or broiler.

3. Season halibut with salt and pepper. Grill or broil for 3 to 5 minutes on each side or until fish flakes easily.

4. Serve 1 fish fillet with 2 tablespoons avocado sauce, 2 tablespoons each red onion and diced tomato and 1 tablespoon cilantro.

MAKES 4 SERVINGS
EACH SERVING CONTAINS APPROXIMATELY:
235 calories | 15 gm. carbohydrate
8 gm. fat | 38 mg. cholesterol
37 gm. protein | 400 mg. sodium | 4 gm. fiber

MEAL SUGGESTION:
Mexican Rice and carrots

Ingredients

FOR THE AVOCADO SAUCE:

1 medium avocado, peeled and sliced

¼ cup nonfat sour cream

2 tablespoons fresh lime juice

¼ teaspoon hot sauce, such as Tabasco

1 teaspoon ground cumin

1 tablespoon white wine

FOR THE HALIBUT:

4 4-ounce halibut fillets

1 teaspoon salt

½ teaspoon black pepper

½ cup diced red onion

½ cup peeled, seeded and diced tomatoes

¼ cup chopped fresh cilantro

Cook's Note:

Toast whole cumin seeds for 3 to 5 minutes in a dry sauté pan over medium heat, then grind them in a spice grinder or crush with a mortar and pestle for truly astounding flavor.

Created by Steve Matson

**FOR THE CARAMELIZED
PINEAPPLE SAUCE:**

1 teaspoon butter

3 tablespoons finely minced
   onions

½ cup diced fresh pineapple

¼ cup frozen concentrated
   pineapple juice

1½ tablespoons rice vinegar

1 teaspoon peeled and minced
   ginger

1½ cups Vegetable Stock
    (see recipe)

1 vanilla bean

½ teaspoon low-sodium tamari
   sauce

Pinch cayenne pepper

FOR THE MAHI MAHI:

¼ cup all-purpose flour

4 4-ounce mahi mahi fillets

2 beaten egg whites

¼ cup crushed macadamia nuts

Macadamia-Crusted Mahi Mahi

1. Preheat oven to 400°.

2. In a medium sauté pan, melt butter over low heat. Add onions and cook until translucent. Add pineapple and cook until all ingredients are browned, about 15 to 20 minutes. Add pineapple juice and rice vinegar. Cook sauce for 5 to 10 minutes, or until thick and golden.

3. Add ginger and vegetable stock and bring to a boil. Add vanilla bean, tamari sauce and cayenne pepper. Simmer for 15 to 20 minutes. Remove vanilla bean and puree pineapple mixture and reserve.

4. While sauce simmers, place flour in a small bowl. Dredge fish in flour, dip in beaten egg whites and roll in crushed macadamia nuts. Place in greased baking dish and bake for 10 to 15 minutes, or until fish is cooked through.

5. Serve 1 fish fillet with ¼ cup caramelized pineapple sauce.

MAKES 4 SERVINGS
EACH SERVING CONTAINS APPROXIMATELY:
230 calories | 15 gm. carbohydrate
12 gm. fat | 139 mg. cholesterol
17 gm. protein | 275 mg. sodium | 1 gm. fiber

MEAL SUGGESTION:
Red Himalayan rice and
sautéed baby yellow squash

Cook's Note:

Do not over-chop macadamia nuts – they'll become oily and sticky if you do.

Created by Scott Uehlein

Macadamia-Crusted Mahi Mahi

FOR THE AVENETO SALSA:

2 teaspoons olive oil

⅓ cup water-packed artichoke hearts, drained and diced

¼ cup diced red bell pepper

¼ cup diced fresh fennel

4 cloves roasted garlic, chopped

¼ cup diced tomatoes

2 tablespoons diced kalamata olives

¼ cup peeled and diced cucumber

½ teaspoon black pepper

3 tablespoons champagne vinegar

1 teaspoon fresh lemon juice

FOR THE TROUT:

6 4-ounce trout fillets

3 teaspoons olive oil

1 teaspoon salt

½ teaspoon black pepper

Trout with Aveneto Salsa

1. Combine all ingredients for salsa, cover and place in refrigerator for at least 2 hours.

2. Preheat grill. Lightly coat trout fillets with olive oil, salt and pepper. Grill for 2 to 3 minutes on each side or until cooked through.

3. Serve 1 trout fillet with ¼ cup salsa.

MAKES 6 SERVINGS
EACH SERVING CONTAINS APPROXIMATELY:
205 calories | 5 gm. carbohydrate
11 gm. fat | 58 mg. cholesterol
22 gm. protein | 321 mg. sodium | 2 gm. fiber

MEAL SUGGESTION:
Whole-wheat couscous
and grilled fennel

Created by Carlos Guzman

Grilled Fish Sandwich with Olive Tapenade

 30 MIN

1. In a small bowl combine all ingredients for olive tapenade and mix well. Set aside.

2. Preheat grill or broiler.

3. Grill or broil fish fillets 3 to 5 minutes on each side.

4. Slice and grill the sourdough rolls. Spread 1 tablespoon of the tapenade on each roll, then add a fish fillet and garnish with lettuce, tomato, onion and serve with lemon wedge.

MAKES 6 SERVINGS
EACH SERVING CONTAINS APPROXIMATELY:
380 calories | 49 gm. carbohydrate
6 gm. fat | 49 mg. cholesterol
33 gm. protein | 601 mg. sodium | 5 gm. fiber

Ingredients

FOR THE OLIVE TAPENADE:
- 1 teaspoon minced fresh garlic
- 2 tablespoons minced black olives
- 1 tablespoon minced green olives
- 2 tablespoons minced sun-dried tomatoes
- 2 teaspoons olive oil
- Pinch black pepper
- 1½ teaspoons chopped fresh basil

FOR THE FISH:
- 1½ pounds whitefish fillets
- 6 3-ounce sourdough French rolls
- 6 lettuce leaves
- 6 tomato slices
- 6 onion slices
- 1 lemon sliced into 6 wedges

Cook's Note:

Savory tapenade hails from Provence, in the south of France. Make extra and serve it with a plate of raw vegetables or spread a bit on crusty, fresh bread.

Created by
Scott Uehlein/Touria Semingson

FOR THE GREEN APPLE CHIPOTLE SALSA:

½ cup diced Granny Smith apple

¼ cup diced red onion

¼ cup diced red bell pepper

2 tablespoons chopped fresh cilantro

2 tablespoons apple juice

2 tablespoons red wine vinegar

Pinch chipotle chili powder

FOR THE SPICE MIX:

6 tablespoons paprika

2 tablespoons black pepper

2 tablespoons salt

1 tablespoon chili powder

2 teaspoons brown sugar

Pinch cayenne

12 large shrimp, peeled, deveined and butterflied

1 tablespoon olive oil

Shrimp with Green Apple Chipotle Salsa

1. Combine all ingredients for salsa in a medium bowl and mix well. Refrigerate covered for at least 1 hour.

2. Combine all ingredients for spice mix in a small bowl. Leftover spice mix may be stored in an airtight container for future use.

3. Lightly dust shrimp with spice mix. If grilling, coat shrimp with olive oil and cook until pink, about 1 minute on each side. If sautéing, add olive oil to sauté pan and heat to medium. Sauté for about 1 minute on each side.

4. Serve ¼ cup salsa with three shrimp.

MAKES 4 SERVINGS
EACH SERVING CONTAINS APPROXIMATELY:
155 calories | 9 gm. carbohydrate
5 gm. fat | 129 mg. cholesterol
18 gm. protein | 568 mg. sodium | 2 gm. fiber

MEAL SUGGESTION:
Red beans and rice, sautéed
red and yellow bell peppers

Created by Steve Matson

Shrimp with Green Apple Chipotle Salsa

2 tablespoons olive oil

2 teaspoons minced fresh garlic

½ teaspoon black pepper

½ cup low-sodium ketchup

½ cup balsamic vinegar

2 tablespoons Worcestershire Sauce

Pinch crushed red chili flakes

½ cup chopped fresh parsley

1 pound shrimp, peeled and deveined

4 8-inch wooden skewers

Spicy Grilled Shrimp

1. Combine all ingredients except shrimp in a shallow glass dish.

2. Add shrimp and stir to coat. Marinate, uncovered, in refrigerator, for at least 2 hours.

3. Pour marinade from shrimp into a small saucepan. Boil and set aside.

4. Prepare hot coals for grilling or preheat broiler. Soak skewers in water for 10 minutes.

5. Thread 3 shrimp onto each skewer. Grill and baste shrimp with boiled marinade until color changes to pink, about 2 minutes on each side. Do not overcook.

MAKES 4 SERVINGS
EACH SERVING CONTAINS APPROXIMATELY:
220 calories | 11 gm. carbohydrate
9 gm. fat | 172 mg. cholesterol
24 gm. protein | 259 mg. sodium | 1 gm. fiber

MEAL SUGGESTION:
Wild rice and Glazed Baby Carrots

Cook's Note:

Smaller portions make a terrific, easy-to-eat appetizer.

Shrimp with Garlic Sauce

 30 MIN

1. In a medium saucepan, combine garlic, shallots and wine and simmer until wine is evaporated. Add chicken stock and simmer until reduced by half, about 5 minutes.

2. In a small bowl or cup, combine cornstarch and 1½ teaspoons water to make a paste. Add to sauce and simmer until thickened, about 2 to 3 minutes. Remove from heat and add remaining ingredients. Cover.

3. In a large sauté pan, heat olive oil over medium heat. Add shrimp and sauté until pink, about one minute on each side. Do not overcook!

4. Serve 1½ tablespoons sauce over 3 ounces cooked shrimp.

MAKES 4 SERVINGS

EACH SERVING CONTAINS APPROXIMATELY:
170 calories | 5 gm. carbohydrate
6 gm. fat | 179 mg. cholesterol
20 gm. protein | 504 mg. sodium | Trace fiber

MEAL SUGGESTION:
White Corn Polenta and
sautéed rapini (broccoli raab)

Ingredients

GARLIC SAUCE:

1½ tablespoons minced fresh garlic

1 tablespoon diced shallots

½ cup white wine

1 cup Chicken Stock (see recipe)

1½ teaspoons cornstarch

½ cup peeled, seeded and diced tomatoes

2 tablespoons nonfat sour cream

2 tablespoons heavy cream

2 tablespoons chopped fresh parsley

1 teaspoon fresh lemon juice

½ teaspoon salt

Pinch pepper

1 pound shrimp, peeled and deveined

2 teaspoons olive oil

Created by Scott Uehlein

FOR THE AVOCADO RELISH:

¼ cup diced onions

1 cup peeled and diced avocado

¼ cup diced tomatoes

Pinch ground cumin

Pinch salt

Pinch black pepper

FOR THE QUESADILLA:

4 medium flour tortillas, about 9" in diameter

4 teaspoons canned green chile peppers, diced

½ cup chopped crab meat

4 tablespoons shredded low-fat Monterey Jack cheese

8 tablespoons Pico de Gallo (see recipe)

4 tablespoons nonfat sour cream

Crab and Avocado Quesadilla

This is a delicate, upscale version of a universally beloved Southwestern snack or appetizer, tortilla with melted cheese – or, more properly, quesadilla (kay-suh-DEE-yuh).

1. In a small sauté pan lightly sprayed with canola oil, cook onions until translucent.

2. In a large bowl, combine avocado, tomatoes, and cooked onion. Season mixture with cumin, salt and pepper. Mix well.

3. Lay tortilla flat on work surface. On one half, spread 6 tablespoons avocado mixture, 1 teaspoon green chile peppers, 2 tablespoons crab meat and 1 tablespoon cheese. Fold the tortilla in half.

4. Lightly spray a large sauté pan with canola oil. Cook each tortilla for 3 to 5 minutes per side, or until cheese is melted.

5. Cut each quesadilla into three triangle-shaped pieces. Serve with 2 tablespoons relish and 1 tablespoon non-fat sour cream on the side.

MAKES 4 SERVINGS

EACH SERVING CONTAINS APPROXIMATELY:
395 calories | 61 gm. carbohydrate
10 gm. fat | 20 mg. cholesterol
16 gm. protein | 598 mg. sodium | 8 gm. fiber

Nutrition Note:

Avocados are rich in calories from heart-healthy, monounsaturated fat. They also contain a fair helping of vitamins C, B1 and B2.

Created by Barry Correia

Crab and Avocado Quesadilla

FOR THE SCALLOPS:

3 tablespoons olive oil

2 tablespoons grated lemon peel

1 pound large scallops

FOR THE PAPAYA RELISH:

1 teaspoon honey

½ teaspoon fresh lime juice

½ papaya, cleaned and diced

2 teaspoons chopped fresh cilantro

1 teaspoon chopped scallions

1½ tablespoons minced red bell pepper

1 teaspoon minced red onion

Pinch salt

Scallops with Lemon Oil

1. In a small bowl, combine olive oil and grated lemon peel. Cover and let sit overnight at room temperature. Strain mixture, using a fine sieve.

2. In a small bowl, combine honey and lime juice. Add remaining ingredients for papaya relish and mix well.

3. Lightly spray a large sauté pan with olive oil. Sauté scallops over medium heat until cooked through, about 2 to 3 minutes on each side. Do not overcook.

4. Serve with 2 teaspoons lemon oil and 2 tablespoons papaya relish.

MAKES 4 SERVINGS
EACH SERVING CONTAINS APPROXIMATELY:
215 calories | 9 gm. carbohydrate
11 gm. fat | 37 mg. cholesterol
19 gm. protein | 223 mg. sodium | 1 gm. fiber

MEAL SUGGESTION:
Baby zucchini and black rice

Cook's Note:

If you would like to use the lemon oil right away, place oil and lemon peel in a blender, puree and strain.

Created by Scott Uehlein

Scallops with Lemon Oil

Ingredients

- 4 4-ounce ahi tuna fillets
- 2 teaspoons olive oil
- 2 green tea bags
- 3 cups hot water
- 1 tablespoon ginger juice
- 3 tablespoons low-sodium tamari sauce
- 2 teaspoons pineapple juice concentrate
- 3 cups garlic shoots or leeks, cut into 1-inch pieces
- 2 teaspoons olive oil
- 2 cups cooked brown rice

Ahi Tuna with Green Tea Soy Broth

 30 MIN

1. Prepare hot coals for grilling or preheat broiler.

2. Brush each tuna fillet with ½ teaspoon of olive oil and grill 3 to 5 minutes on each side or to desired doneness. Keep warm.

3. Brew the green tea in hot water for 4 to 6 minutes. In a large saucepan, combine the tea, ginger juice, tamari sauce and pineapple juice concentrate, creating a broth.

4. In a large sauté pan, heat the olive oil to medium heat. Add garlic shoots and sauté briefly.

5. Reheat broth to a simmer. Pour ¾ cup broth into a 12 ounce bowl. Add ½ cup cooked brown rice.

6. Top with grilled ahi tuna fillet and ¾ cup sautéed garlic shoots.

7. Fill the remaining 3 bowls with broth, rice, tuna and garlic shoots.

MAKES 4 SERVINGS
EACH SERVING CONTAINS APPROXIMATELY:
330 calories | 33 gm. carbohydrate
9 gm. fat | 49 mg. cholesterol
31 gm. protein | 648 mg. sodium | 3 gm. fiber

Created by Scott Uehlein

Cook's Note:

A simple way of preparing ginger juice is to grate enough fresh ginger root, skin and all, to fit in the palm of your hand. Squeeze the juice into a bowl and throw away the fibers.

Ahi Tuna with Green Tea Soy Broth

FOR THE PICKLED ONIONS:

1 large onion, thinly sliced in rounds

2 tablespoons water

2 tablespoons white wine vinegar

Pinch salt

FOR THE SLAW:

4 cups shredded cabbage

½ teaspoon salt

½ teaspoon black pepper

1 tablespoon fresh lime juice

1 tablespoon chopped fresh cilantro

FOR THE FISH TACO:

4 4-ounce grouper or halibut fillets

4 large whole-wheat flour tortillas, about 9-inches in diameter

½ cup Pico de Gallo (see recipe)

Created by Touria Semingson

Fish Taco

This classic Mexican beach food tastes especially good on a hot day.

1. In a large saucepan or kettle, boil 1 quart of water. Place onion slices in a colander. Pour boiling water over onions and drain well. Set aside.

2. In a small bowl, combine water, vinegar and salt. Add onions and marinate covered for at least 1 hour at room temperature.

3. In a medium bowl, combine all ingredients for slaw. Set aside.

4. Preheat oven for grilling or broiling. Grill fish 3 to 5 minutes on each side to desired doneness.

5. Place tortilla flat on plate. Place fish in center of tortilla and fold into a cone shape. Garnish with ¼ cup pickled onions, 1 cup slaw and 2 tablespoons Pico de Gallo.

MAKES 4 SERVINGS

EACH SERVING CONTAINS APPROXIMATELY:
295 calories | 32 gm. carbohydrate
7 gm. fat | 40 mg. cholesterol
27 gm. protein | 521 mg. sodium | 5 gm. fiber

Cook's Note:

At the Ranch we use halibut cheeks for this recipe; see if your fishmonger can find some for you.

Poultry

MORE GREAT TASTES

COOKING IS LIKE LOVE. IT SHOULD BE

ENTERED WITH ABANDON OR NOT AT ALL

– Harriet Van Horne

Poultry is a favorite source of protein – it's low in fat, relatively inexpensive and tasty, and its mild flavor makes it a perfect backdrop for interesting treatment in the kitchen. Our chefs have drawn inspiration from around the world to marinate, sauce, stuff, dredge and grind chicken, turkey and duck with dozens of other ingredients.

As with the other foods you buy, it pays to know your merchant, and to ask about means of production. Humanely raised poultry is probably safer, and certainly tastes better than factory-farmed birds.

Once you get poultry home, be careful how you handle it to prevent contamination. Keep it cold and keep it clean. Wash cutting surfaces and hands thoroughly with soap after handling raw poultry. Never taste a marinade in which poultry has soaked.

The experts all agree that poultry is done when juices from the center run clear. If you use a thermometer to monitor doneness, position it deep in the side or center of the breast. When the thermometer reads 165-170° Fahrenheit, you can be sure poultry is thoroughly cooked.

Szechuan Chicken

Szechuan is a province in Western China that's famous – along with neighboring Hunan – for hot, spicy cooking. Adjust the heat in this dish to your taste.

1. Combine marinade ingredients in a baking dish.

2. Place chicken breasts in marinade and turn to coat evenly. Cover and refrigerate for at least 2 hours.

3. Prepare coals for grilling or preheat broiler.

4. Remove chicken from marinade and grill or broil 3 to 4 minutes a side.

5. Chicken is done when juices run clear when pierced with a fork.

MAKES 4 SERVINGS
EACH SERVING CONTAINS APPROXIMATELY:
165 calories | 5 gm. fat
2 gm. carbohydrate | 72 mg. cholesterol
27 gm. protein | 364 mg. sodium | Trace fiber

MEAL SUGGESTION:
Basmati rice and stir-fry broccoli

Ingredients

FOR THE MARINADE:

3 tablespoons low-sodium tamari sauce

1½ tablespoons white wine

1 teaspoon rice vinegar

1 teaspoon peeled and minced fresh ginger

1 teaspoon minced fresh garlic

1 tablespoon chili sauce

Pinch of black pepper

1 tablespoon sesame oil

4 skinless chicken breast halves, boned and defatted

FOR THE BLACKBERRY SAUCE:

1½ cups Chicken Stock (see recipe)

2 tablespoons diced shallots

¼ cup white wine

½ cup crushed fresh or frozen blackberries, strained

FOR THE MEDALLIONS:

½ cup all-purpose flour

½ cup cornmeal

¾ teaspoon ground cumin

¾ teaspoon chili powder

¾ teaspoon ground coriander

¾ teaspoon garlic powder

¼ teaspoon salt (optional)

Pinch black pepper

1 pound boneless turkey breast, fat removed

4 teaspoons butter

Turkey Breast Medallions with Blackberry Sauce

1. In a small saucepan, bring 1½ cups of chicken stock to a boil and reduce by half. Set aside.

2. Lightly coat a medium sauté pan with canola oil and sauté shallots until translucent. Add white wine and cook until wine is almost evaporated.

3. Add strained blackberries and chicken stock. Cook until liquid is reduced by half. Keep warm.

4. In a shallow bowl, combine flour, cornmeal, cumin, chili powder, coriander, garlic powder, salt and pepper. Set aside.

5. Slice turkey breasts into 2-ounce portions. Pound with meat mallet between sheets of wax paper until ¼-inch thick.

6. Melt butter in a large sauté pan. Dredge turkey medallions in seasoned flour and sauté in butter for 3 to 5 minutes on each side, or until golden brown. Serve 2 turkey medallions with 2 tablespoons blackberry sauce.

MAKES 4 SERVINGS

EACH SERVING CONTAINS APPROXIMATELY:
285 calories | 29 gm. carbohydrate
7 gm. fat | 78 mg. cholesterol
28 gm. protein | 406 mg. sodium | 1 gm. fiber

MEAL SUGGESTION:
Mashed Yukon gold potatoes and green beans

Cook's Note:

Other fruits or even fruit juices may be used if blackberries are not available.

Created by Jim Massey

Turkey Breast Medallions with Blackberry Sauce

FOR THE SAUCE:

⅔ cup water

2 tablespoons peeled and sliced ginger

2 tablespoons sliced lemon grass

2 tablespoons low-sodium tamari sauce

2 tablespoons seasoned rice vinegar

4 teaspoons fresh lemon juice

2 teaspoons wasabi powder

FOR THE STIR-FRY:

4 teaspoons canola oil

1 pound boneless, skinless chicken breast, cut into 1-inch strips

1½ cups peeled and sliced carrots

¾ cup broccoli florets

1 cup julienne red bell pepper

2 cups julienne yellow squash

1½ cups snow peas

1 cup julienne shiitake mushrooms

2 cups chopped bok choy

2 cups cooked white basmati rice

4 teaspoons sesame seeds

2 scallions, cut on the bias

Created by Frank Cañez

Chicken Stir-fry

Lots of chopping and a few exotic ingredients result in a brilliant, nourishing medley of flavors and colors. Shiitake mushrooms are often available fresh at well-stocked supermarkets and Asian markets; look for wasabi (Japanese horseradish) powder in the Oriental foods aisle.

1. Combine all ingredients for the sauce in a small saucepan. Bring to a boil and reduce liquid to ½ cup.

2. Heat wok to medium heat and add canola oil. When oil is hot, add chicken and sauté, until cooked through, about 1 to 2 minutes. Remove chicken from wok and add carrots. Stir-fry until just tender, about 1 minute. Add broccoli, bell peppers and yellow squash. Sauté until tender, but crisp. Add snow peas, mushrooms and bok choy. Add the sauce and chicken and stir-fry until chicken and vegetables are coated.

3. Serve 1½ cups stir-fry over ½ cup cooked rice. Sprinkle with 1 teaspoon sesame seeds and garnish with scallions.

MAKES 4 SERVINGS
EACH SERVING CONTAINS APPROXIMATELY:
400 calories | 44 gm. carbohydrate
10 gm. fat | 72 mg. cholesterol
35 gm. protein | 202 mg. sodium | 7 gm. fiber

Cook's Note:

Complete preparation – everything chopped in advance – and a hot wok are the keys to tender-crisp stir-fried vegetables. Vegetables that cook more slowly, like carrots, go in first. Snow peas, bok choy and mushrooms need very little cooking time and should be added last.

Sesame-Crusted Chicken

30 MIN

This easy recipe is a terrific base for a salad or an entrée – use your imagination.

1. With a meat mallet, pound chicken breasts to ½-inch thick between 2 sheets of wax paper.

2. In a shallow bowl, combine sesame seeds and salt and sprinkle over chicken breasts.

3. In a large sauté pan, heat sesame oil over medium heat. When oil is hot, sauté chicken breasts until golden brown and cooked through, about 3 to 5 minutes on each side. Juices will run clear when meat is pierced with a fork.

MAKES 4 SERVINGS
EACH SERVING CONTAINS APPROXIMATELY:
205 calories | Trace carbohydrate
10 gm. fat | 72 mg. cholesterol
28 gm. protein | 205 mg. sodium | Trace fiber

MEAL SUGGESTION:
Japanese Stir-fry Vegetables
and brown rice

Ingredients

4 skinless chicken breast halves, boned and defatted

1 tablespoon sesame seeds

1 tablespoon black sesame seeds

¼ teaspoon salt

1 tablespoon sesame oil

Nutrition Note:

Sesame seeds are high in heart-healthy oils that can help raise "good" HDL cholesterol. Look for the black ones in Asian markets and health-food stores.

Created by Scott Uehlein

Ingredients

FOR THE MARINADE:

1/3 cup rice vinegar

2 tablespoons sesame oil

4 teaspoons reduced-sodium tamari

1 cup pineapple juice concentrate

1/2 teaspoon ground ginger

1 teaspoon minced fresh garlic

FOR THE KABOBS:

1 medium yellow bell pepper

1/2 red onion

1 pound skinless chicken breast halves, boned and defatted

8 cherry tomatoes, washed

8 medium mushrooms, washed

8 8-inch wooden skewers

Asian Chicken Kabobs

These make great appetizers.

1. Combine marinade ingredients in a shallow baking dish and mix well. Place wooden skewers in water to soak 10 to 15 minutes.

2. Cut peppers and onions into 1" x 1" pieces and set aside. Cut chicken into 1-ounce cubes.

3. Alternately skewer vegetables and chicken, placing two pieces of each vegetable and 2 cubes of chicken on each skewer.

4. Place kabobs in marinade, turning to coat evenly. Marinate covered for at least 2 hours in the refrigerator.

5. Transfer kabobs to grill or broiler and discard marinade. Cook for 3 to 4 minutes or until cooked through.

MAKES 4 SERVINGS

EACH 2 KABOB SERVING CONTAINS APPROXIMATELY:

340 calories | 39 gm. carbohydrate

6 gm. fat | 72 mg. cholesterol

32 gm. protein | 277 mg. sodium | 3 gm. fiber

MEAL SUGGESTION:
Jasmine rice

Asian Chicken Kabobs

Ingredients

FOR THE SAUCE:

1 cup Chicken Stock (see recipe)

⅓ cup diced shallots

3 tablespoons minced
  fresh garlic

1 teaspoon olive oil

½ cup diced red bell pepper

2 tablespoons cider vinegar

1 cup apple juice

½ teaspoon ground cinnamon

¼ teaspoon ground ginger

¼ teaspoon ground nutmeg

½ teaspoon salt

½ teaspoon black pepper

1 tablespoon butter

FOR THE CHICKEN:

4 skinless chicken breasts halves,
  boned and defatted

1½ cups peeled and julienne
  apples

¼ cup all-purpose flour

1 tablespoon ground cinnamon

1 tablespoon olive oil

Spiced Apple Chicken

This dish emphasizes the affinity of poultry for fruit and "sweet" spices.

1. In a small saucepan, bring 1 cup chicken stock to a boil, reduce to simmer and reduce by half. Set aside.

2. Sauté shallots and garlic with olive oil until translucent. Add red bell pepper and sauté until tender. Add cider vinegar and apple juice and reduce the liquid by half. Add chicken stock and heat to a simmer. Remove from heat. Stir in cinnamon, ginger, nutmeg, salt, pepper and butter. Set aside.

3. Preheat oven to 350°. Lightly coat a baking sheet with canola oil.

4. Place chicken breasts between sheets of waxed paper and pound with the flat side of meat mallet until ½-inch thick.

5. Place apple strips in the middle of each chicken breast and roll tightly. Secure seams with wooden toothpicks.

6. In a large bowl, mix the flour and cinnamon. Dredge rolled chicken breast in the flour mixture.

7. Heat a sauté pan with olive oil, and sauté the chicken breasts cut side down until golden brown. Transfer to a baking pan, cover and bake in oven for 8 to 10 minutes, or until chicken is cooked through. Serve with 2 tablespoons warm sauce.

MAKES 4 SERVINGS
EACH SERVING CONTAINS APPROXIMATELY:
355 calories | 34 gm. carbohydrate
12 gm. fat | 80 mg. cholesterol
29 gm. protein | 664 mg. sodium | 4 gm. fiber

MEAL SUGGESTION:
Garlic mashed potatoes
and green beans

Created by Andrew Hall

Raspberry Mustard-Crusted Chicken Breast

1. Combine ingredients for raspberry mustard in a blender until smooth. Cover tightly and refrigerate overnight to let flavors mingle.

2. In a small saucepan, combine ingredients for fig vinegar. Bring to a boil, reduce heat and simmer over low heat for 1 minute. Cool, cover tightly and refrigerate overnight. Strain.

3. With a meat mallet, pound chicken breasts between sheets of wax paper to ½-inch thick.

4. In a medium bowl, combine breadcrumbs, pistachios, salt and pepper. In a shallow pan, place chicken breasts in raspberry mustard sauce and turn to coat. Roll each one in breadcrumb mixture.

5. Heat a large sauté pan with olive oil. Sauté chicken breasts over medium heat until chicken is cooked through and crust is light brown, about 3 to 5 minutes on each side. Juices will run clear when meat is pierced with a fork.

6. Reheat fig vinegar in a small pan. Serve 1 chicken breast with 2 tablespoons fig vinegar.

MAKES 4 SERVINGS
EACH SERVING CONTAINS APPROXIMATELY:
295 calories | 24 gm. carbohydrate
9 gm. fat | 85 mg. cholesterol
30 gm. protein | 620 mg. sodium | 3 gm. fiber

MEAL SUGGESTION:
Saffron Rice and
Glazed Baby Carrots

Ingredients

FOR THE RASPBERRY MUSTARD:
- 4 tablespoons Dijon mustard
- 4 tablespoons fresh or frozen raspberries
- 3 teaspoons honey

FOR THE FIG VINEGAR:
- ⅔ cup balsamic vinegar
- 6 tablespoons chopped dried figs
- 2 teaspoons honey

FOR THE CHICKEN BREAST:
- 4 skinless chicken breast halves, boned and defatted
- ½ cup dry breadcrumbs
- 2 tablespoons minced pistachio nuts
- ½ teaspoon salt
- ¼ teaspoon black pepper
- 2 teaspoons olive oil

Cook's Note:

You can use a variety of dried fruits – and various vinegars – to make your own fruited vinegars. Cherries, blackberries and apricots are all possibilities, but the figs used in this version contribute sweetness, flavor and produce a sauce with a thicker consistency than most other fruits.

Created by Steve Matson

Ingredients

- 2 tablespoons olive oil
- 4 skinless chicken breast halves, boned and defatted
- ¼ cup all-purpose flour
- 2 tablespoons diced shallots
- 2 cups sliced mushrooms, mixed varieties
- 4 tablespoons Marsala wine
- ½ cup diced tomatoes
- 1 tablespoon chopped fresh tarragon
- 2 cups Chicken Stock (see recipe)
- ½ teaspoon salt
- ¼ teaspoon black pepper

Chicken Scaloppine with Mushrooms and Tarragon

This calls for a mixed variety of mushrooms. We recommend oyster, cremini, portobello and traditional button mushrooms, but you can use whatever types are in season.

1. With a meat mallet, pound chicken breast on a flat surface between sheets of wax paper until ½ inch thick. Cut each pounded breast in half.

2. Heat olive oil in a large sauté pan over medium heat. Dust chicken with flour and sauté in olive oil until lightly browned on both sides. Remove chicken from pan and add shallots and mushrooms. Add wine and cook until wine has almost evaporated, about 1 to 2 minutes.

3. Add tomatoes, tarragon, chicken stock, salt and pepper. Bring to a simmer and cook until sauce is reduced by half. Serve ¼ cup sauce with 2 breast pieces.

MAKES 4 SERVINGS
EACH SERVING CONTAINS APPROXIMATELY:
260 calories | 13 gm. carbohydrate
8 gm. fat | 72 mg. cholesterol
29 gm. protein | 370 mg. sodium | 2 gm. fiber

MEAL SUGGESTION:
Spinach noodles and asparagus

Created by Steve Matson

Chicken Scaloppine with Mushrooms and Tarragon

Ingredients

4 skinless chicken breast halves, boned and defatted

¼ cup buttermilk

Pinch black pepper

FOR THE SWEET CORN SAUCE:

½ cup fresh or frozen corn kernels

1 tablespoon minced fresh garlic

¼ cup diced onion

1¼ teaspoons olive oil

1 teaspoon minced jalapeño pepper

2 tablespoons minced red bell pepper

1½ cups Chicken Stock (see recipe)

1 tablespoon honey

½ teaspoon salt

Pinch black pepper

¼ teaspoon chopped fresh thyme

2 teaspoons fresh lemon juice

FOR THE BATTER:

¾ cup all-purpose flour

1¼ teaspoons paprika

¾ teaspoon salt

½ teaspoon garlic powder

½ teaspoon onion powder

¼ teaspoon celery seed

½ teaspoon dry mustard

1 teaspoon olive oil

Created by Scott Uehlein

Buttermilk-Battered Chicken Breast with Sweet Corn Sauce

A soak in buttermilk and pepper is the secret to incomparably moist chicken, paired up here with a summery sweet corn sauce.

1. With a meat mallet, pound chicken breast on a flat surface between sheets of wax paper until about ½-inch thick. In a shallow glass baking dish, combine chicken with buttermilk and black pepper. Cover and refrigerate for at least 2 hours.

2. In a medium sauté pan, sauté corn, garlic and onions in olive oil over medium heat until onions begin to turn translucent. Add jalapeño and red bell pepper and cook for 30 more seconds. Add chicken stock and reduce liquid by half. Season with honey, salt and pepper, thyme and lemon juice. Transfer to blender container and puree briefly. Set aside.

3. In a medium bowl, combine flour with paprika, salt, garlic powder, onion powder, celery seed and dry mustard. Dredge each marinated chicken breast in seasoned flour until all sides are coated generously.

4. Heat olive oil in a large sauté pan and add chicken breasts. Over medium heat, cook chicken for 3 to 5 minutes on each side until golden. When chicken is fully cooked, juices run clear when meat is pierced with a fork. Serve with ¼ cup sweet corn sauce.

MAKES 4 SERVINGS

EACH MEAL CONTAINS APPROXIMATELY:
260 calories | 23 gm. carbohydrate
7 gm. fat | 73 mg. cholesterol
30 gm. protein | 496 mg. sodium | 2 gm. fiber

MEAL SUGGESTION:
Scallion Mashed Potatoes and
Sautéed Mustard Greens

Sautéed Thai Duck Breast with Coconut Sauce

Save extra curry paste for use on vegetables or meats. This amazing condiment keeps in the refrigerator for about two weeks.

1. Combine all ingredients for the Thai red curry paste in a blender container and puree until smooth. Rub 2 teaspoons paste on each duck breast and let sit for 5 minutes. Store unused paste in an airtight container in the refrigerator.

2. In a small sauté pan, combine vegetable stock, cream and sugar. Bring to a boil and add cornstarch mixture. Cook until very thick, about 30 seconds. Remove from heat and cool to room temperature. Add remaining ingredients and whisk to combine.

3. Lightly spray a large sauté pan with canola oil. Sauté duck breasts over medium heat to desired doneness, about 3 to 5 minutes on each side, or until juices run clear when the center is pierced with a fork. Serve each breast with 3 tablespoons coconut sauce.

MAKES 4 SERVINGS
EACH SERVING CONTAINS APPROXIMATELY:
205 calories | 6 gm. carbohydrate
10 gm. fat | 7 mg. cholesterol
23 gm. protein | 402 mg. sodium | Trace fiber

MEAL SUGGESTION:
Red Himalayan rice and grilled yellow squash

Ingredients

FOR THE THAI RED CURRY PASTE:

1 medium red bell pepper, roasted

1 jalapeño pepper, roasted

1 Thai chile, diced

1 green chile, roasted

1 tablespoon grated lime peel

1 tablespoon ground coriander

1 tablespoon peeled and chopped fresh ginger

1 tablespoon minced fresh cilantro stems

2 cloves fresh garlic

1 tablespoon fresh lime juice

1 teaspoon salt

1 tablespoon chopped lemon grass

1 pound skinless duck breasts, boned and defatted

FOR THE COCONUT SAUCE:

1½ tablespoons Vegetable Stock (see recipe)

1½ tablespoons heavy cream

1 tablespoon sugar

1 teaspoon cornstarch mixed with 2 teaspoons water

2 teaspoons fresh lime juice

½ cup light coconut milk

¼ teaspoon bottled fish sauce

Created by Justin Morrow

Cook's Note:

Lemon grass is a key ingredient in Thai cooking. It's available fresh or dried at Asian markets.

2 Cornish game hens

FOR THE MARINADE:

1 cup fresh or frozen raspberries

2 cloves minced fresh garlic

1 tablespoon olive oil

1 teaspoon low-sodium tamari sauce

⅓ cup raspberry vinegar

⅓ cup plum wine

2 teaspoons chopped fresh mint

2 teaspoons cornstarch

2 teaspoons water

Raspberry Cornish Hen

1. Cut thawed hens in half lengthwise and remove skin and wing bone. Place in a large shallow bowl.

2. In a blender container, puree the raspberries, garlic, olive oil, tamari sauce, vinegar and wine until smooth. Add the fresh mint and mix by hand.

3. Pour ½ marinade over hens and marinate covered in the refrigerator for at least 2 hours.

4. Preheat oven to 350°. Lightly coat a baking pan with olive oil.

5. Place marinated hens in a the baking pan, cover and bake for 30 to 40 minutes until golden brown, or until juices run clear when thigh is pierced with a fork.

6. Pour remaining marinade through a fine mesh strainer into a small saucepan. In a small bowl or cup, combine cornstarch and water to form a thin paste. Stir into marinade, bring to a boil, reduce heat and simmer until sauce is thickened, about 2 minutes. Serve 2 tablespoons sauce over each ½ hen.

MAKES 4 SERVINGS
EACH SERVING CONTAINS APPROXIMATELY:
150 calories | 5 gm. carbohydrate
5 gm. fat | 90 mg. cholesterol
20 gm. protein | 118 mg. sodium | Trace fiber

MEAL SUGGESTION:
Glazed Baby Carrots
and Saffron Rice

Cook's Note:

You can sometimes find fresh Cornish hens at the market, but they usually come frozen. Thaw in the refrigerator overnight to decrease the chance of bacterial growth.

Created by Barry Correia

Raspberry Cornish Hen

Ingredients

FOR THE CHICKEN MEATBALLS:

2 skinless chicken breast halves, boned and defatted

1 tablespoon raisins

1 teaspoon minced fresh garlic

Pinch red chili flakes

1 teaspoon fennel seed

¼ large carrot, peeled and sliced

2 tablespoons chopped fresh parsley

1 tablespoon chopped pine nuts

½ teaspoon salt

1 tablespoon olive oil

1 whole egg, beaten

FOR THE SUB:

4 whole-wheat baguettes, about 3 ounces each

1 cup Classic Marinara Sauce, heated (see recipe)

4 ounces mozzarella cheese, shredded

Chicken Meatball Sub

These meatballs go just as well in sauce over pasta. Raisins and fennel give unique flavor to a traditional Sicilian favorite.

1. Dice chicken into 1-inch pieces. Place in a meat grinder or food processor. Grind or chop to ground-beef consistency. Add raisins, garlic, chili flakes, fennel seed, carrots, parsley and pine nuts and grind or chop together.

2. Place in a medium bowl and add salt, olive oil and egg. Mix well. Cover tightly and refrigerate overnight.

3. Preheat oven to 375°. Lightly coat a baking pan with canola oil.

4. Form ground chicken mixture into 1-ounce balls, about 2 tablespoons each. Place 2 inches apart in a baking pan and bake for 10 to 15 minutes, or until cooked through.

5. Slice bun ¾ of the way through. Place 3 meatballs in bun and top with ¼ cup warm marinara sauce. Sprinkle with 1 ounce of mozzarella cheese.

MAKES 4 SERVINGS

EACH SERVING CONTAINS APPROXIMATELY:
420 calories | 47 gm. carbohydrate
14 gm. fat | 86 mg. cholesterol
28 gm. protein | 698 mg. sodium | 4 gm. fiber

MEAL SUGGESTION:
Chuckwagon Coleslaw

Created by Scott Uehlein

Chicken Meatball Sub

FOR THE ENCHILADA SAUCE:

- 3 tablespoons all-purpose flour
- 1 tablespoon chili powder
- ½ teaspoon paprika
- ¼ teaspoon ground cumin
- ½ teaspoon ground oregano
- Pinch dried thyme
- Pinch black pepper
- ¼ teaspoon garlic powder
- ½ teaspoon onion powder
- 3½ cups Vegetable Stock (see recipe)
- 1 tablespoon chopped fresh cilantro
- 1 teaspoon honey
- 1 teaspoon fresh lime juice
- 1 teaspoon salt

FOR THE ENCHILADAS:

- ½ cup minced onion
- 12 ounces cooked chicken breast, diced
- 1 teaspoon dried oregano
- 1 teaspoon chili powder
- 1 cup Vegetable Stock (see recipe)
- 8 corn tortillas
- 4 ounces low-fat cheddar cheese, shredded
- 4 ounces shredded green leaf lettuce

Created by Scott Uehlein

Chicken Enchiladas

This popular Mexican specialty is made by rolling a softened corn tortilla around a seasoned meat or cheese filling, covering with sauce and baking. Lots of ingredients, but worth the trouble!

1. In a large sauté pan, combine flour with dry herbs and spices and cook over medium heat until golden brown. Add remaining ingredients for sauce and whisk to combine. Bring to a boil, reduce heat to low, and simmer for 45 minutes, stirring frequently to prevent scorching.

2. Lightly coat a medium sauté pan with canola oil and sauté onion, chicken, oregano and chili powder until chicken is lightly browned. Add 1 cup vegetable stock and simmer until liquid has evaporated.

3. Preheat oven to 350°.

4. Soak a tortilla briefly in warm water, lay on flat work surface and spoon 3 tablespoons chicken filling inside one edge. Roll tightly and place into 8" x 8" baking pan. Repeat. Ladle sauce on top and sprinkle with cheddar cheese. Bake for 15 minutes or until cheese is melted and sauce is bubbly.

5. Garnish with lettuce.

MAKES 4 SERVINGS
EACH 2 ENCHILADA SERVING CONTAINS APPROXIMATELY:
430 calories | 55 gm. carbohydrate
9 gm. fat | 76 mg. cholesterol
35 gm. protein | 482 mg. sodium | 6 gm. fiber

Chicken Enchiladas

FOR THE MARINADE:

- 2 tablespoons thinly sliced lemon grass
- 1 tablespoon low-sodium tamari sauce
- 2 tablespoons mirin wine
- 1 tablespoon rice vinegar
- 1 pound skinless duck breasts, boned and defatted

FOR THE PONZU SAUCE:

- 2 tablespoons fresh lime juice
- 2 tablespoons low-sodium tamari sauce
- 2 tablespoons water
- 1 tablespoon rice vinegar
- 1 teaspoon peeled and minced fresh ginger
- 2 teaspoons sugar

Lemon Grass-Marinated Duck Breast with Ponzu Sauce

1. In a shallow glass baking dish, combine lemon grass, tamari, mirin wine and rice vinegar. Add duck breasts, turn to coat, and marinate covered for at least two hours in the refrigerator.

2. Preheat grill or broiler.

3. Grill or broil marinated duck breast 3 to 5 minutes on each side or until cooked through. Juices will run clear when meat is pierced with a fork.

4. Combine all ingredients for ponzu sauce in a blender container and puree. Strain, if desired.

5. In a small saucepan, heat ponzu sauce and serve 2 tablespoons over each duck breast.

MAKES 4 SERVINGS
EACH SERVING CONTAINS APPROXIMATELY:
160 calories | 4 gm. carbohydrate
8 gm. fat | 63 mg. cholesterol
17 gm. protein | 517 mg. sodium | Trace fiber

MEAL SUGGESTION:
Rice noodles and snow peas

Cook's Note:

Mirin, or rice wine, is widely available in Oriental markets, wine shops and well-stocked supermarkets. If you cannot find fresh lemon grass, fresh ginger will do.

Created by Scott Uehlein

Duck Wrap with Apple-Raisin Chutney

1. In a baking dish, mix pepper, cinnamon, ginger, brown sugar, vinegar, oils, chili powder and diced chipotle pepper.

2. Add duck to baking dish, turning to coat each piece with seasoning mix. Cover and refrigerate for at least one hour.

3. For chutney, rehydrate raisins with ½ cup apple cider in a small bowl. Let sit for 5 minutes. Strain. Discard cider.

4. In a small saucepan, heat apples, sugar and ¼ cup cider over medium heat. Stir in rehydrated raisins, chiles, allspice, cinnamon and salt. Remove from heat, cover and keep warm.

5. Roast duck in a baking pan in a 450° oven for 12 minutes, or until cooked through. Juices will run clear when meat is pierced with a fork at the center.

6. Remove duck from oven and let rest for at least 5 minutes. Carve each breast thinly, on the bias.

7. Spread ¼ cup chutney on each warm tortilla, top with one sliced duck breast and ¼ cup greens. Roll tortilla, folding ends in, and cut in half on the diagonal.

MAKES 4 SERVINGS
EACH SERVING CONTAINS APPROXIMATELY:
380 calories | 56 gm. carbohydrate
9 gm. fat | 59 mg. cholesterol
22 gm. protein | 284 mg. sodium | 5 gm. fiber

Cook's Note:

To warm tortillas, stack and wrap in foil. Heat at 350° for 10 minutes.

Ingredients

FOR THE ROASTED DUCK BREAST:
- 1½ teaspoons black pepper
- 2 teaspoons cinnamon
- 2 teaspoons ground ginger
- 4 tablespoons brown sugar
- 2 tablespoons red wine vinegar
- 1½ teaspoons sesame oil
- 1½ teaspoons peanut oil
- ¾ teaspoon chili powder
- ¼ teaspoon canned chipotle pepper, diced
- 4 skinless duck breasts, boned and defatted

FOR THE APPLE-RAISIN CHUTNEY:
- ¼ cup raisins
- ¾ cup apple cider
- 1 cup sliced apples
- ¾ teaspoon sugar
- 1½ teaspoons diced green chiles
- Pinch allspice
- ¼ teaspoon cinnamon
- Pinch salt

FOR THE WRAP:
- 4 whole-wheat tortillas
- 1 cup mixed greens

FOR THE HERB VINAIGRETTE DRESSING:

2 teaspoons minced shallots

¾ teaspoon chopped fresh basil

½ teaspoon chopped fresh oregano

¼ teaspoon minced fresh garlic

2 tablespoons balsamic vinegar

1 tablespoon olive oil

Pinch salt

Pinch black pepper

FOR THE SANDWICH:

8 slices multi-grain bread

10 ounces thinly sliced breast of turkey

4 ounces thinly sliced Swiss cheese

1 Roma tomato, thinly sliced

1 cup fresh spinach

Turkey and Swiss Cheese Sandwich

30 MIN

1. In a small bowl, whisk together all dressing ingredients. Set aside.

2. Arrange 2½ ounces turkey, 1 ounce Swiss cheese, 1 ounce tomato slices, and ¼ cup spinach on a slice of multi-grain bread and drizzle 1 teaspoon dressing over spinach. (Cover remaining dressing and refrigerate for future use.) Top with slice of multi-grain bread.

3. Repeat process for remaining sandwiches.

MAKES 4 SANDWICHES
EACH SERVING CONTAINS APPROXIMATELY:
410 calories* | 34 gm. carbohydrate
15 gm. fat | 60 mg. cholesterol
38 gm. protein | 588 mg. sodium | 6 gm. fiber

*Calories and fat grams will vary depending upon the type of multi-grain bread you use.

Created by Shelly Pulcini-Corso

Meat

MORE GREAT TASTES

A GOOD COOK IS LIKE A SORCERESS

WHO DISPENSES HAPPINESS

– Elsa Schiapirelli

Protein is important, and meat is an efficient source of it – although, of course, there are many others.

Environmental, ethical and safety concerns about meat are very much in the news these days; we'll limit our focus to health. Know your butcher, know how the animals you choose to eat were fed and raised, and always take care in handling and storing meat. Be sure that any ground meats you consume are freshly ground – not produced in a giant plant, frozen and shipped – and that they are cooked through.

Our main health concern about meat at Canyon Ranch, however, is that most of us simply eat too much of it. Meat is nourishing – and an excellent source of important minerals – but it's high in both calories and saturated fat. Our recipes called for lean cuts, trimmed of all visible fat, and for portions a fraction of the size of a typical restaurant serving. A 4-ounce portion of meat – about the size of pack of playing cards – is about right, and using our recipes will help you learn to better judge the portions served in restaurants.

Beef Tenderloin with Apple Bourbon Sauce

1. Spray a medium saucepan lightly with canola oil. Over medium heat, sauté shallots for 1 minute. Add bourbon and cook 30 more seconds, stirring to get all the juices dissolved. Add veal stock, apple juice concentrate and sachet. Bring to a boil and cook 5 minutes.

2. Remove sachet and strain off shallots. In a small cup, mix cornstarch with 1 teaspoon water to make a thin paste. Blend into sauce using a wire whip. Remove from heat. Add diced apples, salt and pepper.

3. Prepare hot coals for grilling or preheat broiler.

4. Grill or broil meat to desired doneness. Serve with 2 tablespoons sauce.

MAKES 4 SERVINGS
EACH SERVING CONTAINS APPROXIMATELY:
220 calories | 22 gm. carbohydrate
6 gm. fat | 56 mg. cholesterol
19 gm. protein | 524 mg. sodium | Trace fiber

MEAL SUGGESTION:
Scallion Mashed Potatoes
and baby carrots.

Ingredients

FOR THE APPLE BOURBON SAUCE:
2 tablespoons chopped shallots
1 tablespoon bourbon
1 cup Veal Stock (see recipe)
1½ tablespoons apple juice concentrate
Sachet of 1 tablespoon each thyme, bay leaf and peppercorn
1 teaspoon cornstarch
4 small apples, peeled and diced
¼ teaspoon salt
¼ teaspoon black pepper

1 pound lean beef tenderloin, cut into 4-ounce fillets

Cook's Note:

A cooking sachet is a small bag made from a circle of cheesecloth filled with herbs, added to a cooking liquid, and simmered. The result is a clear, flavorful sauce.

Created by Justin Morrow

FOR THE ADOBADO PASTE:

1 tablespoon packed
   brown sugar

1 tablespoon fresh lime juice

1 clove fresh garlic, minced

2 teaspoons olive oil

3 tablespoons chili powder

1 pound lean beef tenderloin,
   cut into 4-ounce fillets

Beef Tenderloin with Adobado Paste

1. Preheat grill or broiler.

2. In a small bowl, combine brown sugar, lime juice, garlic, olive oil and chili powder. Mix to a smooth paste.

3. Spread 1 teaspoon paste on each side of beef tenderloin fillet. Grill or broil to desired doneness, about 3 to 5 minutes on each side.

MAKES 4 SERVINGS
EACH SERVING CONTAINS APPROXIMATELY:
215 calories | 7 gm. carbohydrate
10 gm. fat | 71 mg. cholesterol
25 gm. protein | 112 mg. sodium | Trace fiber

MEAL SUGGESTION:
Chipotle Mashed Potatoes
and Calabacitas

Cook's Note:

Make adobado paste in quantity and store it, tightly covered, in the refrigerator for up to 2 weeks. It's also terrific with chicken and fish.

Created by Frank Cañez

Beef Tenderloin with Adobado Paste

Ingredients

FOR THE STEW:

¼ cup all-purpose flour

¼ teaspoon salt

¼ teaspoon black pepper

1½ pounds veal, cubed

4 cups Veal Stock (see recipe)

1½ cups chopped celery

1½ cups peeled and chopped carrots

1½ cups peeled and chopped parsnips

1 tablespoon minced fresh garlic

½ cup chopped fresh basil

1 cup diced tomatoes

½ cup sherry

½ cup tomato paste

½ teaspoon salt (optional)

FOR THE POTATOES:

3 large potatoes, peeled and cubed

2 tablespoons olive oil

¼ cup nonfat milk

¼ cup heavy cream

½ teaspoon salt

½ teaspoon black pepper

1 teaspoon curry powder

2 tablespoons chopped fresh chives

1 cup Caramelized Onions (see recipe)

Created by Barry Correia

Veal Stew

You can make this sumptuous yet homey dish with beef or chicken, if you prefer.

1. In a large bowl, combine flour with salt and pepper. Coat veal cubes in flour mixture.

2. Lightly coat a large saucepan with olive oil. Sauté veal over medium heat until golden brown.

3. Add veal stock, celery, carrots, parsnips and garlic. Simmer over low heat for 20 to 25 minutes. Add remaining stew ingredients and cook for 10 minutes.

4. Place potatoes in a large saucepan and cover with cold water. Bring to a boil and cook on medium heat until potatoes are tender, about 10 to 15 minutes. Drain and add olive oil, milk, cream, salt, black pepper and curry powder. Whip with a mixer until smooth and fluffy. Stir in chives.

5. To serve, place ⅓ cup potatoes in each bowl. Top with 1 cup stew and garnish with 2 tablespoons Caramelized Onions.

MAKES 8 SERVINGS

EACH SERVING CONTAINS APPROXIMATELY:
355 calories | 41 gm. carbohydrate
10 gm. fat | 68 mg. cholesterol
23 gm. protein | 471 mg. sodium | 7 gm. fiber

Veal Stew

FOR THE VEAL:

2 pounds veal tenderloin

1 teaspoon salt

1 teaspoon black pepper

FOR THE ASPARAGUS SALAD:

2 pounds fresh asparagus, trimmed and washed

2 tablespoons chopped fresh basil

2 tablespoons grated lemon peel

2 tablespoons fresh lemon juice

1 teaspoon salt

FOR THE CAPER OIL:

¼ cup olive oil

1 tablespoon drained and rinsed capers

Veal Tenderloin with Asparagus Salad

This is a perfect hot weather meal with chilled slices of veal.

1. Preheat oven to 350°. Tie tenderloin with kitchen string into a round roast. Season with salt and pepper and sear the outside of meat in a large, hot sauté pan until light brown. Place in baking pan. Place in oven and roast until internal temperature reaches 120°, about 1½ hours. Remove from oven and cool. Cover and refrigerate.

2. Bring 2 quarts water to boil in a medium saucepan. Add asparagus and blanch for 8 to 10 minutes or until tender. Drain water and plunge into a bowl of ice water. Chop asparagus into 1-inch pieces. Combine with basil, lemon peel, lemon juice and salt in a large bowl. Mix well.

3. Combine olive oil and capers, using a mortar and pestle to form a thin paste.

4. Serve 3 ounces sliced cold veal tenderloin with ½ cup asparagus salad. Drizzle veal with 1 teaspoon caper oil.

MAKES 8 SERVINGS

EACH SERVING CONTAINS APPROXIMATELY:
210 calories | 5 gm. carbohydrate
10 gm. fat | 90 mg. cholesterol
25 gm. protein | 444 mg. sodium | 2 gm. fiber

MEAL SUGGESTION:
Crisp breadsticks or
small sourdough rolls

Created by Scott Uehlein

Veal Tenderloin with Asparagus Salad

 *Ingredients*

6 4-ounce lamb chops, trimmed of all fat

1 tablespoon ground sumac

¾ teaspoon salt

¾ teaspoon black pepper

2 tablespoons pomegranate molasses (or pomegranate syrup)

Lamb Chops with Pomegranate Molasses

30 MIN

1. Preheat grill or broiler.

2. In a small bowl, mix sumac, salt and pepper.

3. Dust lamb chop on each side with sumac mixture.

4. Grill or broil lamb chops until cooked through, about 3 to 5 minutes per side.

5. Serve 1 lamb chop with 1 teaspoon pomegranate molasses.

MAKES 6 SERVINGS
EACH SERVING CONTAINS APPROXIMATELY:
200 calories | 5 gm. carbohydrate
9 gm. fat | 81 mg. cholesterol
25 gm. protein | 377 mg. sodium | 1 gm. fiber

MEAL SUGGESTION:
Tabbouli and patty pan squash

Cook's Note:

The purple-red berries of the sumac bush are dried and ground to produce a mildly astringent, fruity spice popular throughout the Middle East. Look for ground sumac and pomegranate molasses at Middle Eastern markets or online.

Created by Scott Uehlein

Lamb Chops with Pomegranate Molasses

Ingredients

1 tablespoon Burgundy

1 teaspoon chopped fresh
   rosemary

1 cup Chicken Stock (see recipe)

1 cup Veal Stock (see recipe)

1 teaspoon salt

¼ teaspoon black pepper

1 pound lean rack of lamb

Lamb with Rosemary Jus

1. In a medium sauté pan, bring wine and rosemary to a boil. Reduce heat and simmer until wine has evaporated. Add stocks, salt and pepper. Continue to simmer until sauce has reduced by half.

2. Preheat broiler.

3. Slice lamb rack into 4-ounce portions, leaving the bone in. Place in broiling pan and broil to desired doneness, about 3 to 5 minutes.

4. Serve with ¼ cup rosemary jus.

MAKES 4 SERVINGS
EACH SERVING CONTAINS APPROXIMATELY:
205 calories | Trace carbohydrate
9 gm. fat | 83 mg. cholesterol
26 gm. protein | 230 mg. sodium | Trace fiber

MEAL SUGGESTION:
Scalloped Potatoes and
grilled zucchini and
yellow squash

Created by Justin Morrow

Fennel-Crusted Lamb
with Olive Relish

Fat is an essential nutrient in a healthy diet; all fats, however, are not created equal. Our focus on healthy fats and oils emphasizes using vegetable sources like olive and canola oils, and avocado, olives and nuts.

1. Prepare hot coals for grilling or preheat broiler.

2. Grind fennel seed, peppercorns and salt together in a spice grinder. Dust lamb chops on each side with fennel mixture. Broil or grill until cooked through, about 3 to 5 minutes on each side.

3. Combine ingredients for olive relish in a medium bowl and mix well.

4. Serve ¼ cup relish with 3 ounces cooked lamb chop.

MAKES 4 SERVINGS
EACH SERVING CONTAINS APPROXIMATELY:
155 calories | 5 gm. carbohydrate
8 gm. fat | 207 mg. cholesterol
17 gm. protein | 351 mg. sodium | 2 gm. fiber

MEAL SUGGESTION:
Roasted Yukon gold potatoes
and asparagus

Ingredients

FOR THE LAMB:

1½ teaspoons fennel seed

½ teaspoon peppercorns

½ teaspoon salt

4 4-ounce lamb chops, trimmed of all fat

FOR THE OLIVE RELISH:

¼ cup minced red onion

¼ cup minced red bell pepper

2 teaspoons grated lemon peel

1½ tablespoons fresh lemon juice

¾ cup chopped kalamata olives

2 tablespoons chopped fresh basil

2 teaspoons chopped fresh mint

Pinch black pepper

Created by Scott Uehlein

Pasta & Pizza

MORE GREAT TASTES

A CRUST EATEN IN PEACE IS BETTER

THAN A BANQUET PARTAKEN IN ANXIETY

– Aesop

Pasta, that dependable, infinitely versatile staple, comes in dozens of shapes and is made from a variety of grains. Try soba (buckwheat noodles), and rice, corn and lentil noodles for a break from wheat.

Cook all pasta in a large quantity of rapidly boiling water and watch carefully. Pasta should be cooked al dente – to the point at which noodles are cooked through but still offer slight resistance "to the tooth." This law of Italian cooking not only results in appealing texture, it produces healthier noodles: A meal of mushy, overcooked pasta is followed by a bigger surge in blood sugar levels than a meal of properly cooked pasta.

Our pasta serving size is 1 cup (210 calories and 1 gram of fat) – about a third to a quarter of what you'll get in most restaurants. You can build a wonderful, balanced meal around that cup of pasta – colorful vegetables, flavorful grilled chicken, shrimp or beef, various sauces – our recipes show you how.

Mediterranean Sauce

30 MIN

Vegetable sauce for pasta need not be dense and long-cooked. This quick sauce has fresh-from-the-garden appeal.

1. In a large sauté pan, sauté garlic in olive oil over medium heat for about 30 seconds. Add zucchini and continue to sauté until zucchini is tender.

2. Add tomatoes and basil and simmer for approximately 10 minutes. Season with salt.

3. Serve ⅓ cup sauce over 1 cup cooked pasta. Garnish each plate with 1 teaspoon of feta cheese and 1 teaspoon of black olives.

MAKES 8 SERVINGS
EACH ½ CUP SERVING CONTAINS APPROXIMATELY:
70 calories | 7 gm. carbohydrate
4 gm. fat | 25 mg. cholesterol
2 gm. protein | 104 mg. sodium | 4 gm. fiber

Ingredients

¾ teaspoon minced fresh garlic

1 tablespoon olive oil

4 cups julienne zucchini, about 1 pound

2 cups peeled and chopped tomatoes

2 tablespoons chopped fresh basil

½ teaspoon salt

8 teaspoons crumbled feta cheese

8 teaspoons chopped kalamata olives

Created by Carlos Guzman

Ingredients

2 teaspoons olive oil

1 teaspoon minced fresh garlic

1 tablespoon minced shallots

2 tablespoons diced onion

⅓ cup finely diced red bell pepper

¼ cup finely diced fennel

2 cups 2% milk

4 teaspoons cornstarch

1 tablespoon chopped fresh basil

1 tablespoon fresh lemon juice

Pinch salt

Pinch black pepper

1½ teaspoons pure anise extract

4 ounces chopped lobster meat

Lobster Sauce with Fennel

 30 MIN

1. Place oil in a large sauté pan, sauté garlic, shallots, onion, red bell pepper, and fennel until onions and shallots are translucent and vegetables are tender, about 2 to 3 minutes.

2. In a cup, mix the cornstarch with 4 teaspoons of the milk to form a thin paste. In a medium bowl, add remaining milk, and stir in cornstarch mixture. Add to sautéed vegetables and stir. Bring to a simmer and cook until sauce thickens.

3. Add remaining ingredients and cook until just heated through.

4. Serve ½ cup sauce over 1 cup cooked pasta.

MAKES 4 SERVINGS
EACH ½ CUP SERVING CONTAINS APPROXIMATELY:
100 calories | 5 gm. carbohydrate
3 gm. fat | 16 mg. cholesterol
5 gm. protein | 203 mg. sodium | 1 gm. fiber

Cook's Note:

Fennel is a celery-like vegetable with a mild licorice flavor that becomes even milder with cooking. You may substitute celery for fennel in this recipe.

Lobster Sauce with Fennel

Ingredients

- 2 skinless chicken breast halves, boned and defatted
- 2 tablespoons butter
- 2 cups diced portobello mushroom caps
- 2 tablespoons all-purpose flour
- ⅓ cup white wine
- 1 cup 2% milk
- ¼ bay leaf
- Pinch saffron threads
- ½ teaspoon black pepper
- 1 teaspoon salt

Chicken and Portobello Mushroom Cream Sauce with Saffron

1. Cut chicken in 1-inch cubes.

2. Melt 1 tablespoon butter in a large saucepan and add chicken. Cook over medium heat until chicken is cooked through and lightly browned, about 2 to 3 minutes.

3. Remove chicken from pan and add remaining 1 tablespoon butter. Add mushrooms and cook for about 2 minutes. Mix in flour and simmer for 1 minute. Add wine and simmer briefly, about 20 seconds, mixing with a wire whip.

4. Add milk and bay leaf and mix with whip until mixture begins to thicken. Reduce heat and add saffron, pepper and salt. Add cooked chicken and simmer 5 minutes. Remove bay leaf.

5. Serve ½ cup over 1 cup cooked pasta.

MAKES 4 SERVINGS
EACH ½ CUP SERVING CONTAINS APPROXIMATELY:
185 calories | 8 gm. carbohydrate
9 gm. fat | 56 mg. cholesterol
16 gm. protein | 376 mg. sodium | Trace fiber

Created by Steve Betti

Italian Garden Ragu

1. In a medium sauté pan, sauté onions, garlic, and mushrooms in olive oil until soft.

2. Add tomatoes, vegetable stock, oregano, salt and pepper. Bring sauce to a boil, reduce heat and simmer for 30 minutes, stirring occasionally.

3. Add zucchini and cook for 5 minutes. Stir in tomato paste and basil.

4. Serve ½ cup sauce over 1 cup cooked pasta.

MAKES 4 SERVINGS
EACH ½ CUP SERVING CONTAINS APPROXIMATELY:
70 calories | 14 gm. carbohydrate
2 gm. fat | 0 mg. cholesterol
3 gm. protein | 262 mg. sodium | 2 gm. fiber

Ingredients

½ cup diced onion

2 tablespoons minced fresh garlic

1 cup sliced fresh mushrooms

¾ teaspoon olive oil

1 cup diced tomato

1½ cups Vegetable Stock (see recipe)

¾ teaspoon dried oregano

½ teaspoon salt

½ teaspoon black pepper

½ cup julienne zucchini

6 tablespoons tomato paste

2½ teaspoons chopped fresh basil

Created by Joe Botz

- 1 teaspoon olive oil
- 1 tablespoon minced fresh garlic
- 2 pounds fresh clams, rinsed and scrubbed with a brush
- ¼ cup white wine
- 1½ tablespoons fresh lemon juice
- 1½ cups clam juice
- ¼ teaspoon black pepper
- 2 teaspoons cornstarch
- 2 tablespoons chopped fresh parsley

Fresh Clam Sauce

Clams in the shell impart the unmistakable scent of the sea to this simple, classic preparation. An age-old dish that cannot be improved upon.

1. In a large sauté pan, combine olive oil and garlic. Sauté for about 30 seconds over medium heat. Add clams and continue to sauté. Add white wine and cook until most of wine has evaporated. Add lemon juice, clam juice and black pepper. Simmer until clams open, about 5 minutes. Remove clams. (Discard any that do not open.)

2. In a small bowl or cup, combine cornstarch with 2 teaspoons water and mix to form a thin paste. Add to sauce and cook until thickened. Add fresh parsley.

3. Divide clams into 4 portions. Serve clams over 1 cup cooked pasta with ½ cup sauce.

MAKES 4 SERVINGS
EACH SERVING CONTAINS APPROXIMATELY:
190 calories | 9 gm. carbohydrate
3 gm. fat | 77 mg. cholesterol
30 gm. protein | 343 mg. sodium | Trace fiber

Cook's Note:

When you chop fresh parsley – flat-leaved Italian parsley is best – include plenty of tender stems. They hold most of the flavor.

Created by Justin Morrow

Fresh Clam Sauce

⅔ cup diced onion

1½ teaspoons olive oil

½ tablespoon minced fresh garlic

¼ teaspoon red chili flakes

1 teaspoon dried basil

½ teaspoon dried oregano

¼ teaspoon dried thyme

6 cups canned whole tomatoes

1½ cups canned tomato puree

1 tablespoon honey

1 tablespoon chopped fresh basil

1 tablespoon chopped fresh oregano

Classic Marinara Sauce

Versatile, popular and easy to make, this staple of Italian cooking has developed an even better reputation in the last few years – the antioxidants in tomatoes, particularly when combined with olive oil, have important health benefits for men.

1. In a large saucepan, sauté onion in olive oil over low heat. Add garlic and brown slightly. Add red chili flakes, dried herbs and sauté for about 30 seconds.

2. Immediately add whole tomatoes and tomato puree. Simmer for approximately 1 hour or until sauce has thickened. Add honey, fresh basil and fresh oregano. Puree slightly in a blender, if desired.

3. Serve ½ cup sauce over 1 cup cooked pasta.

MAKES 12 SERVINGS
EACH ½ CUP SERVING CONTAINS APPROXIMATELY:
50 calories | 11 gm. carbohydrate
Trace fat | 0 mg. cholesterol
2 gm. protein | 334 mg. sodium | 1 gm. fiber

Cook's Note:

Rub dried herbs between your hands before adding to other ingredients to release their volatile oils.

Created by Scott Uehlein

Fresh Tomato, Olive and Caper Sauce

 30 MIN

1. Place olive oil in a large sauté pan. Sauté carrots, celery and onions over medium heat until onions begin to turn translucent. Add vegetable stock and bring back to a simmer.

2. Reduce heat to low and add remaining ingredients. Simmer for 10 to 15 minutes. Add additional vegetable stock if sauce becomes too thick. Remove bay leaf.

3. Serve ½ cup sauce over 1 cup cooked pasta.

MAKES 6 SERVINGS
EACH ½ CUP SERVING CONTAINS APPROXIMATELY:
50 calories | 7 gm. carbohydrate
3 gm. fat | 0 mg. cholesterol
2 gm. protein | 460 mg. sodium | 2 gm. fiber

Ingredients

2 teaspoons olive oil

¼ cup peeled and diced carrots

¼ cup diced celery

¼ cup diced onion

1 cup Vegetable Stock (see recipe)

1 tablespoon minced fresh garlic

1½ cups diced tomatoes (about 4 medium)

¼ cup tomato paste

1 tablespoon chopped fresh basil

1 teaspoon chopped fresh oregano

¼ bay leaf

3 tablespoons chopped kalamata olives

3 tablespoons drained and rinsed capers

Cook's Note:

Kalamata olives – dark, eggplant-colored olives from Greece – have a rich and fruity flavor. Look for those packed in vinegar.

Created by Justin Morrow

Ingredients

1 medium eggplant, peeled and thinly sliced, and grilled

½ cup diced onions

1 tablespoon minced fresh garlic

1 tablespoon olive oil

1 tablespoon chopped fresh basil

1 tablespoon chopped fresh oregano

Pinch red chili flakes

½ cup white port wine

1 15-ounce can diced tomatoes, drained

1 tablespoon chopped black olives

¼ teaspoon fresh lemon juice

½ teaspoon salt

Eggplant and White Port Wine Sauce

1. Dice grilled eggplant and set aside.

2. In a large sauté pan, sauté onions and garlic in olive oil over medium heat until translucent. Add fresh herbs and chili flakes. Reduce heat and sauté for 1 to 2 minutes or until aromatic. Add wine and bring to a boil. Simmer until liquid has reduced by half.

3. Add eggplant, tomatoes and olives and continue to cook for 5 to 10 minutes. Add lemon juice and salt. Serve ½ cup sauce over 1 cup cooked pasta.

MAKES 4 SERVINGS
EACH ½ CUP SERVING CONTAINS APPROXIMATELY:
125 calories | 12 gm. carbohydrate
4 gm. fat | 0 mg. cholesterol
2 gm. protein | 465 mg. sodium | 1 gm. fiber

Cook's Note:

To remove bitterness and excess liquid from eggplant, lightly salt and cover with parchment paper. Weigh down with a baking sheet for 30 minutes or more, until liquid drains off. Rinse and blot dry. Coat lightly with olive oil before grilling.

Mixed Herb Pesto Sauce

 30 MIN

Combine all ingredients in food processor or blender container and puree until smooth. Serve 2 tablespoons with 1 cup cooked pasta.

MAKES 6 SERVINGS
EACH 2 TABLESPOON SERVING CONTAINS
APPROXIMATELY:
95 calories | 3 gm. carbohydrate
9 gm. fat | 0 mg. cholesterol
2 gm. protein | 89 mg. sodium | Trace fiber

Ingredients

4 tablespoons chopped pine nuts

1 tablespoon chopped fresh basil

1 tablespoon chopped fresh oregano

3 tablespoons shredded arugula

3 tablespoons chopped chives

2 tablespoons grated Parmesan cheese

1 tablespoon olive oil

1 tablespoon Vegetable Stock (see recipe)

2 teaspoons chopped fresh garlic

Pinch salt

Cook's Note:

Pesto is more than a pasta sauce. It's also great as a pizza topping, tossed with vegetables before roasting, spread on crusty bread in place of garlic butter, and drizzled over boiled or baked potatoes. It's one of the good things in life.

Created by Justin Morrow

½ cup diced onions

1 tablespoon minced fresh garlic

½ teaspoon red chili flakes

½ teaspoon paprika

2 teaspoons olive oil

3 cups clam juice

¼ cup thinly sliced lemon grass

½ cup chopped Roma tomatoes

¼ cup tomato sauce

2 teaspoons chopped fresh basil

Pinch salt

¾ cup cooked shellfish (shrimp, lobster or scallops)

Shellfish Sauce with Tomato and Lemon Grass

 30 MIN

1. In a medium sauté pan, sauté onions, garlic, chili flakes and paprika in olive oil.

2. Add clam juice and simmer until liquid has reduced by half. Add lemon grass, tomatoes, tomato sauce, basil and salt. Mix well and simmer 5 more minutes. Just before serving, add shellfish and warm briefly. Do not overcook!

3. Serve ½ cup sauce over 1 cup cooked pasta.

MAKES 8 SERVINGS
EACH ½ CUP SERVING CONTAINS APPROXIMATELY:
155 calories | 6 gm. carbohydrate
4 gm. fat | 106 mg. cholesterol
22 gm. protein | 433 mg. sodium | Trace fiber

Created by James Boyer

Shellfish Sauce with Tomato and Lemon Grass

Pizza

Pizza is a wonderful food that's all about freedom and creativity. In the following pages you'll find a recipe for crust, three full pizza recipes and nutritional information for some of our favorite toppings. And just to get you started, here are some combinations we particularly enjoy.

- Diced sun-dried tomatoes, goat cheese and sliced red onions

- Diced tomatoes, basil, roasted garlic and sliced mushrooms

- Eggplant Port Wine Sauce, roasted red bell pepper and chopped yellow squash

- Classic Marinara Sauce and mixed, sliced mushrooms

- Roasted garlic, feta cheese, kalamata olives, caramelized onion

- Mixed Herb Pesto Sauce, roasted peppers, grilled eggplant and pine nuts

- Diced Roma tomatoes, basil, chopped artichoke hearts and cooked, chopped shrimp

- Fresh Tomato, Olive and Caper Sauce, fresh garlic and grilled eggplant

- Roasted garlic, cooked diced chicken, feta cheese, kalamata olives and red chili flakes

- Classic Marinara Sauce, cooked Breakfast Sausage, red onion and mozzarella cheese

- Sweetened ricotta cheese, mango, peaches, pineapple (a great dessert)

Whole-Wheat Pizza Crust

Ingredients

1 cup water

½ teaspoon active dry yeast

½ teaspoon sugar

½ teaspoon salt

¾ teaspoon olive oil

1 cup whole-wheat flour

1 cup all-purpose flour

1. Mix water, yeast, sugar, salt and olive oil in a large mixing bowl. Using an electric mixer with a dough hook, add flour gradually and mix on medium low until dough separates from the sides of the bowl. Add more flour if too sticky. (If you don't have a dough hook, mix by hand, then turn out on a floured board and knead until dough is smooth and elastic.)

2. Form into a ball and place in a medium bowl which has been lightly coated with olive oil. Cover and let sit in a warm place for 1 hour.

3. Preheat oven to 400°. Lightly coat a baking sheet with olive oil.

4. Punch down dough and lightly knead for 30 seconds. Divide into 6 3-ounce balls. Lightly flour a flat surface and roll out dough to 6-inch rounds, flouring lightly to keep rolling pin from sticking to dough.

5. Place crusts on a greased baking sheet and add toppings (see pizza recipes for ideas). Place in oven for 10 minutes or until crust is golden.

MAKES 6 PIZZA CRUSTS
EACH CRUST CONTAINS APPROXIMATELY:
175 calories | 36 gm. carbohydrate
1 gm. fat | 0 mg. cholesterol
6 gm. protein | 150 mg. sodium | 4 gm. fiber

Created by Frank Cañez

1 recipe Whole-Wheat Pizza Crust

¾ cup Classic Marinara Sauce (see recipe)

3 cups fresh spinach leaves

12 ounces shredded mozzarella cheese

2 egg whites, beaten (optional)

Spinach and Cheese Calzone

1. Preheat oven to 400°. Lightly coat a baking sheet with olive oil.

2. Place crusts on baking sheet and spread each with 2 tablespoons Marinara sauce. Top with ½ cup spinach leaves and 2 ounces cheese. Fold in half to form a half moon and crimp edges. Brush with egg whites, if desired.

3. Place in oven and bake until crust is golden, about 10 to 15 minutes.

MAKES 6 SERVINGS
EACH SERVING CONTAINS APPROXIMATELY:
360 calories | 44 gm. carbohydrate
11 gm. fat | 33 mg. cholesterol
23 gm. protein | 549 mg. sodium | 6 gm. fiber

Mexican Pizza

1. Preheat oven to 400°. Lightly coat a baking sheet with olive oil.

2. Place crusts on baking sheet and spread each with ¼ cup Pico de Gallo. Sprinkle with 1 ounce chicken sausage and 1 ounce cheese.

3. Place in oven and bake until crust begins to turn golden and cheese is melted, about 10 minutes.

MAKES 6 INDIVIDUAL PIZZAS
EACH PIZZA CONTAINS APPROXIMATELY:
350 calories | 43 gm. carbohydrate
10 gm. fat | 40 mg. cholesterol
23 gm. protein | 645 mg. sodium | 1 gm. fiber

Ingredients

1 recipe Whole-Wheat Pizza Crust

1½ cups Pico de Gallo (see recipe)

6 ounces ground chicken sausage with Southwestern seasoning

6 ounces shredded low-fat Monterey Jack cheese

Cook's Note:

Be sure the sausage you buy, whether fresh or frozen, is low-fat, made from wholesome meat and free of nitrites, nitrates and other unnecessary additives.

Ingredients

1 recipe Whole-Wheat Pizza Crust

6 tablespoons roasted garlic

1 large red onion, sliced and grilled

1 large yellow squash, sliced and grilled

1 large red bell pepper, sliced and grilled

12 ounces shredded mozzarella cheese

Pizza with Grilled Vegetables and Roasted Garlic

1. Preheat oven to 400°. Lightly coat a baking sheet with olive oil.

2. Place pizza crusts on baking sheet and spread 1 tablespoon roasted garlic on each crust. Layer with 1 ounce each of grilled red onion, yellow squash and red bell pepper, and 2 ounces shredded mozzarella cheese.

3. Place in oven and bake until crust is golden and cheese melts, about 10 minutes.

MAKES 6 INDIVIDUAL PIZZAS
EACH PIZZA CONTAINS APPROXIMATELY:
375 calories | 48 gm. carbohydrate
11 gm. fat | 33 mg. cholesterol
23 gm. protein | 526 mg. sodium | 6 gm. fiber

Pizza with Grilled Vegetables and Roasted Garlic

Create-a-Pizza Toppings

Create a different pizza every night, or a custom pizza for each member of the household, while still being able to judge exactly how the nutritive value is stacking up. V=vegan (contains no animal products).

INGREDIENTS	CALORIES	CARBOHYDRATE GM	PROTEIN GM	FAT GM	CHOLESTEROL MG	SODIUM MG	CALCIUM MG	FIBER GM
PIZZA CRUST								
Whole-Wheat Pizza Crust (V)	175	36	6	1	0	150	9	4
SAUCE								
Eggplant & Port Wine Sauce (V), ¼ cup	60	6	1	2	0	230	10	1
Fresh Tomato, Olives & Caper Sauce (V), ¼ cup	25	4	1	2	0	230	11	2
Italian Garden Ragout (V), ¼ cup	35	7	2	1	0	131	12	2
Lobster and Fennel Sauce, ¼ cup	50	3	3	2	16	101	20	1
Classic Marinara Sauce (V), ¼ cup	25	6	tr	tr	0	145	27	1
Mediterranean Sauce, ¼ cup	35	4	1	2	12	52	45	4
Mixed Herb Pesto Sauce, 2 T	95	3	2	9	2	89	33	tr
Pico de Gallo (V), ¼ cup	20	4	tr	tr	0	226	19	tr
CHEESES:								
Mozzarella cheese, part skim, 1 oz.	70	tr	7	4	16	132	183	0
Feta cheese, 1 oz.	75	1	4	6	25	316	139	0
Parmesan cheese, ¼ oz.	30	tr	3	2	5	132	97	0
Colby cheese, reduced fat, 1 oz.	85	tr	8	5	18	209	224	0
Chèvre cheese, ½ oz.	40	tr	3	3	10	23	20	0
Goat cheese, ½ oz.	65	tr	4	5	15	49	127	0
Ricotta cheese, low-fat, 1 oz.	40	2	3	2	9	35	77	0

INGREDIENTS	CALORIES	CARBOHYDRATE GM	PROTEIN GM	FAT GM	CHOLESTEROL MG	SODIUM MG	CALCIUM MG	FIBER GM
CHICKEN AND FISH:								
Chicken breast, cooked, 2 oz.	95	0	18	2	48	42	9	0
Shrimp, cooked, 2 oz.	55	0	12	tr	111	127	22	0
Lobster, cooked, 2 oz.	80	2	15	1	51	129	36	0
Lox (smoked salmon), cooked, 1 oz	40	0	6	2	16	104	6	0
VEGETABLES:								
Onions (V), chopped, 2 T.	10	2	tr	0	0	1	4	tr
Squash, zucchini (V), chopped, 2 T.	5	tr	tr	tr	0	1	2	tr
Tomatoes (V), chopped, 2 T.	5	1	tr	tr	0	3	1	tr
Garlic cloves (V), chopped, 1 t.	5	1	tr	tr	0	1	6	tr
Spinach (V), shredded, ¼ c.	5	tr	tr	tr	0	11	14	tr
Shallots (V), chopped, 2 T.	15	3	tr	0	0	2	7	tr
Bell Peppers–red, green, yellow–(V), chopped, 2 T.	5	1	tr	tr	0	tr	2	tr
Mushrooms (V), chopped, ¼ c.	5	1	tr	tr	0	1	1	tr
Eggplant (V), chopped, ¼ c.	5	1	tr	tr	0	1	1	tr
Peppers, green chili (V), chopped, 2 T.	5	1	tr	tr	0	2	1	tr
Olives (V), chopped, 1 T.	10	1	tr	1	0	74	7	tr
Cucumber (V), chopped, 2 T.	5	tr	tr	tr	0	1	2	tr
Artichokes (V), chopped, 2 T.	10	2	tr	0	0	14	6	tr
FRUITS								
Papaya (V), chopped, 2 T.	5	1	tr	0	0	1	4	tr
Mango (V), chopped, 2 T.	15	3	tr	tr	0	0	2	tr
Pineapple (V), chopped, 2 T.	10	2	tr	tr	0	0	1	tr

Desserts

MORE GREAT TASTES

Dessert? At Canyon Ranch? Of course.

Eating for good health need not and

should not mean deprivation.

Our sugar guideline is no more than two to

three teaspoons of added sugar per serving

– a rule that makes our chefs' creations all

the more delectable. The natural sweetness

of fruits and nuts, the rich goodness of

milk, butter and eggs, the seductive flavors

of chocolate and vanilla come through all

the more clearly when they're not

overwhelmed by excessive sugar. We think

you'll agree – and we think you'll enjoy the

concept of the nutritionally virtuous

dessert.

ONE CANNOT THINK WELL, LOVE WELL, SLEEP

WELL, IF ONE HAS NOT DINED WELL

–Virginia Woolf

Gingerbread Pudding

1. Preheat oven to 325°.

2. In a large mixing bowl, whisk brown sugar, molasses, egg, egg white and prune puree until light and fluffy. Add flour, salt, baking powder, cinnamon, ginger, nutmeg and cloves and stir to combine. Add milk and mix well.

3. Lightly coat the bottom of a 15" x 10" x 1" baking sheet with canola oil and line with parchment paper. Pour batter over paper and bake for 20 to 25 minutes or until toothpick inserted in the center comes out clean. Remove from oven and let cool on rack. Leave oven at 325°.

4. In a medium saucepan, combine milk, sugar and vanilla on medium heat and stir until sugar is dissolved. Cool slightly.

5. Beat eggs in a large bowl. Slowly whisk in warm milk mixture. Strain through a fine mesh strainer if mixture is lumpy.

6. Turn gingerbread out of baking sheet and remove parchment paper. Cut into ½" squares and evenly divide among 12 4-ounce custard cups. Pour ¼ cup custard over gingerbread in each ramekin.

7. Arrange custard cups in a deep baking pan. Place in oven and carefully pour hot water into the pan until it comes up to the level of the custard in the cups. Bake for 45 minutes in 325° oven until custard is set and a knife inserted in the center comes out clean. Serve warm.

MAKES 12 SERVINGS
EACH ½ CUP SERVING CONTAINS APPROXIMATELY:
120 calories | 18 gm. carbohydrate
2 gm. fat | 49 mg. cholesterol
3 gm. protein | 142 mg. sodium | 1 gm. fiber

Ingredients

FOR THE GINGERBREAD:

- 2 tablespoons brown sugar
- 2 tablespoons blackstrap molasses
- 1 whole egg
- 1 egg white
- ¼ cup prune puree
- ¾ cup whole-wheat pastry flour
- ½ teaspoon salt
- 1 teaspoon baking powder
- ¼ teaspoon ground cinnamon
- ¼ teaspoon ground ginger
- ¼ teaspoon ground nutmeg
- ¼ teaspoon ground cloves
- ¼ cup skim milk

FOR THE PUDDING:

- 1½ cups 2% milk
- ⅓ cup sugar
- 1 tablespoon pure vanilla extract
- 4 whole eggs

Created by Laurie Erickson

2 cups dried pears (about 8 ounces)

1½ cups dried figs (about 6 ounces)

2½ cups water

¼ teaspoon grated lemon peel

½ teaspoon pure vanilla extract

½ teaspoon ground cinnamon

¼ teaspoon ground cloves

8 full sheets phyllo pastry

1 tablespoon sugar

¼ teaspoon ground cinnamon

Spiced Pear and Fig in Phyllo

1. Preheat oven to 375°. Lightly coat the cups of a 12-cup muffin tin with canola oil.

2. Slice pears and figs into strips. Place in a medium saucepan with water, lemon peel, vanilla, cinnamon and cloves. Cover and bring to a boil over medium heat.

3. Reduce heat and simmer until most of the water is absorbed, stirring frequently. Remove the cinnamon sticks. Cover and set aside.

4. In a small bowl, mix the sugar and ground cinnamon.

5. Using 4 sheets of phyllo, lay one sheet on a work surface (keep remaining sheets covered with a damp towel to prevent drying out). Mist with canola oil and sprinkle with a pinch of sugar mixture. Top with another phyllo sheet and repeat the process for 2 more layers. Cut into 6 equal squares. Repeat process with 4 more phyllo sheets.

6. Arrange squares in lightly oiled muffin tins, to form cups. Mist tops with canola oil spray and bake in a 375° oven for 5 minutes or until golden brown. Remove and let cool on a rack.

7. Fill each phyllo cup with ⅓ cup of the warm fig and pear compote.

MAKES 12 SERVINGS
EACH SERVING CONTAINS APPROXIMATELY:
150 calories | 33 gm. carbohydrate
2 gm. fat | 0 mg. cholesterol
2 gm. protein | 66 mg. sodium | 5 gm. fiber

Spiced Pear and Fig in Phyllo

1 cup plus 2 tablespoons nonfat milk

2½ tablespoons polenta

⅔ cup semi-sweet chocolate chips, about 4 ounces

3 tablespoons sugar

2 whole eggs

4 egg whites

1 tablespoon unsweetened applesauce

½ teaspoon baking powder

Chocolate Polenta Cake

This wheat- and gluten-free cake is an interesting use of polenta, the cornmeal mush of Northern Italy. If you can't find polenta, substitute stone-ground cornmeal.

1. Preheat oven to 350°. Lightly coat an 8" round cake pan with canola oil.

2. In a medium saucepan, bring milk to a boil, then whisk in polenta with a wire whip. Cook until thickened, stirring constantly, about 10 minutes. Cool slightly.

3. In a medium saucepan, slowly melt the chocolate. Blend in polenta mixture and set aside.

4. In a double boiler, combine sugar, eggs and egg whites. Whisk until warm or until eggs are a lemon yellow color. Transfer egg mixture to a medium bowl and beat with an electric mixer on high speed for 8 to 10 minutes. Mixture will become pale yellow.

5. Stir applesauce into the chocolate polenta mixture and mix well. Sprinkle the baking powder over the mixture, then gently fold in half of the egg mixture until just combined.

6. Gently fold in remaining egg mixture. Pour batter into pan. Bake for 25 to 30 minutes. Cool. Cut into 8 slices.

MAKES 8 SERVINGS
EACH SERVING CONTAINS APPROXIMATELY:
135 calories | 18 gm. carbohydrate
6 gm. fat | 56 mg. cholesterol
5 gm. protein | 58 mg. sodium | Trace fiber

Dried Cherry and Nut Torte

1. Preheat oven to 300°. Lightly coat a 9" x 13" baking pan with canola oil.

2. In a medium bowl, sift together flour and baking powder. Set aside.

3. In a large bowl, cream butter, applesauce and honey until smooth. Add almond extract and mix well. Add egg yolks and beat until creamy.

4. Add flour mixture in thirds, alternately with milk, to egg mixture. Mix well after each addition. Spread evenly into baking pan.

5. In a medium mixing bowl, beat egg whites until foamy with an electric mixer. Add sugar, 2 tablespoons at a time, and continue to beat on high speed until stiff peaks form.

6. Pour batter in pan and sprinkle with dried cherries. Spread beaten egg whites over batter and sprinkle with pecans. Bake for 30 to 45 minutes, or until cake is cooked through and meringue is lightly brown. Cut into 18 equal portions.

MAKES 18 SERVINGS
EACH SERVING CONTAINS APPROXIMATELY:
135 calories | 21 gm. carbohydrate
5 gm. fat | 56 mg. cholesterol
2 gm. protein | 43 mg. sodium | Trace fiber

Ingredients

1 cup all-purpose flour
1 teaspoon baking powder
¼ cup butter
¼ cup unsweetened applesauce
¼ cup honey
1 teaspoon pure almond extract
4 whole eggs, separated
3 tablespoons 2% milk
½ cup sugar
½ cup dried cherries
¼ cup chopped pecans

Created by Laura Stanton

Ingredients

FOR THE FILLING:

3 tablespoons cornstarch

4 tablespoons water

1½ pounds apples, peeled and sliced

3 tablespoons sugar

¾ teaspoon ground cinnamon

½ cup raisins

FOR THE PÂTE BRISÉE:

1 cup all-purpose flour

¼ teaspoon salt

3 tablespoons sugar

¼ cup cold butter

6 tablespoons ice cold water

1 egg white, beaten

1 teaspoon sugar

Apple Strudel

Replace the apples with seasonal fruits, as you wish.

1. Preheat oven to 375°. Lightly coat a baking sheet with a small amount of canola oil and set aside.

2. Mix cornstarch and 2 tablespoons water in a small bowl. Set aside.

3. Lightly coat a sauté pan with a small amount of canola oil. Over medium heat, sauté apples with sugar, cinnamon, and remaining water. When apples are tender, stir in raisins.

4. Add cornstarch mixture to apples and cook until thickened. Remove from heat and cool. Set aside.

5. Place flour in a medium bowl. Add salt and sugar and mix well. Add butter and cut into flour, using a pastry cutter, until butter is the size of small peas. Add water, 1 tablespoon at a time, mixing gently and briefly after each addition. Dough will begin to form a ball when enough water has been added. Gather dough with dry hands and form into an even ball. Let rest for 5 minutes.

6. On a lightly floured surface, roll out dough into a 8" x 12" rectangle. Spoon filling along the long edge of the dough, about 1 inch from edge. Roll the dough and filling over itself and seal the ends to form the strudel. Score into 10 1-inch slices.

7. Brush top of strudel with beaten egg white. Sprinkle with sugar and transfer to greased baking sheet.

8. Bake in preheated oven for 35 to 40 minutes, or until top is lightly browned. Remove from oven and trim any extra pastry off the ends. Let cool slightly on a rack. Cut and serve.

MAKES 10 SERVINGS
EACH SERVING CONTAINS APPROXIMATELY:
150 calories | 31 gm. carbohydrate
3 gm. fat | 7 mg. cholesterol
2 gm. protein | 101 mg. sodium | 3 gm. fiber

Apple Strudel

1 cup graham cracker crumbs (about 15 graham cracker squares)

2 tablespoons unsweetened applesauce

1 cup water

1 vanilla bean

2 cups nonfat cottage cheese

2 cups light cream cheese

½ cup yogurt cheese

3 whole eggs

1 tablespoon all-purpose flour

¾ cup sugar

1 tablespoon pure vanilla extract

1 cup unsweetened frozen cherries

¼ cup sugar

French Vanilla Cheesecake

This not-as-wicked-as-it-tastes treat gets its flavor straight from the vanilla bean. The vanilla paste inside the bean is a mass of tiny spheres – the minute seeds of a celadon-colored orchid.

1. Preheat oven to 325°. Lightly coat a 10" springform pan with canola oil.

2. In a medium bowl, combine graham cracker crumbs and applesauce. Mix well. Press into the bottom of springform pan. Set aside.

3. Bring water to boil in a small saucepan. Add vanilla bean and simmer until softened, about 1 minute. Remove from water and when bean is cool enough to handle, slit lengthwise. Scrape out vanilla bean paste inside with a knife and reserve.

4. In a blender container, puree cottage cheese until smooth. In a large mixing bowl, combine pureed cottage cheese, cream cheese and yogurt cheese and blend with electric mixer on high until smooth, about 2 minutes. Add eggs, one at a time and blend well. Add flour, sugar, vanilla bean paste and vanilla extract. Blend well. Pour into graham cracker crust.

5. Bake for 40 minutes. Turn oven off and allow cheesecake to cool slowly, still in the oven, for another 30 minutes. Remove from oven and let cool for 20 minutes before refrigerating.

6. In a medium saucepan, combine cherries with sugar and bring to a boil. Reduce heat and simmer until sugar is dissolved and cherries begin to soften, about 10 minutes. Add water, if necessary, to keep from scorching. Remove from heat, cool, cover, and refrigerate.

7. When cheesecake is cold, remove springform sides and slice into 16 portions. Serve 1 tablespoon cherries over each slice.

MAKES 16 SERVINGS

EACH SERVING CONTAINS APPROXIMATELY:
175 calories | 20 gm. carbohydrate
6 gm. fat | 59 mg. cholesterol
9 gm. protein | 328 mg. sodium | Trace fiber

Created by Touria Semingson

Lemon Blackberry Pie

This is a true seasonal dish. Use whatever fresh berries are available – raspberries, boysenberries or blueberries will do nicely. Frozen berries are too juicy and will ruin the crust.

1. Preheat oven to 400°.

2. Place flour in a medium bowl. Add salt and sugar and mix well. Add butter and cut into flour, using a pastry cutter, until butter is the size of small peas. Add water, 1 tablespoon at a time, mixing gently and briefly with a fork after each addition. Dough will begin to form a ball when enough water has been added. Gather dough with dry hands and form into an even ball. Let rest for 5 minutes.

3. On a lightly floured surface, roll into a 12-inch circle. Gently drape over a 9" pie pan and flute edges. Lightly prick bottom of crust with a fork. Bake for about 8 minutes or until puffy, but not browned. Remove from oven and set aside. Reduce oven temperature to 350°.

4. In a large bowl, combine lemon juice and sugar. In medium mixing bowl, beat eggs and egg whites together with an electric mixer until combined. Add to lemon juice mixture and beat until a bright lemon color forms. Add lemon peel and melted butter and mix well.

5. Spread berries evenly in the bottom of pie shell. Pour lemon mixture over blackberries and bake for 30 minutes. Let cool and cut into 16 slices.

MAKES 16 SERVINGS
EACH SERVING CONTAINS APPROXIMATELY:
135 calories | 20 gm. carbohydrate
5 gm. fat | 53 mg. cholesterol
3 gm. protein | 37 mg. sodium | Trace fiber

Ingredients

FOR THE PÂTE BRISÉE:

1 cup all-purpose flour

¼ teaspoon salt

3 tablespoons sugar

¼ cup cold butter

6 tablespoons ice cold water

FOR THE FILLING:

¾ cup fresh lemon juice

¾ cup sugar

3 whole eggs

2 egg whites

4 tablespoons grated lemon peel

¼ cup melted butter

1 cup fresh blackberries

Created by Touria Semingson

1 vanilla bean

1 cup half and half

1⅓ cups evaporated skim milk

⅔ cup sugar

4 egg yolks

1 tablespoon Grand Marnier liqueur

1½ teaspoons grated orange peel

¼ teaspoon pure orange extract

2½ teaspoons sugar

Created by Touria Semingson

Grand Marnier Crème Brûlée

The very last step – broiling the sugar on top of the custard until it caramelizes – gives this elegant dessert its name.

1. Preheat oven to 300°

2. Bring 1 cup of water to boil in a small saucepan. Add vanilla bean and simmer until softened, about 1 minute. Remove from water and when bean is cool enough to handle, slit lengthwise. Scrape out vanilla paste inside with a knife and reserve.

3. Combine half and half with milk in a large saucepan. Add vanilla paste to milk mixture and heat to just below a simmer over medium heat. Add sugar and heat to a simmer, stirring constantly. Remove from heat.

4. Place egg yolks in a small bowl. Temper egg yolks with milk mixture by adding a small amount of milk – about ¼ cup – to egg yolks while stirring. Repeat process a few times and then add mixture back to milk mixture on the stove, stirring constantly. Do not allow mixture to come to a boil. When thickened, add Grand Marnier, orange peel and orange extract and remove from heat.

5. Pour approximately ⅓ cup into each of 10 4-ounce custard cups and arrange in a deep baking pan. Place in oven and carefully pour hot water into the pan around the cups until it comes up to the level of the custard. Bake for 30 to 45 minutes, until custard is set or until a knife inserted in the center comes out clean. Cool, cover and refrigerate.

6. When ready to serve, preheat broiler. Sprinkle ¼ teaspoon sugar on top of custard. Place under broiler for 1 minute or until sugar is caramelized. Watch carefully – sugar burns quickly.

MAKES 10 SERVINGS
EACH SERVING CONTAINS APPROXIMATELY:
155 calories | 18 gm. carbohydrate
6 gm. fat | 154 mg. cholesterol
5 gm. protein | 54 mg. sodium | 0 mg. fiber

Cook's Note:

Tempering beaten eggs with small additions of a hot mixture warms them for even incorporation. If you simply poured eggs straight into the milk on the stove, they'd cook instantly and form blobs of cooked egg in milk – instead of this rich, lustrous cream.

Grand Marnier Crème Brûlée

2 medium limes
½ cup sugar
4 whole eggs
½ cup 2% milk
2 kiwis, peeled and sliced

Lime Pots de Crème

1. Preheat oven to 275°.

2. Using a vegetable peeler or paring knife, cut the green peel from the limes, being careful not to cut into white pith. Place peel in a small saucepan of boiling water and boil for 5 minutes. While peel is boiling, juice limes and discard membranes and pith. Strain peel from the boiling water. Place lime juice, lime peel, sugar, eggs and milk in a blender container and blend on high for 5 minutes. Strain through a fine sieve.

3. Fill six 4-ounce custard cups ¾ of the way with lime mixture. Place in large baking pan, place in oven, then carefully pour in hot water to the level of the custard in the cups.

4. Bake for 30 minutes or until a knife inserted in the center comes out clean. Garnish with a slice of kiwi.

MAKES 6 SERVINGS
EACH SERVING CONTAINS APPROXIMATELY:
145 calories | 24 gm. carbohydrate
4 gm. fat | 140 mg. cholesterol
5 gm. protein | 55 mg. sodium | Trace fiber

Created by Laurie Erickson

Almond Pear Torte

Also good made with lightly poached apples.

1. Preheat oven to 400°.

2. Place flour in a medium bowl. Add salt and sugar and mix well. Add butter and cut into flour, using a pastry cutter, until butter is the size of small peas. Add water, 1 tablespoon at a time, mixing gently and briefly with a fork after each addition. Dough will begin to form a ball when enough water has been added. Gather dough with dry hands and form into an even ball. Let rest for 5 minutes.

3. On a lightly floured surface, roll dough into a 12-inch circle. Gently drape over a 9" tart pan or 9" x 9" square baking pan and press into the pan. Lightly prick bottom of crust with a fork. Bake for about 8 minutes or until puffy, but not browned. Remove from oven and set aside.

4. In a large mixing bowl, combine sugar with almond paste with an electric mixer until sugar is dissolved, about 5 minutes. Add butter, whole-wheat pastry flour, almond milk and vanilla. Mix well. Continue mixing, adding eggs, one at a time. Pour mixture into crust. Arrange pears symmetrically over filling. Reduce heat to 350° and bake for 30 to 40 minutes or until crust is golden brown and filling is set.

5. Remove from oven and cool before slicing.

MAKES 16 SERVINGS
EACH SERVING CONTAINS APPROXIMATELY:
170 calories | 25 gm. carbohydrate
7 gm. fat | 35 mg. cholesterol
3 gm. protein | 29 mg. sodium | 1 gm. fiber

Cook's Note:

Almond milk, which has sweet, light almond flavor, can be purchased at natural food stores.

Ingredients

FOR THE PÂTE BRISÉE:
1 cup all-purpose flour
¼ teaspoon salt
3 tablespoons sugar
¼ cup cold butter
6 tablespoons ice cold water

FOR THE FILLING:
½ cup sugar
¾ cup almond paste
2 tablespoons melted butter
½ cup whole-wheat pastry flour
¼ cup almond milk
1 teaspoon pure vanilla extract
2 whole eggs
2 cups juice-packed canned pears, drained and sliced

Created by Touria Semingson

2 egg yolks

¼ cup sugar

1 tablespoon Marsala wine

2 tablespoons white chocolate chips

½ vanilla bean, scraped

½ tablespoon gelatin

⅓ cup Neufchâtel cheese

2 egg whites

1 tablespoon sugar

⅓ cup heavy cream

½ cup brewed coffee

20 ladyfingers

Dash cocoa powder

Tiramisu

1. In a double boiler, combine egg yolks, sugar, wine, white chocolate and vanilla bean. Mix well. Heat until thickened, about 8 to 10 minutes. Do not let simmer. Set aside to cool.

2. Combine gelatin and 1 tablespoon water in a small saucepan and let sit for 5 minutes to soften gelatin. Heat over low, stirring, to dissolve. Cool and add to egg mixture.

3. In a small bowl, whip Neufchâtel cheese with an electric mixer and add to cooled egg mixture.

4. In a medium bowl, whip egg whites with electric mixer until frothy. Increase speed and gradually add sugar. Whip until stiff peaks form. Set aside. In another, small bowl, whip cream until soft peaks form. Do not over mix. Fold egg mixture into egg whites. Then gently fold in whipped cream.

5. Lay half the ladyfingers on bottom of a 8½" x 4½" x 2½" loaf pan. Brush with coffee. Spread half of cream mixture over ladyfingers. Soak remaining ladyfingers in coffee and layer over cream mixture. Top with remaining cream mixture. Sprinkle with cocoa powder.

6. Place in freezer for at least 2 hours or overnight to set. Cut into 12 slices.

MAKES 12 SERVINGS
EACH SERVING CONTAINS APPROXIMATELY:
145 calories | 18 gm. carbohydrate
7 gm. fat | 114 mg. cholesterol
4 gm. protein | 55 mg. sodium | Trace fiber

Cook's Note:

Look for ladyfingers –
a delicate sponge cake –
made without hydrogenated
vegetable oil.

Created by Touria Semingson

Tiramisu

⅓ cup fresh lemon juice

2 tablespoons butter

3½ tablespoons sugar

2 egg yolks, beaten

½ cup diced fresh organic strawberries

1½ tablespoons sugar

1½ tablespoons water

1½ pints fresh organic strawberries, hulled and sliced

Berries with Lemon Curd

June in a dish.

1. In a small saucepan, combine lemon juice, butter and sugar. Bring to a boil, stirring constantly. Remove from heat. Cool.

2. Place beaten egg yolks in a small bowl. Spoon 2 tablespoons lemon juice mixture into egg yolks, mix well then add back to remaining lemon juice mixture. Return to heat and slowly bring to a boil over medium heat, stirring constantly. Once mixture is boiling, remove from heat and cool.

3. In a blender container, combine ½ cup diced strawberries, sugar and water. Puree until smooth.

4. Place 2 tablespoons strawberry sauce on plate. Top with ½ cup sliced strawberries and 1½ tablespoons lemon curd.

MAKES 6 SERVINGS
EACH SERVING CONTAINS APPROXIMATELY:
120 calories | 19 gm. carbohydrate
5 gm. fat | 71 mg. cholesterol
2 gm. protein | 4 mg. sodium | 3 gm. fiber

Created by Touria Semingson

Chocolate Cake with Raspberry Filling

1. Preheat oven to 350°. Lightly coat a 9" cake pan with canola oil. Dust with flour.

2. In a large bowl, combine flour, cocoa, sugar, baking powder, baking soda and salt.

3. In a medium bowl, combine buttermilk, carrot and prune puree, extracts, coffee and egg. Mix on low with an electric mixer until smooth. Add in dry ingredients and continue to mix on low. Add melted unsweetened chocolate and beat on medium until glossy and smooth. Fold in chocolate chips.

4. Pour into prepared cake pan and bake for 25 to 30 minutes or until toothpick inserted at the center comes out clean. Place on rack and cool.

5. Invert cake onto dry surface and slice in half horizontally using a serrated knife. Spread raspberry preserves on bottom layer. Replace top and frost with nonfat fudge sauce. Slice into 16 servings.

MAKES 16 SERVINGS
EACH SERVING CONTAINS APPROXIMATELY:
135 calories | 26 gm. carbohydrate
3 gm. fat | 15 mg. cholesterol
3 gm. protein | 153 mg. sodium | 2 gm. fiber

Ingredients

1¼ cups all-purpose flour

⅓ cup cocoa

¾ cup sugar

1 teaspoon baking powder

1 teaspoon baking soda

Pinch salt

½ cup buttermilk

1 4-ounce jar baby food carrot puree

1 4-ounce jar baby food prune puree

1 tablespoon pure vanilla extract

1 tablespoon pure almond extract

2 tablespoons brewed coffee

1 whole egg

1 egg white

1 1-ounce square unsweetened baking chocolate, melted

¼ cup semi-sweet chocolate chips

½ cup raspberry all-fruit preserves

¼ cup nonfat fudge sauce

Created by Jayne Shaulis

FOR THE RASPBERRY CONSOMMÉ:

2 pints fresh or frozen raspberries

3 tablespoons sugar

2 tablespoons raspberry liqueur

½ vanilla bean

FOR THE PHYLLO COOKIE:

3 phyllo sheets

2 tablespoons melted butter

1 tablespoon granulated sugar

FOR THE LEMON CHIFFON:

½ cup lemon juice

⅓ cup granulated sugar

2 egg yolks

½ tablespoon unflavored gelatin

1 tablespoon water

2 tablespoons sugar

2 tablespoons water

2 egg whites

¼ cup heavy cream

Created by Touria Semingson

Lemon Chiffon

1. Combine all ingredients for raspberry consommé in a medium bowl. Let sit at room temperature for at least 3 hours. Place in double boiler and cook for 15 minutes until all liquid has seeped out of berries. Remove vanilla bean and slice lengthwise, scraping out bean pulp and mixing into sauce. Cool, strain, cover and refrigerate.

2. Cut phyllo sheets in half, brush with melted butter, sprinkle with sugar, and layer one on top of the other to make 6 layers. Place on baking sheet then lay another sheet pan over stacked phyllo sheets. Top with a heavy object. Refrigerate for 3 hours.

3. Combine lemon juice, ⅓ cup sugar and egg yolks in a small saucepan. Beat until foamy and lemon colored. Place on stove and cook over low heat until just thickened. Combine gelatin and water in a small bowl and set aside for 5 minutes. Add to egg yolk mixture.

4. Combine 2 tablespoons sugar and water and place in a small saucepan. Cook over medium heat until sugar is dissolved, about 1 to 2 minutes. Place egg whites in a medium mixing bowl and begin whipping with an electric mixer on medium speed until soft peaks form. Add hot sugar water slowly to egg whites while beating on high to form stiff peaks. Set aside. In a small bowl, whip heavy cream to soft peaks.

5. Place lemon custard in a medium bowl. Gently fold in egg whites. Fold in whipped cream last. Pour chiffon into a 8½" x 4½" x 2½" glass baking dish lined with plastic wrap and place in freezer for 2 hours to set.

6. Preheat oven to 350°. Using a 3-inch cookie cutter, cut phyllo dough sheets into rounds and place on greased baking sheet. Bake for 10 minutes or until crispy. Cool.

7. Remove chiffon from freezer about 15 minutes before serving. Invert the dish over a plate and remove plastic wrap. Cut into 10 triangles or squares. Serve with 2 tablespoons raspberry consommé and a phyllo cookie.

MAKES 10 SERVINGS
EACH SERVING CONTAINS APPROXIMATELY:
140 calories | 22 gm. carbohydrate
5 gm. fat | 65 mg. cholesterol
2 gm. protein | 37 mg. sodium | 1 gm. fiber

Cook's Note:

To remove bubbles from plastic wrap lining the baking dish, fill with water which presses the plastic wrap against the dish walls. Pour out water, dry and use.

Lemon Chiffon

FOR THE PÂTE BRISÉE:

1 cup all-purpose flour

¼ teaspoon salt

3 tablespoons sugar

¼ cup cold butter

6 tablespoons ice cold water

FOR THE FILLING:

½ cup sugar

½ cup corn syrup

2 whole eggs

1 teaspoon butter, melted

1 cup chopped pecans

1½ teaspoons pure vanilla extract

2 large red apples, cored, peeled and chopped

1 teaspoon fresh lemon juice

Pecan Tart

1. Preheat oven to 350°.

2. In a medium bowl, combine flour, salt and sugar and mix well. Add butter and cut into flour, using a pastry cutter, until butter is the size of small peas. Add water, 1 tablespoon at a time, mixing gently and briefly with a fork after each addition. Dough will begin to form a ball when enough water has been added. Gather dough with dry hands and form into an even ball. Let rest for 5 minutes. Roll pâte brisée to a 12-inch circle. Gently drape over a 9" tart pan and lightly press into pan.

3. In a large bowl, combine sugar and corn syrup. Add eggs and beat until smooth. Add melted butter and continue to beat. Add pecans and vanilla and mix well. Set aside.

4. In a small bowl, mix apples with lemon juice. Spread apples onto bottom of pan and pour egg mixture over apples. Bake tart for 45 minutes to 1 hour or until set.

5. Cool on rack before cutting into 16 pieces.

MAKES 16 SERVINGS
EACH SERVING CONTAINS APPROXIMATELY:
155 calories | 22 gm. carbohydrate
7 gm. fat | 32 mg. cholesterol
2 gm. protein | 167 mg. sodium | 1 gm. fiber

Created by Touria Semingson

Pecan Tart

1½ cups low-fat milk
½ cup half and half
1 teaspoon pure vanilla extract
1 vanilla bean
½ cup sugar
¼ cup beaten egg yolks

Canyon Ranch Homemade Vanilla Ice Cream

An ice cream freezer and a candy thermometer make this a snap.

1. Place egg yolks in a medium bowl.

2. In a large saucepan, combine remaining ingredients and cook over medium heat, stirring constantly.

3. When milk mixture is scalded (about 165 degrees), remove vanilla bean and let cool. Then remove milk from heat and start adding ¼ cup at a time to egg yolks, stirring constantly. Mix well after each addition.

4. Slice vanilla bean lengthwise, scrape out vanilla paste and add to custard mixture. Mix well. Return to saucepan.

5. Place saucepan back on heat. Stirring constantly, heat to just under a simmer – about 170 degrees. Do not boil! Immediately transfer to an ice bath and cool completely.

6. Place in an ice cream freezer and follow directions to freeze the ice cream.

MAKES 10 SERVINGS
EACH ⅓ CUP SERVING CONTAINS APPROXIMATELY:
90 calories | 12 gm. carbohydrate
3 gm. fat | 117 mg. cholesterol
3 gm. protein | 27 mg. sodium | 0 mg. fiber

Cook's Note:

For chocolate ice cream, add ¾ ounce melted unsweetened baking chocolate to hot milk and egg mixture before placing in ice bath.

For peanut butter ice cream, add 2 tablespoons natural creamy peanut butter to hot milk and egg mixture before placing in ice bath.

For coffee ice cream, add 1 tablespoon espresso concentrate to hot milk and egg mixture before placing in ice bath.

For fruit-based ice cream, add 2 to 4 tablespoons of fruit puree to hot milk and egg mixture before placing in ice bath.

Created by Touria Semingson

Canyon Ranch Homemade Vanilla Ice Cream

1 box firm silken organic tofu, about 10½ ounces, drained

½ cup sugar

½ cup brown sugar

⅓ cup canola oil

1 tablespoon pure vanilla extract

¼ teaspoon pure almond extract

1½ cups rolled oats

1 cup all-purpose flour

½ teaspoon salt

1½ teaspoons ground cinnamon

1 teaspoon baking powder

½ cup raisins

Vegan Oatmeal Cookies

These cookies are free of all animal products – no butter or eggs. And they're good.

1. Preheat oven to 375°. Lightly coat a baking sheet with canola oil.

2. Puree tofu in a blender container. Transfer to a mixing bowl and add sugars and oil. Add extracts and mix well. Add oatmeal and stir to combine.

3. Combine flour, salt, ground cinnamon, and baking powder in a medium bowl and mix well. Add dry ingredients to tofu mixture in thirds, mixing after each addition until all ingredients are moistened. Add raisins last.

4. Roll about 2 tablespoons (1 ounce) dough into a ball and set on prepared baking sheet. Repeat for remaining dough. Wet hands and lightly flatten cookies before baking. Bake for 10 to 12 minutes or until just golden.

MAKES 36 COOKIES
EACH COOKIE CONTAINS APPROXIMATELY:
85 calories | 14 gm. carbohydrate
3 gm. fat | 0 mg. cholesterol
2 gm. protein | 78 mg. sodium | Trace fiber

Created by Scott Uehlein

Holidays & Special Occasions

MORE GREAT TASTES

NO MAN CAN BE WISE ON AN

EMPTY STOMACH

– George Eliot

No holiday or party is complete unless
we eat and drink good things together.

Our sumptuous recipes for holidays and
entertaining are proof that a joyous table
need not be a weight-management
Waterloo. From hors d'oeuvres made with
Tuscan White Bean Spread, pleasantly
accompanied by one of our non-alcholic
"mocktails," through Turkey Roulade with
Dried Apricot Rosemary Dressing served
with Potato Kugel, and on to Pumpkin
Pecan Pie, a holiday feast Canyon Ranch-
style combines the savor of tradition
with sound nutritional common sense.
And our Chocolate Birthday Cake is, well,
exactly what a birthday cake ought to be.

Eat, drink and be very merry indeed!

Matzo Ball Soup

A traditional part of the Passover meal. We've substituted canola oil for the usual chicken fat.

1. In a medium bowl, combine eggs, salt and oil. Stir in matzo meal and mix until well blended. Gradually add stock and stir until mixture reaches a dough consistency. Chill in refrigerator 2 to 3 hours.

2. Shape chilled dough into 10 balls, about 2 inches in diameter.

3. In a large saucepot, heat broth to a boil. Drop matzo balls into stock and simmer for 30 to 45 minutes.

4. Ladle ¾ cup broth and 1 matzo ball into each serving bowl.

MAKES 10 SERVINGS
EACH ¾ CUP SERVING CONTAINS APPROXIMATELY:
85 calories | 6 gm. carbohydrate
5 gm. fat | 55 mg. cholesterol
4 gm. protein | 166 mg. sodium | Trace fiber

Ingredients

2 whole eggs, slightly beaten
1 teaspoon salt
2 tablespoons canola oil
½ cup matzo meal
2 tablespoons Chicken Stock (see recipe)
10 cups Chicken Consommé or Stock (see recipe)

Cook's Note:

To save time, use best-quality, organic canned chicken stock or broth.

Created by Scott Uehlein

6 squares whole-wheat matzo, crumbled

3 cups nonfat milk (enough to cover matzo)

3 whole eggs

6 egg whites

Pinch salt (to taste)

Pinch cinnamon (optional)

2 teaspoons canola oil

Matzo Brei

A traditional Passover dish that's also great for breakfast.

1. Place crumbled matzo into a large mixing bowl. Add milk to cover and soak for 15 minutes.

2. Beat eggs and whites with a fork to blend. Add salt and cinnamon. Squeeze matzo dry and add to egg mixture. Let soak another 15 minutes.

3. Heat canola oil in a large sauté pan over medium heat. Pour in egg and matzo mixture. Scramble as you would eggs or allow to cook pancake-style, browning on both sides.

4. Serve immediately with honey or maple syrup.

MAKES 6 SERVINGS
EACH SERVING CONTAINS APPROXIMATELY:
190 calories | 28 gm. carbohydrate
5 gm. fat | 111 mg. cholesterol
10 gm. protein | 144 mg. sodium | Trace fiber

Matzo Brei, Potato Kugel and Potato Latkes

Ingredients

4 large russet baking potatoes, peeled and grated

1 cup diced onion

2 whole eggs, beaten

¾ teaspoon salt

¼ teaspoon black pepper

2 teaspoons olive oil

3 tablespoons all-purpose flour

Created by Scott Uehlein

Potato Latkes

1. In a medium bowl combine potatoes and onions and mix well. Add eggs, salt, pepper and olive oil. Sift in flour last and mix well.

2. Lightly spray a large sauté pan with canola oil. Portion a scant ¼ cup potato mixture for each latke, then flatten and cook 3 latkes in pan at a time. Cook for about three minutes, or until golden brown on the bottom, then flip and finish browning on the other side.

3. Serve 3 latkes with nonfat yogurt, nonfat sour cream or applesauce.

MAKES 8 SERVINGS
EACH 3 LATKE SERVING CONTAINS APPROXIMATELY:
130 calories | 22 gm. carbohydrate
3 gm. fat | 42 mg. cholesterol
4 gm. protein | 302 mg. sodium | 2 gm. fiber

Ingredients

5 medium potatoes, peeled and diced

1 cup diced onions

½ cup peeled and diced carrots

2 tablespoons chopped fresh parsley

¼ cup matzo meal

1 teaspoon salt

¼ teaspoon pepper

2 whole eggs plus 4 egg whites, beaten

2 tablespoons olive oil

Potato Kugel

1. Preheat oven to 375°. Lightly coat the cups of a 12-cup muffin tin with olive oil, then dust with matzo meal.

2. Place vegetables in a large bowl. Add remaining ingredients and mix well.

3. Fill muffin tins and place in oven. Bake 45 to 50 minutes or until golden brown.

MAKES 12 MUFFINS
EACH MUFFIN CONTAINS APPROXIMATELY:
115 calories | 18 gm. carbohydrate
3 gm. fat | 35 mg. cholesterol
4 gm. protein | 137 mg. sodium | 2 gm. fiber

Cook's Note:

For a crispier kugel, turn onto cookie sheet and bake in oven for 10 more minutes.

Tzimmes

Tzimmes is a popular casserole of fruit and/or vegetables that's usually served on the Sabbath or holidays.

1. Preheat oven to 375°. Lightly coat an 8" x 8" baking pan with canola oil.

2. Place 1 cup hot water in a medium bowl and add prunes. Re-hydrate for about 5 minutes, drain water and dice.

3. In a large bowl, combine cinnamon, nutmeg and brown sugar. Save half of mixture for topping.

4. Toss sweet potatoes, carrots, prunes and pineapple with other half of cinnamon sugar mixture. Place in baking pan and drizzle with pineapple juice concentrate. Sprinkle with remaining cinnamon sugar mixture, cover and bake 1 hour.

MAKES 8 SERVINGS
EACH ½ CUP SERVING CONTAINS APPROXIMATELY:
105 calories | 26 mg. carbohydrate
Trace fat | 0 mg. cholesterol
1 gm. protein | 10 mg. sodium | 3 gm. fiber

Ingredients

¾ cup diced prunes

Pinch ground cinnamon

Pinch ground or fresh grated nutmeg

2 tablespoons brown sugar

1 pound sweet potatoes, diced, about 2 cups

¾ cup peeled and diced carrots

½ cup diced fresh pineapple

2 tablespoons pineapple juice

Created by Justin Morrow

Haroset

Haroset is one of the symbolic foods on the Passover Seder plate – it represents the mortar the Israelites were forced to carry as Pharoah's slaves in Egypt. Without the wine it makes a tasty breakfast accompaniment.

Combine all ingredients and mix well.

MAKES 8 SERVINGS
EACH 3 TABLESPOON SERVING CONTAINS APPROXIMATELY:
65 calories | 9 gm. carbohydrate
3 gm. fat | 0 mg. cholesterol
1 gm. protein | 41 mg. sodium | 2 gm. fiber

Ingredients

2 medium red apples, cored, peeled and shredded

4 tablespoons chopped almonds

1 tablespoon sugar

¼ teaspoon ground cinnamon

¾ teaspoon grated fresh lemon peel

2 tablespoons red wine

Ingredients

1 16-ounce can white beans, preferably cannellini

½ cup water

2 tablespoons olive oil

1 tablespoon fresh chopped thyme

2 teaspoons fresh lemon juice

3 cloves roasted garlic

1 cup julienne arugula leaves

½ teaspoon salt

¼ teaspoon pepper

Tuscan White Bean Spread

30 MIN

Terrific on thin slices of fresh bread or crackers, with a bowl of olives on the side.

1. Place all ingredients, except arugula, in a blender container or bowl of food processor and blend until smooth.

2. Transfer bean mixture to a serving bowl and stir in arugula, salt and pepper.

MAKES 12 SERVINGS
EACH 2 TABLESPOON SERVING CONTAINS APPROXIMATELY:
75 calories | 10 gm. carbohydrate
3 gm. fat | 0 mg. cholesterol
4 gm. protein | 2 mg. sodium | 2 gm. fiber

Ingredients

1 tablespoon olive oil

½ cup diced onions

½ cup diced mushrooms

¾ cup chopped, canned chestnuts

1 teaspoon minced fresh rosemary

1 teaspoon minced fresh thyme

¼ teaspoon salt

2 tablespoons raisins

¾ cup water

1½ cups dried bread cubes

Chestnut Stuffing

1. In a large saucepan, sauté onions in olive oil until translucent. Add mushrooms, chestnuts, herbs and salt and sauté for about 30 seconds. Add raisins and water and mix well. Remove from heat and fold in bread cubes. Mixture should be moist, but not wet.

2. Transfer to an 8" x 8" baking pan, which has been lightly coated with olive oil and bake for 20 to 30 minutes, or until heated through.

MAKES 8 SERVINGS
EACH ½ CUP SERVING CONTAINS APPROXIMATELY:
95 calories | 17 gm. carbohydrate
2 gm. fat | 0 mg. cholesterol
2 gm. protein | 38 mg. sodium | 3 gm. fiber

Nutrition Note:

Unlike most other nuts, chestnuts are nearly fat-free. Nonetheless, they have a sweet, buttery flavor that makes this dressing sumptuous. Chestnuts are a good source of folate, vitamin C and fiber.

Turkey Roulade with Dried Apricot Rosemary Stuffing

1. Preheat oven to 350°

2. Toast bread cubes in baking pan for 10 minutes or until golden brown and crisp. Place in a medium bowl.

3. Lightly spray a non-stick skillet with olive oil and cook onion, celery and rosemary over moderate heat for 5 minutes or until onion is soft. Stir in apricots and ¼ cup of the chicken stock and cook until liquid is absorbed, about 2 minutes. Add mixture to bread cubes and lightly mix.

4. In a small bowl whisk together apricot nectar, mustard, and remaining stock. Reserve.

5. Place one cutlet at a time between sheets of wax paper. Gently pound with a meat mallet. Remove from paper and spoon 2 tablespoons of stuffing down long side of each cutlet, leaving a ½ inch border along edge. Roll up cutlets and secure seam with a wooden toothpick.

6. Place cornmeal in a shallow bowl and coat roulades evenly. Heat oil in a large skillet over medium high heat until hot, but not smoking. Brown roulades for 3 minutes. Transfer to a baking dish and arrange in a single layer.

7. Deglaze skillet with wine and bring to a boil over medium heat. Add nectar mixture and mix well. Pour sauce around roulades and place in oven for 30 minutes or until cooked through.

8. Remove roulades from baking pan and transfer to a cutting board. Transfer liquid in baking pan to a small saucepan and boil until reduced to 1 cup. Whisk in arrowroot, salt and pepper and cook until thickened. Remove toothpicks from roulades and cut into ½ inch slices. Serve with 2 tablespoons sauce.

MAKES 4 SERVINGS
EACH SERVING CONTAINS APPROXIMATELY:
200 calories | 19 gm. carbohydrate
6 gm. fat | 51 mg. cholesterol
21 gm. protein | 509 mg. sodium | 1 gm. fiber

Ingredients

1½ slices whole-wheat bread, cut into ½-inch cubes

½ cup chopped onion

¼ cup chopped celery

1 teaspoon chopped fresh rosemary

1 ounce dried apricots

1¼ cups Chicken Stock (see recipe)

½ cup canned apricot nectar

1½ tablespoons Dijon mustard

4 4-ounce turkey cutlets

2 tablespoons yellow cornmeal

1 tablespoon olive oil

¼ cup white wine

½ teaspoon arrowroot

Pinch salt

Pinch black pepper

FOR THE CAKE:

1 cup all-purpose flour

½ cup cocoa

¾ cup sugar

1 teaspoon baking soda

1 teaspoon baking powder

Pinch salt

2 tablespoons unsweetened applesauce

½ cup buttermilk

2 teaspoons pure vanilla extract

1 teaspoon pure almond extract (optional)

2 tablespoons brewed coffee

½ cup baby food prunes

2 egg whites

1 whole egg

½ ounce semi-sweet chocolate mini chips

FOR THE TOPPING:

1 recipe Cream Cheese Frosting (see recipe below)

2 tablespoons nonfat fudge sauce

½ pound Neufchâtel cream cheese

¼ cup powdered sugar

½ teaspoon pure vanilla extract

Created by Jayne Shaulis

Chocolate Birthday Cake

We celebrate our guests' birthdays with this delicious cake. The baby food prunes make it lusciously moist.

1. Preheat oven to 300°. Spray a 10" round cake pan with nonstick vegetable coating and lightly dust with cocoa.

2. Sift together dry ingredients in a large mixing bowl.

3. In a small bowl, mix applesauce, milk, vanilla extract and almond extract (if desired), coffee, prunes, egg whites and egg. Pour into dry ingredients and stir until smooth. Stir in chocolate chips.

4. Spread batter in prepared pan. Bake for 25-30 minutes, or until a toothpick inserted in middle of cake comes out clean.

5. When cake is cool, spread with Cream Cheese Frosting and drizzle decoratively with nonfat fudge sauce. Cut into 12 equal pieces.

MAKES 12 SERVINGS
EACH SERVING CONTAINS APPROXIMATELY:
150 calories | 33 gm. carbohydrate
2 gm. fat | 19 mg. cholesterol
4 gm. protein | 199 mg. sodium | 3 gm. fiber

Cream Cheese Frosting

Combine all ingredients in a large bowl and blend on medium with an electric mixer until smooth and creamy.

EACH 1 OUNCE SERVING CONTAINS APPROXIMATELY:
65 calories | 3 gm. carbohydrate
5 gm. fat | 16 mg. cholesterol
3 gm. protein | 160 mg. sodium | Trace fiber

Chocolate Birthday Cake with Cream Cheese Frosting

1 cup toasted and chopped macadamia nuts

¼ cup finely chopped crystallized ginger

3 egg whites

Pinch salt

Pinch cream of tartar

½ cup sugar

½ teaspoon pure vanilla extract

Holiday Meringue Cookies

1. Preheat oven to 200°

2. In a small bowl, combine macadamia nuts and ginger.

3. Place egg whites in a large mixing bowl and add salt and cream of tartar. Beat with electric mixer on medium until foamy. Add 1 tablespoon sugar and beat on high. Gradually add remaining sugar a tablespoon at a time. Add vanilla when egg whites form stiff peaks. Fold in nut and ginger mixture.

4. Spoon meringue on ungreased baking sheet to form 1½ inch cookies. Bake in oven for 1 hour or until meringue begins to crust. Turn off oven and allow cookies to remain in oven 1 more hour to dry.

MAKES 40 COOKIES
EACH COOKIE CONTAINS APPROXIMATELY:
40 calories | 4 gm. carbohydrate
3 gm. fat | 0 mg. cholesterol
Trace protein | 8 mg. sodium | Trace fiber

Cook's Note:

Crystallized ginger is peeled ginger root that has been boiled in sugar syrup and coated with coarse sugar. The best crystallized ginger comes from Australia. A slice of it in a cup of hot tea – instead of sugar – adds wonderful flavor and settles the stomach. Crystallized ginger also pairs up nicely with melon.

Cherry Almond Biscotti

1. Preheat oven to 350°. Lightly coat a baking sheet with canola oil.

2. In a large bowl, cream sugar and butter until smooth. Add egg and egg white, vanilla, almond extract and applesauce.

3. In another bowl, mix flour, baking powder, fennel seed, salt, cherries and almonds. Add to butter mixture. Using a dough hook, mix with electric mixer on low speed until no longer sticky. (If your mixer does not come with a dough hook, mix by hand, turn out on a floured board and knead for 30 seconds.) Add additional flour a tablespoon at a time if necessary.

4. Place dough on lightly floured clean surface. Form into 10" x 1" log. Place on baking sheet and bake for 25 to 30 minutes. Remove from oven and cool slightly. Using a serrated knife, cut into 1 inch slices.

5. Decrease oven temperature to 275°. Place slices on baking sheet and bake 10 to 15 more minutes, or until very dry and slightly browned.

MAKES 10 SERVINGS
EACH SERVING CONTAINS APPROXIMATELY:
150 calories | 25 gm. carbohydrate
4 gm. fat | 17 mg. cholesterol
3 gm. protein | 60 mg. sodium | 1 gm. fiber

Ingredients

¼ cup sugar
2 tablespoons butter
1 whole egg
1 egg white
¾ teaspoon pure vanilla extract
½ teaspoon pure almond extract
¼ cup unsweetened applesauce
1½ cups all-purpose flour
¾ teaspoon baking powder
½ teaspoon fennel seed, toasted
Pinch salt
½ cup chopped dried cherries
3 tablespoons chopped almonds

Created by Touria Semingson

¼ cup sugar

2 tablespoons butter

1 whole egg

1 egg white

¾ teaspoon pure vanilla extract

½ teaspoon pure anise extract

1 teaspoon grated fresh
lemon peel

¼ cup unsweetened applesauce

1½ cups all-purpose flour

¾ teaspoon baking powder

½ teaspoon fennel seed, toasted

Pinch salt

½ cup dried chopped figs

3 tablespoons chopped
pistachio nuts

Fig and Pistachio Biscotti

The name of these delectable little Italian cookies means "twice cooked" – it's the second baking that gives them their inimitable crunch.

1. Preheat oven to 350°. Lightly coat a baking sheet with canola oil.

2. In a large bowl, cream sugar and butter until smooth. Add egg and egg white, vanilla extract, anise extract, lemon peel and applesauce.

3. In another bowl, mix flour, baking powder, fennel seed, salt, figs and pistachios. Add to butter mixture. Using a dough hook, mix with electric mixer on low speed until no longer sticky. (If your mixer does not come with a dough hook, mix by hand and knead for 30 seconds.) Add additional flour a tablespoon at a time, if necessary.

4. Place dough on lightly floured clean surface. Form into 10" x 1" log. Place on baking sheet and bake for 25 to 30 minutes. Remove from oven and cool slightly. Using a serrated knife, cut into 1 inch slices.

5. Decrease oven temperature to 275°. Place slices on baking sheet and bake 10 to 15 more minutes, until very dry and slightly browned.

MAKES 10 SERVINGS
EACH SERVING CONTAINS APPROXIMATELY:
145 calories | 25 gm. carbohydrate
4 gm. fat | 17 mg. cholesterol
3 gm. protein | 39 mg. sodium | 2 gm. fiber

Cook's Note:

Toast fennel seed in a small, dry sauté pan over medium heat for a moment or two, stirring until seeds are fragrant and just beginning to brown.

Created by Touria Semingson

Pumpkin Pie
with Pecan Crust

1. Preheat oven to 350°.

2. In a medium bowl, combine graham cracker crumbs with pecans and applesauce. Press into the bottom and halfway up the sides of a 9" pie plate, coated with a small amount of canola oil. Set aside.

3. Combine remaining ingredients, except pecan halves and syrup, in a large bowl. Mix until blended.

4. Pour pumpkin mixture into pie crust.

5. Bake for 20 to 30 minutes or until a knife inserted in the middle comes out clean. Refrigerate pie when cool; cut into 12 equal pieces.

6. In a small bowl, coat pecan halves with syrup. Transfer to a lightly oiled baking sheet, reduce heat to 325° and bake for 4 to 5 minutes. Remove from oven. Place one pecan on the outer edge of each slice of pie before serving.

MAKES 12 SERVINGS
EACH SERVING CONTAINS APPROXIMATELY:
125 calories | 17 gm. carbohydrate
5 gm. fat | 10 mg. cholesterol
4 gm. protein | 81 mg. sodium | 2 gm. fiber

Ingredients

1 cup graham cracker crumbs
2 tablespoons pecans, toasted and ground
1 tablespoon unsweetened applesauce
2 whole eggs
1 cup canned pumpkin
¾ cup evaporated skim milk
¼ cup apple juice concentrate
¼ cup brown sugar
½ teaspoon ground cinnamon
¼ teaspoon ground ginger
Pinch ground cloves
Pinch salt
12 pecan halves
1 teaspoon maple syrup

1 tablespoon horseradish

1½ teaspoons Old Bay® seasoning

2 teaspoons celery seed

2 teaspoons distilled white vinegar

4 tablespoons fresh lemon juice

Pinch black pepper

3 tablespoons Worcestershire sauce

4 cups low-sodium tomato juice

Created by Scott Uehlein

Bloody Mary

Combine all ingredients except for tomato juice in a blender container. Puree briefly. Add tomato juice and blend well. Serve over ice.

MAKES 6 SERVINGS

EACH ¾ CUP SERVING CONTAINS APPROXIMATELY:

35 calories | 8 gm. carbohydrate

Trace fat | 0 mg. cholesterol

2 gm. protein | 311 mg. sodium | 1 gm. fiber

⅓ cup sugar

1½ cups water

⅔ cup fresh lime juice

⅔ cup orange juice

1 tablespoon fresh lemon juice

Created by Scott Uehlein

Margarita

For a beautiful, fuschia-toned prickly pear margarita, add ¼ cup prickly pear syrup.

Combine sugar and water in a medium pitcher and allow to dissolve. Add remaining ingredients and mix well. Serve cold or over ice.

MAKES 4 SERVINGS

EACH ¾ CUP SERVING CONTAINS APPROXIMATELY:

100 calories | 26 gm. carbohydrate

Trace fat | 0 mg. cholesterol

Trace protein | 7 mg. sodium | Trace fiber

Cook's Note:

Prickly pears are the fruit of a common Sonoran Desert cactus. The rather tart juice is a deep pinkish purple, with a melon-like aroma and a flavor something like plums. Southwesterners often brave the stickers and collect ripe fruit to make jewel-toned jellies and syrups. The syrup is available from specialty stores in the Southwest, including Arizona Cactus Ranch, 800-582-9903.

Strawberry Daiquiri, Margarita, and Bloody Mary

1   cup frozen organic
    strawberries

1   cup orange juice

3   tablespoons apple juice
    concentrate

1   teaspoon fresh lemon juice

Strawberry Daiquiri

Combine all ingredients in a blender
container and puree until smooth.

MAKES 2 SERVINGS
EACH 1 CUP SERVING CONTAINS APPROXIMATELY:
110 calories | 26 gm. carbohydrate
Trace fat | 0 mg. cholesterol
1 gm. protein | 9 mg. sodium | 2 gm. fiber

Created by Scott Uehlein

Appendices

MORE GREAT TASTES

GIVE A MAN A FISH AND HE WILL EAT FOR

A DAY. TEACH A MAN TO FISH AND HE WILL

EAT FOR THE REST OF HIS LIFE.

– Chinese Proverb

Basic Food Prep 101

Cooking Beans

Dozens of varieties of dried beans – including newly available, flavorful heirloom beans from all over the world – are great for adding protein and fiber to any meal. For all the nutrition they provide, beans are incredibly economical and easy on the environment.

There are a few simple tricks to dealing with dried beans. Always pick over beans, looking for stones and dirt, and rinse in a colander before soaking.

We recommend soaking rinsed, picked-over beans for 6 to 8 hours (or overnight) before cooking: Place them in a bowl, add enough water to cover plus 3 inches and let sit in a cool place.

(A note on garbanzo beans, also known as chickpeas: Garbanzos are very firm. For a softer bean, add 1 teaspoon of baking soda to soaking water, and let soak overnight or longer. Be sure to pour off soaking water and rinse, and don't use this method for other beans – it will turn them to mush.)

You can also soak beans quickly this way: Place beans in a large saucepan, cover with 3 inches water and bring to a boil. Remove from heat and let soak for 1 hour.

Whichever method you use, pour off soaking water, rinse beans again and add abundant fresh water before cooking. Bring water to a boil, reduce heat and simmer, uncovered.

The following is a guide to cooking beans:

youBean Cooking Guide

Beans (1 cup) Uncooked	Amount of Boiling Water	Cooking Time After Soaking	Yield
Adzuki	3 cups	45 min. to 1 hour	2½ cups
Anasazi	3 cups	45 min. to 1 hour	2 cups
Black	3 cups	1½ hours	2½ cups
Cannellini	3 cups	1 hour	2½ cups
Kidney	3 cups	1 hour	2½ cups
Garbanzo	3 cups	1½ to 2 hours	2½ cups
Lima	3 cups	1 hour	2½ cups
Navy	3 cups	45 min. to 1 hour	2½ cups
Pinto	3 cups	45 min. to 1 hour	2½ cups
Lentils*	3 cups	20 to 30 minutes	3 cups
Split Peas*	3 cups	¾ hour	2 cups
Black-eyed Peas	3 cups	½ hour	2¼ cups

*Soaking not required

Cooking Grains

Cooking times and proportions of grain-to-liquid vary greatly from one type of grain to the next. Couscous and bulgur wheat don't even require cooking: Just stir in boiling water, cover and let sit until water is absorbed.

Other grains require various amounts of water and a range of simmering times. Bring water to a boil, add grain, cover, reduce heat to low and simmer.

The following is a guide to cooking grain:

Grain Cooking Guide

Grains (1 cup) (raw or uncooked)	Amount of Boiling Water	Cooking Time	Yield
Brown Rice, Black Rice & Himalayan Red Rice	2 cups	35 to 45 minutes	3 cups
Barley	5 cups	1½ hours	3¾ cups
Millet	2 cups	20 minutes	3½ cups
Wild Rice	3 cups	35 to 40 minutes	3 cups
Quinoa	2 cups	15 to 20 minutes	3 cups
Bulgur Wheat	1 cup	Cover and set aside for 20 min.	2½ cups
White Basmati Rice	2¼ cups	20 minutes	3 cups
Jasmine Rice	1¾ cup	20 minutes	2¾ cups
Polenta	3 cups	15 minutes	3 cups
Couscous	1 cup	Cover and set side for 5 min.	2 cups

Try substituting chicken or vegetable stock or herbal tea for the water.

Cooking Pasta

Pasta cooked al dente not only tastes better, it's also recommended nutritionally for better digestion and metabolism. Always add pasta to a large quantity of water at a full, rolling boil to prevent sticking. Most pasta is cooked for 8 to 10 minutes; however, if you are fortunate enough to come across fresh pasta, usually 2 to 3 minutes is adequate cooking time.

Grilling Chicken, Fish and Red Meat

We often think of grilling as something that happens outside over coals or gas flames during warm weather, but these days you can grill inside with a cast iron grill pan. This is a quick, low-fat way to cook chicken, fish and red meat. Make sure to heat grill or pan hot enough so that the meat sizzles when placed on the surface. It is also advisable to lightly coat the grill rack or pan with olive oil or canola oil before adding meat to prevent sticking.

Cook chicken and red meat for 3 to 5 minutes on each side per inch of thickness. Chicken is done when juices run clear when the center is pierced with a fork. When cooking fish, watch carefully after 2 minutes to make sure it is not cooking too fast. Fish becomes dry and rubbery when cooked too long.

Grilling or Roasting Vegetables

One of our favorite ways of cooking vegetables is to grill or roast them. After you taste the caramelized sweetness of a zucchini squash cooked this way, you may never steam again.

When grilling vegetables, we recommend cutting them in pieces that are large enough not to fall through the rack. However, vegetables do vary in moisture content and when you're cooking several types at once, you may need to slice slower cooking varieties – such as root vegetables – thinner. Lightly spray with olive oil and season with salt and pepper and then grill until tender, about 5 minutes per side. (The beautiful grill marks enhance the eye appeal of any meal.)

Roasting vegetables is just as easy. Preheat oven to 400° and spread vegetables on a baking sheet. Lightly spray with olive oil and season with salt and pepper. Roast for 10 to 15 minutes or until vegetables are lightly browned, turning once or twice if desired.

Grinding Spices

Grinding whole spices just before using maximizes flavors. Small coffee grinders or spice mills work well for this. A mortar and pestle is a more primitive form of grinding, but we recommend it – especially when a very small quantity is called for.

Grinding Flax Seed

The best method for grinding flax seed is a small coffee or spice grinder. Grinding the seed helps release the omega-3 fatty acids, so the ground product has a limited shelf-life. Flax seed can be purchased ground as flax seed meal, but it must be kept in the refrigerator, then discarded after 3 months. Whole flax seeds can be kept in the refrigerator up to 6 months. Grind them as needed for maximum flavor and nutrition.

Making Bread Crumbs

Day-old whole-wheat bread makes the best bread crumbs. Break bread into small pieces and place in blender or food processor, then blend or pulse on low until crumbs are uniform in size. If bread is too moist it will clump together, so dry moist bread in a 200° oven for 1 hour before making crumbs.

Making an Herb Sachet or Bouquet Garni

Sachets are often used in soups and stocks to add unique flavor when cooking over a long period of time. Cheesecloth is the best wrapper for a sachet of herbs and spices. Generally, dried ingredients such as whole peppercorns, dried thyme, rosemary, parsley and bay leaves make the best sachets. Wrap approximately 1 tablespoon each of the desired herbs and spices in a 6-inch square piece of cheesecloth and tie with string. Immerse in stock or soups while simmering to release flavors. Another technique is to place herbs in a tea ball instead of cheesecloth. This method works particularly well for fresh herbs, but note that the cooking time must be short when you use fresh herbs.

Making Yogurt Cheese

Many of our recipes call for yogurt cheese as an ingredient. For best results, line a colander with dampened cheesecloth and add yogurt. Place colander over a large bowl, store in refrigerator and let drain overnight. Discard liquid, place yogurt cheese in covered container and refrigerate for up to 1 week.

1 quart yogurt = 1½ cups yogurt cheese

Poaching Fish

When poaching fish, place enough liquid to cover food in a large sauté or saucepan, heat to a simmer, add fish, cover and remove from heat source. Fish will cook in hot liquid in about 5 to 10 minutes: a general rule is 10 minutes per inch of thickness. Poaching is often done in stock or wine to add flavor.

Poaching Fruit

When poaching fruit, place enough liquid to cover food in a large saucepan, heat to just under a simmer and add fruit. Tiny bubbles will break the surface of poaching liquid, as if it's just about to begin to simmer. (French cooks say that when the water is at this stage "the pot smiles.") Reduce heat slightly if water comes to a simmer. Fruit typically takes 5 to 10 minutes to poach. You can poach fruit in fruit juice, wine or lightly sugared water for great flavor. If you wish, you can save the poaching liquid, reduce it by boiling and use it as a sauce.

Roasting Garlic

Roasted garlic lends a mellow garlic flavor to many of our recipes. Separate cloves from the bulb and peel. Spread on a baking sheet, coat with a small amount of olive oil and roast in a 400° oven for 10 to 15 minutes. Roasted garlic can be minced or pureed, depending upon the application.

Separating Eggs

To separate egg yolks from whites for dessert recipes, carefully crack an egg, hold it over a bowl, and gently break it crosswise into halves, cupping the yolk in the bottom half of the shell. Allow the white to drain off into the bowl as you gently slip the yolk from one half of shell to the other, being careful not to break it. (Even a speck of yolk, or any other food containing fat or oil, will keep whites from beating up into an airy froth. It's a good idea to give your bowl and mixer or wire whip an extra, hot-water wash before beating egg whites.)

Steaming Vegetables

Steaming vegetables is a great way to retain all the important nutrients contained in plant foods. Bamboo steamer baskets are fine, as are metal steamer baskets that fit in the bottom of a saucepan. You can also find small, electric steamers in any department store. The bottom line on steaming is that you're just suspending vegetables over boiling water in a covered pan. Steaming takes from 5 to 8 minutes, depending on the type and size of the vegetable.

Toasting Nuts and Seeds

Toasting gives a new and richer flavor to nuts and seeds. Spread whole nuts and seeds on a baking sheet and toast at 400° for 5 minutes in a small toaster or conventional oven. If the nuts are not completely toasted after 5 minutes, continue to cook, but watch closely – they burn in a flash. If you don't want to heat up the oven, another toasting technique is to dry-sauté in a sauté pan over medium heat. Again, watch closely so they don't burn.

Toasting Spices

Toasting spices to release flavor and aroma is a secret of great cooks the world over. A small toaster oven allows for more even toasting, but a conventional oven works too. Spread whole spices on a baking sheet and place in a 400° oven. Start by setting the timer for 5 minutes and then watch closely to make sure they don't burn. As our chefs say in our demo kitchen, "not done...not done...burned." You may also dry sauté spices (see Toasting Nuts and Seeds).

Cooking Terms and Techniques

Al Dente

A term applied to pasta or other foods that refers to cooking until tender but with a firm bite. Pasta cooked al dente is nutritionally superior for digestion and metabolism.

Bake

To cook by free-circulating dry air. It is very important to preheat the oven, especially when baking for proper rising. Do not crowd food in the oven; give it room to bake evenly.

Beat

To mix ingredients rapidly, incorporating air for a smooth, creamy texture.

Blanch

To plunge in boiling water briefly to tenderize, and then submerge in ice water to instantly stop the cooking process. Blanching is used to loosen skins of tomatoes and peaches and to partially cook vegetables before roasting or stir-frying. It sets the color and flavor of vegetables and ensures even cooking of ingredients. To ensure loosening of the skin, cut an "X" in the bottom of fruit or vegetable before placing in boiling water.

Blend

To combine ingredients to a desired consistency, usually until smooth. This is often, but not always, done in a blender.

Braise

To brown and then simmer in a covered pan on the stove top or in the oven in a small amount of liquid, over a long period of time, usually 1½ to 3 hours. When braising red meat, remove all visible fat and brown without added oil when possible.

Broil

To cook with intense, direct heat in an oven, under a broiler. The high heat seals in the juices, browns the outside and keeps food tender.

Caramelize

To heat sugar until it liquefies and becomes a clear golden to dark syrup. In the case of fruits and vegetables, caramelizing refers to the process of cooking in a small amount of oil or liquid on low heat for a long period of time until the natural sugars are released and browned.

Chiffonade

To slice in very thin strips or shreds. Flat leaf vegetables such as spinach, basil and leaf lettuce are good subjects. To chiffonade, tightly roll leaves lengthwise and then thinly slice crosswise to produce ribbons of greens.

Chop

To cut foods, usually with a chef's knife, into uniform-sized pieces, about ½ to 1-inch. As a rule of thumb, chop vegetables intended for stews and stir-frys more coarsely than vegetables intended for soups and sauces.

Dash

A small quantity, usually one or two quick shakes from a small hole in a bottle.

Deglaze

To add liquid, such as broth or wine to a pan in which food, usually meat or poultry, has been cooked. Cooking and stirring loosens bits of caramelized food from the bottom and sides of the pan, enriching the flavor of the sauce.

Dice

To cut, usually with a chef's knife, into small cubes ranging from ⅛ to ½-inch. The smaller dice is often referred to as brunoise.

Emulsify

To make a uniform mixture from two ingredients which would normally not combine smoothly – for example, oil and water. Emulsifying is done by slowly adding one ingredient to another while mixing rapidly. This disperses minute droplets of one liquid through the other. Often egg yolk or other lecithin-containing ingredients are used to bind the combative ingredients, as in mayonnaise.

Fold

To incorporate one ingredient into another by gently turning one part of the mixture over the other part with a spoon or rubber spatula. Folding is a gentle way of incorporating fluffy ingredients – whipped cream and beaten egg whites, for instance – without knocking the air out of them.

Garnish

To decorate food with fresh herbs, edible flowers, fresh vegetables or fruit to enhance the look of the dish.

Grill

To cook food on a rack, rapidly, with dry heat over gas, wood coals, charcoal or electric coil. Grilling is an intense, rapid cooking method that gives food a crisp exterior and moist, flavorful interior.

Julienne

To slice fruits or vegetables into 2 to 3-inch strips, usually ⅛-inch wide, also referred to as matchsticks. A chef's knife is the best tool for this cutting method. There's also a classic cutting device called a mandoline that can be used to julienne.

Marinate

To tenderize and flavor food by placing it in a seasoned liquid, usually composed of some combination of vinegar, lemon juice, wine, oil, herbs and spices.

Mash

To break down whole cooked foods, such as beans or potatoes, into a smooth evenly textured mixture. A potato masher is a great tool for this purpose.

Mince

To dice foods such as garlic and ginger very fine. Mincing requires a very sharp knife and patience.

Pinch

As much of a dry ingredient as you can hold between your thumb and forefinger – roughly ⅛ teaspoon.

Poach

To cook food gently in liquid just below the boiling point, just when tiny bubbles break the surface of the liquid. Fish is usually poached in a stock or court-bouillon, eggs in lightly salted water with a small amount of vinegar, and fruit in a light sugar syrup.

Puree

To blend food into a creamy, smooth consistency with a blender or food processor.

Reduce

To simmer with the aim of reducing the volume of a liquid by evaporation. Reducing concentrates flavor.

Roast

To oven-cook food in an uncovered pan to produce a well-browned exterior and a moist interior. Roasting meat and chicken requires tender cuts. Vegetables for roasting should be cut into uniform sizes so they cook evenly.

Sauté

To cook food quickly in a small amount of hot oil or liquid in a skillet or sauté pan over direct heat. Sautéing seals in natural juices, sets colors and preserves the integrity of each ingredient.

Seeding

To remove the seeds of vegetables and fruits such as peppers, tomatoes and cantaloupe by cutting in half and scooping out seeds.

Simmer

To cook gently over low heat at a very low boil.

Slice

To cut food into pieces, either crosswise or lengthwise depending upon the intended use. Slices in a given recipe should be of uniform thickness to ensure uniform cooking.

Steam

To cook food, covered, over a small amount of boiling or simmering water. This is a classic low-fat method of cooking vegetables. It retains foods' flavor, shape, texture and nutrients. Bamboo steamer baskets are a great way of accomplishing this, as are metal baskets that fit in the bottom of a saucepan.

Temper

To introduce a hot food into a cool food without causing the cool food to change chemically. Tempering eggs with a hot mixture is a good example. To accomplish this, gradually add small amounts of the hot mixture, while stirring, to the cool mixture. This "tempers" or gradually heats the cool mixture so it can be added to the rest of the hot mixture.

Toss

To quickly and gently mix ingredients together using a large spoon and fork or salad tongs.

Ingredient Conversions

Food	Amount	Equivalent
Almonds	1 pound, shelled	4 cups
Apples, Fresh	1 pound, 3 medium	2½ cups, chopped; 3 cups, sliced
Apples, Dried	1 pound	4 cups
Apricots, Fresh	1 pound, 12 medium	2 cups, sliced
Apricots, Dried	1 pound	2½ cups
Asparagus, Fresh	1 pound, 16 medium spears	3½ cups, chopped
Avocado	8 ounces, 1 large, skinned & seeded	1¼ cups, chopped; 1 cup, pureed
Bananas	4 ounces, 1 medium, peeled	¾ cup, sliced; ½ cup, pureed
Barley	1 cup, dry	3¾ cups, cooked
Beans		
Adzuki	1 pound, dried	2½ cups, dried
	1 cup, dried	2½ cups, cooked
Anasazi	1 pound, dried	2 cups, dried
	1 cup, dried	2 cups, cooked
Black	1 pound, dried	2¼ cups, dried
	1 cup, dried	2½ cups, cooked
Fava	1 pound, dried	2 cups, dried
	1 cup, dried	2 cups, cooked
Garbanzo	1 pound, dried	2 cups, dried
	1 cup, dried	2½ cups, cooked
Kidney	1 pound, dried	2 cups, dried
	1 cup, dried	2½ cups, cooked
Lima	1 pound, dried	2 cups, dried
	1 cup, dried	2½ cups, cooked
Navy	1 pound, dried	2¼ cups, dried
	1 cup, dried	2½ cups, cooked
Pinto	1 pound, dried	2 cups, dried
	1 cup, dried	2½ cups, cooked
Beets	1 pound, fresh, sizes vary	2 cups, chopped or sliced
Blackberries	1 pint, fresh	2 cups, fresh
	10-ounce bag, frozen	2 cups, frozen

Food	Amount	Equivalent
Blueberries	1 pint, fresh	2 cups, fresh
	10-ounce bag, frozen	1½ cups, frozen
Bread	1 pound loaf	About 16 ½-inch slices; 7 cups fresh crumbs
	1 slice	½ cup fresh crumbs
Broccoli	1 pound, fresh, bunches vary	2 cups, chopped
	10-ounce bag, frozen	1½ cups, chopped
Brussel Sprouts	1 pound fresh, about 20 sprouts	3 cups, fresh
	10-ounce bag, frozen	2½ cups, frozen
Bulgur Wheat	1 cup dry	3¾ cups, cooked
Butter	1 pound	2 cups, 4 sticks
Cabbage	1 pound, fresh	4 cups, shredded
Cantaloupe	1 medium, 2 pounds	3 cups, diced
Carrots	1 pound, trimmed, 4 medium	3 cups, chopped; 2 cups, grated
	10-ounce bag, frozen	2 cups, frozen, sliced
Cashews	1 pound, shelled	3½ cups
Cauliflower	1 pound, fresh, sizes vary	3 cups florets; 2 cups, chopped
	10-ounce bag, frozen	1½ cups, chopped
Celery	1 pound, stalks vary	3 cups, chopped
	2 medium ribs	½ cup chopped
Cheese		
Blue, Feta, Goat	4 ounces	1 cup crumbled
Cheddar, Jack, Mozzarella	1 pound	4 cups shredded
Parmesan, Romano	1 pound	4 cups grated
	¼ ounce	1 tablespoon
Cherries	1 pound, fresh	3 cups pitted
	10-ounce bag, frozen	1 cup, frozen
Chestnuts	1 pound, shelled, peeled	2½ cups
Chicken	½ breast, 4 ounces	¾ cup, cooked, diced

Food	Amount	Equivalent
Chocolate, All Types	8 ounces chips	1 cup
	1 ounce, melted, or 1 square	2 tablespoons
Clams, Canned	1 pound, drained	2 cups
Clams, Fresh	3 dozen, in shell	4 cups, shucked
Cocoa Powder	8 ounces	2¾ cups
Coconut	8 ounces, shredded	3½ cups
Corn	2 medium ears, fresh	1 cup kernels
	10-ounce bag, frozen	1¾ cups, frozen
Cornmeal	1 pound, dry	3 cups, dry
Cornstarch	1 pound	3 cups
Corn Syrup, light or dark	16 fluid ounces	2 cups
Cottage Cheese	8 ounces	1 cup
Couscous	1 cup, dry	2½ cups, cooked
Crab	1 pound cooked meat	3 cups, cooked
Crackers, Graham	15 squares	1 cup crumbs
Cranberries	12 ounces, fresh	3 cups, fresh
Cream		
Half and Half	1 pint	2 cups
Heavy, Whipping	1 pint	2 cups; 4 cups, whipped
Sour	1 pint	2 cups
Cream Cheese	8 ounces	1 cup
Cucumber	1 medium	1½ cups, chopped
Currants	1 pound, dried	3¼ cups, dried
Dates	1 pound, pitted	2½ cups, pitted
Eggplant, fresh	1 pound, fresh	3½ cups, diced; 2 cups, diced, cooked
Egg Roll Wrappers	1 pound	14 wrappers
Eggs, Whole, Large	1 dozen	2⅓ cups
	5 eggs	1 cup
	1 egg	3 tablespoons
Eggs, Whites, Large	1 dozen	1½ cups
	8 whites	1 cup
	2 whites	2½ cups, stiffly beaten
Eggs, Yolks, Large	1 dozen yolks	1 cup
	1 yolk	1½ tablespoons

Food	Amount	Equivalent
Egg, Hard Cooked	1 whole egg	⅓ cup, chopped
Figs	1 pound, fresh	12 medium 3 cups, chopped
Flour		
All-purpose, Bread, Hi-Gluten	1 pound	3 cups, sifted
Pastry, Cake	1 pound	4½ cups, sifted
Potato	1 pound	3 cups, sifted
Rice	1 pound	3½ cups, sifted
Rye	1 pound	3½ cups, sifted
Tapioca	1 pound	3½ cups, sifted
Whole-Wheat	1 pound	3½ cups, unsifted
Garlic	1 large head	12 cloves; 4 tablespoons, minced
	1 large clove	1 teaspoon, minced
Gelatin, Unflavored	¼-ounce packet	1 tablespoon
Ginger, Fresh	2-inch piece	2 tablespoons, minced; 1 tablespoon juice
Grapefruit	1 pound fresh	1 medium; 1½ cups segments; ¾ cup juice
Grapes	1 pound	3 cups
Green Beans (Haricot Verts)	1 pound, fresh	3½ cups, whole, trimmed
Greens		
Kale, Chard, Mustard	1 pound fresh	1½ cups, cooked
Hazelnuts	1 pound, shelled	1½ cups
Herbs	1 tablespoon, fresh, chopped	1 teaspoon, dried, crumbled
Honey	1 pound	2 cups
Horseradish	1 pound, fresh	3 cups, grated
Ketchup	16-ounce bottle	2 cups
Kiwi	1 pound, 6 medium	2¼ cups, chopped
Leeks	1 pound	2½ cups, chopped 1 cup, cooked
Lemons	1 pound, 6 medium	1 cup juice
	1 medium	3 tablespoons juice; 1 tablespoon grated peel
Lentils	1 pound, dried	2¼ cups, dried
	1 cup, dried	2 cups, cooked

Food	Amount	Equivalent
Lettuce, All Types	1 pound	6 cups, chopped or torn; 4 cups, shredded
Limes	1 pound, 8 medium	¾ cup juice
	1 medium	1½ tablespoons juice; 1½ teaspoons grated peel
Lobster	1 pound	2½ cups meat
Mango, Fresh	12 ounces, 1 medium	1 cup, chopped
Maple Syrup	16 fluid ounces	2 cups
Meat, Ground	1 pound	2 cups
Milk		
Fresh, All Types	1 quart	4 cups
Evaporated Skim	12-ounce can	1½ cups
Sweetened Condensed, Skim	14-ounce can	1¾ cups
Millet	1 cup	3½ cups, cooked
Molasses	16 fluid ounces	2 cups
Mushrooms, All Types	1 pound fresh	6 cups, chopped; 5½ cups, sliced
Mussels, Fresh	1 pound, medium, 12 mussels	1 cup meat
Mustard, All Types	16 fluid ounces	2 cups, prepared
	1 tablespoon, prepared	1 teaspoon, dried
Nectarines	1 pound, 3 to 4 medium	2 cups, chopped; 2½ cups, sliced
Oats, Rolled	1 pound, dry	5 cups, dry
	1 cup, dry	1¾ cups, cooked
Oil, All Types	8 ounces	1 cup
Okra	1 pound, fresh	2¼ cups, chopped, cooked
	10-ounce bag, frozen	1¼ cups, chopped
Onions		
Green, Scallions	1 medium, bulb and top	⅓ cup, chopped
White, Yellow or Red	1 pound, fresh, 4 medium	4 cups, chopped
Oranges	1 pound, 3 medium	1¼ cups juice
	1 medium	¾ cup segments, sliced; 1½ tablespoons grated orange peel
Oranges, Mandarin	11-ounce can	1¼ cups segments, drained

Food	Amount	Equivalent
Oysters	8 ounces, 16 oysters	1 cup, shucked
Papaya	12 ounces, 1 medium	1½ cups, chopped; 2 cups, sliced
Parsnips	1 pound, fresh, 4 medium	2 cups, chopped; 2½ cups, sliced
Pasta		
Macaroni	2 ounces, dry	1 cup, cooked
	1 cup, dry	1¾ cups, cooked
Noodles, 1-inch pieces	2 ounces dry	1 cup, cooked
	1 cup, dry	1¾ cups, cooked
Spaghetti, 12-inch noodles	2 ounces, dry	1 cup, cooked
Peaches	1 pound, fresh, 4 medium	2½ cups, chopped; 2¾ cups, sliced
	10-ounce bag, frozen	1½ cups, sliced
	1 pound, dried	2¾ cups, dried
Peanut Butter	16-ounce jar	1½ cups
Peanuts	1 pound, shelled	3½ cups
Pears	1 pound, fresh, 3 medium	2 cups, sliced
	1 pound, canned, drained	2 cups, sliced
	1 pound, dried	2¾ cups, dried
Peas, Black-eyed	1 pound, dried	2 cups, dried
	1 cup, dried	2 cups, cooked
	10-ounce bag, frozen	1½ cups
Peas, Green	1 pound, fresh, in pod	1 cup, shelled
	10-ounce bag, frozen	2 cups
Peas, Split	1 pound, dried	2¼ cups, dried
	1 cup, dried	2 cups, cooked
Pecans	1 pound, shelled	4 cups halves; 3½ cups, chopped
Peppers, Bell	1 pound, 2 large	2½ cups, chopped; 3 cups, sliced
	1 medium	1 cup, chopped
Phyllo	1 pound package	24 sheets
Pineapple	1 medium, fresh	5 cups, cubed
	15-ounce can, pineapple and juice	1½ cups, drained
Pine Nuts	1 pound, shelled	3 cups
Pistachios	1 pound, shelled	3½ cups

Food	Amount	Equivalent
Plums	1 pound, fresh	2 cups, chopped; 2½ cups, sliced
Potatoes		
Red Bliss	1 pound, 4 medium	3½ cups, chopped; 4 cups, sliced
Russet	1 pound, 2 large	3½ cups, chopped; 4 cups, sliced
Sweet	1 pound, fresh, 3 medium	3½ cups, chopped; 4 cups, sliced
Yukon Gold	1 pound, 4 medium	3½ cups, chopped; 4 cups, sliced
Prunes	1 pound, dried	2½ cups, dried; 4 cups, cooked
Pumpkin	1 pound, fresh	1 cup, cooked and mashed
	15-ounce can	1¾ cups, mashed
Quinoa	1 pound, dried	2½ cups, dried
	1 cup, dried	3 cups, cooked
Radishes	1 pound, fresh, 24 radishes	1½ cups, sliced
Raisins	1 pound, dried	2½ cups, dried
Raspberries	1 pint, fresh	2 cups, fresh
	10-ounce bag, frozen	1¾ cups, frozen
Rhubarb	1 pound, fresh	2 cups, chopped, cooked
	10-ounce bag, frozen	1¼ cups, chopped, frozen
Rice	1 cup, white basmati	3 cups, cooked
	1 cup, brown	3 cups, cooked
	1 cup, wild	3 cups, cooked
Ricotta Cheese	7½ ounces	1 cup
Rutabaga, Fresh	1 pound, fresh	2½ cups, cubed
Sauerkraut	1 pound	2 cups
Scallops	1 pound, medium	2 cups
Shallots	1 pound	2½ cups, chopped
Shrimp	1 pound, shelled	2 cups, cooked
	1 pound, unshelled	12 jumbo / 16 large / 30 medium / 36 small

Food	Amount	Equivalent
Soy Beans, fresh (Edamame)	1 pound, shelled	2 cups, shelled
Spinach	1 pound, fresh	10 cups, fresh; 2 cups, cooked
	10-ounce bag, frozen	1½ cups, frozen
Squash		
Acorn, Yellow, Zucchini	1 pound, 3 medium	3 cups, chopped; 3½ cups, sliced
Butternut	1 pound, fresh	1 cup, cooked, mashed
Strawberries	1 pint, fresh	2 cups, sliced
	10-ounce bag, frozen	1½ cups
Sugar		
Brown	1 pound	2¼ cups, packed
Granulated	1 pound	2 cups
Powdered	1 pound, (confectioners')	4 cups
Tangerines	1 pound, 4 medium	2 cups, segments
Tofu		
Firm	1 pound	2¾ cups, cubed
Silken	1 pound	2½ cups, cubed
Tomatoes	1 pound, 3 medium	1½ cups, chopped; 2 cups, sliced
	15-ounce can	1¾ cups, whole or diced with juice; 2 cups, pureed
Tomato Paste	6-ounce can	¾ cup
Tuna	6-ounce can	¾ cup
Turkey	12 pounds, raw	16 cups cooked meat
Turnips	1 pound, 3 medium	2½ cups, chopped, cooked
Walnuts	1 pound, shelled	3¾ cups, halved; 3½ cups, chopped
Watermelon	10 pounds	20 cups, cubed
Wheat Germ	16 ounces	4 cups
Wine	750 ml	Regular bottle, 3¼ cups
Wonton Skins (Wrappers)	1 pound	60 wrappers
Yeast	¼-ounce package	1 tablespoon
Yogurt	8 ounces	1 cup

Notes

Index

• **Recipes are in bold.**

Index to Cook's and Nutrition Notes

DAIRY-FREE RECIPES